WITH GRATEFUL HEARTS

With thanks and love for

Will and our Children

Jennifer & Charlie
David & Janet
Drew & April

And in memory of
Tom

With Grateful Hearts

These texts, also copyrighted by Glyn Ruppe-Melnyk
originally appeared online in 2013 and 2014 at
http://motherglyn.com

Printed and bound in the United States of America
Cover Photo by Glyn Ruppe Melnyk, 2013

ISBN-13: 978-1503368750
ISBN-10: 1503368750

Published by

Ephods and Pomegranates

WITH GRATEFUL HEARTS

RELFECTIONS ON LECTIONARY READINGS FOR YEAR A

The Rev. Glyn Lorraine Ruppe-Melnyk
November 2014

TABLE OF CONTENTS

Forward

This project began in the summer of 2013 when my vestry suggested that I write and publish a daily online and email devotional series as part of our adult education programming at St. Francis in the Fields.

Because we already had a strong cohort of members attending weekly Lectionary Bible Study Classes, I decided to use this project as a means of expanding that ministry to include those who could not attend a midweek class. As starting texts, I chose the Lectionary readings for the coming week and wrote six meditations per week (Monday through Saturday), hoping that doing so would encourage attendance at Sunday worship (if for no other reason than to hear how the lessons might come together in a sermon!)

We soon discovered that those who followed the posts were not only becoming far more familiar with Scripture than they had been before, they were becoming more regular in Sunday attendance and more engaged in the liturgy.

With encouragement from readers I decided to produce a series of three volumes – one for each of the three years in the lectionary cycle. This is volume one, based on Year A.

The Rev. Glyn Lorraine Ruppe-Melnyk
Malvern, PA
November 30, 2014

ADVENT

What Then Will This Child Become?

All who heard them (these events) pondered them and said, "What then will this child become?" For indeed the hand of the Lord was with him. (Luke 1:66)

The birth of John the Baptist included its own share of the miraculous. His parents' Elizabeth and Zechariah were well beyond child-bearing age, and Elizabeth had long been considered barren. When visited by an angel of the Lord with the announcement that his wife would have a son, Zechariah was incredulous and as a result was punished by not being able to speak until the birth and naming of the child. At that point, the priestly Zechariah was obedient and named the baby John as the angel had directed him.

Apparently these facts were known to the entire community, and inspired a great deal of awe and wonder concerning just who this child might grow up to be. And, of course, John did grow up to be the one who would be the last of the Old Testament Prophets, and the one who prepared the way for the coming of the Messiah.

During these first days of Advent, I wonder...what would our world be like if the birth of every child were marked by such attention and with such questions? How many of us are born, live and die without anyone ever seriously wondering, or taking an active part in helping to determine, what we might become?

How sad. For, all of us are children of God, and every birth contains its own degree of the miraculous. We may not be called to so obvious a role as John's, but God provides purpose for each of us. And that purpose involves our participation in preparing the way of the Lord so that the love and light of God are made present in the world.

How will we know him? We will know him by his authority.

"When he entered Capernaum, a centurion came to him, appealing to him and saying, 'Lord, my servant is lying at home paralyzed, in terrible distress.' And he said to him, 'I will come and cure him.' The centurion answered, 'Lord, I am not worthy to have you come under my roof; but only speak the word, and my servant will be healed. For I also am a man under authority, with soldiers under me; and I say to one, "Go", and he goes, and to another, "Come", and he comes, and to my slave, "Do this", and the slave does it.' When Jesus heard him, he was amazed and said to those who followed him, 'Truly I tell you, in no one in Israel have I found such faith". (Matthew 8:5-10)

As usual, I find myself slightly surprised that the lessons for the season of Advent don't get around to actually talking about the birth of the Messiah until the season is nearly over. But, I don't think the problem is with the lectionary. I think the problem is a symptom of our limited attention spans, and our inability to hold competing ideas in tension. We are like the expectant parent who has the nursery ready, the overnight bag packed and the diaper service on standby – we are ready, whether the baby is or not, and every day's delay is a cause for worry and anxiety. God, however, is talking to us about at least two things at once. Yes, we are about to experience the birth of the Messiah; and yes, we are already experiencing what it is like to have the Messiah in the world. So our lessons during this season are about how Jesus, God in Christ, reveals the Kingdom, acts with the power and authority of his divine nature, and calls forth in us a response of faith.

But most of us hedge our bets about that. We don't like waiting, but most of us have had plenty of experience doing it. So, we are always willing to hope that this year, if we get everything right, if we are really ready by December 24th, we will recognize the baby in the manger as the one who grew up to be the Messiah, and the Kingdom of Heaven will be with us.

The thing is, Advent is about more than the getting the nursery ready. Advent is also about the arrival of the reign of God. The same signs that tell us that the Messiah is coming, are signs that the Messiah is already with us.

How will we know him? Believing is Seeing.

"At that same hour Jesus rejoiced in the Holy Spirit and said, 'I thank you, Father, Lord of heaven and earth, because you have hidden these things from the wise and the intelligent and have revealed them to infants; yes, Father, for such was your gracious will. All things have been handed over to me by my Father; and no one knows who the Son is except the Father, or who the Father is except the Son and anyone to whom the Son chooses to reveal him.' Then turning to the disciples, Jesus said to them privately, 'Blessed are the eyes that see what you see! For I tell you that many prophets and kings desired to see what you see, but did not see it, and to hear what you hear, but did not hear it.'" (Luke 10:21-24)

There is a wonderful example of this kind of faith in the animated movie "Polar Express." On his journey to the North Pole, the main character, a skeptical young man of nine, meets a ghostly hobo travelling on the roof of the train. The hobo has a disconcerting habit of disappearing into thin air, but always showing up in the nick of time when there is danger. He also has an excellent piece of advice for his empirically minded young friend ~ "believing is seeing."

We live in just such a skeptical world. If we cannot prove it, it must not be true. If we cannot replicate the experience, we must have imagined it. That skepticism infects our hearts and our faith.

So why do we go through Advent every year? Why do we continue to read the words of Jesus, the messages of the prophets and the prayers of the Church? Why don't we just accept life with resignation, and move on?

The answer lies in what Jesus is saying in this passage. If we are relying on our wisdom and intelligence we are lost. But hope is the property of the heart, and the trust abides in the realm of love. The truly young have not yet had their innocence challenged. They are able to trust and believe until their trust and belief are disappointed. But that is not the end of it.

Hope and trust are not lost to us – they simply require an act of will. Advent is a time when we are called to trust in the power of love, even when it does not seem possible. Advent is a time when we can choose to see the truth of the miracle of God's love for us, even when it does not meet our immediate expectations. Most of all, Advent is a time when if we are vulnerable enough to believe, we will see. If we let down the guards of our hearts and still the chattering of our minds we will see the possible, and in seeing it, we will know it to be true.

How will we know him? We will know him in abundance.

Then Jesus called his disciples to him and said, 'I have compassion for the crowd, because they have been with me now for three days and have nothing to eat; and I do not want to send them away hungry, for they might faint on the way.' The disciples said to him, 'Where are we to get enough bread in the desert to feed so great a crowd?' Jesus asked them, 'How many loaves have you?' They said, 'Seven, and a few small fish.' Then ordering the crowd to sit down on the ground, he took the seven loaves and the fish; and after giving thanks he broke them and gave them to the disciples, and the disciples gave them to the crowds. And all of them ate and were filled; and they took up the broken pieces left over, seven baskets full. Those who had eaten were four thousand men, besides women and children. (Matthew 15:32-38)

In every generation of the church, one evangelist or another surges to popularity by promising physical financial prosperity to the faithful. "God wants you to be rich, and if you aren't it must be because your faith is insufficient." These so-called Gospels of prosperity miss the point entirely. Being a person of faith is not a promise of riches. In fact, it means that you will most likely have less material wealth than if you were not sharing it with others.

But what does happen when a community recognizes Christ in its midst and is freed from the captivity of fear of loss? Everybody shares and everybody benefits from the sharing. The community realizes that not only is there enough to go around, but that there is an abundance. Everyone is taken care of and there are basketfuls left over.

This sign – Jesus' multiplication of the loaves and fishes – is the guarantee that in God's economy there is always enough. That was one of the first and most important ways that the people saw and recognized Jesus in their midst. His presence changed things – people, food, attitudes – to the extent that the needs of all were met. Of course, it is true that this story is metaphorical. Was it the feeding of the 4000 or of the 5000? Was it on the mount or on the plain? Were there seven baskets left over, or was it twelve? Clearly, those details are not the most important parts of the account. The important part is that the sovereignty of Jesus, and his divine authority are revealed in his ability to make what is at hand sufficient to meet the present need.

How will we know him? We will know him by acting on his word.

'Not everyone who says to me, "Lord, Lord", will enter the kingdom of heaven, but only one who does the will of my Father in heaven. On that day many will say to me, "Lord, Lord, did we not prophesy in your name, and cast out demons in your name, and do many deeds of power in your name?" Then I will declare to them, "I never knew you; go away from me, you evildoers." 'Everyone then who hears these words of mine and acts on them will be like a wise man who built his house on rock. The rain fell, the floods came, and the winds blew and beat on that house, but it did not fall, because it had been founded on rock. And everyone who hears these words of mine and does not act on them will be like a foolish man who built his house on sand. The rain fell, and the floods came, and the winds blew and beat against that house, and it fell—and great was its fall!' (Matthew 7:21-27)

We have all known people who are adept at pretending at friendship and trust. Those are the folks who always agree with you so long as you are in their presence, and then forget what you said the moment you walk away. Or they are the ones who value your friendship so long as it is expedient to do so, and is not too much trouble. They are not the sort who will sit up with you all night at the sickbed of your child, or walk with your through the ravaged landscape of grief or loss.

Those are the types of people that Jesus warns us against becoming ourselves. And just as we can recognize when someone is not fully invested in a relationship with us, Jesus recognizes whether or not we are fully invested in a relationship with him. It is not enough to invoke his name in public, or praise him in prayer or worship. Are we willing to make him the foundation of our lives? Are we willing to build the houses of our spirits on the rock of trust in him? It is easy to "talk the talk", as the saying goes. It is much more difficult to walk the walk. We know that there are storms and challenges in life and that it is only by building on the bedrock of a living and active faith in Christ that we will be able to survive the storms.

In this first week of Advent, do your own "home inspection". What is the condition of your heart's home? It may be weather-beaten, but that does not mean that it is not solid. It may be cosmetically perfect but that glorious exterior may hide a foundation that is subject to cracking and erosion. Now is the time to shore up your faith, and your relationship with the One in whom you may safely and eternally place your trust.

How will we know him? We will know him when we trust him.

As Jesus went on from there, two blind men followed him, crying loudly, 'Have mercy on us, Son of David!' When he entered the house, the blind men came to him; and Jesus said to them, 'Do you believe that I am able to do this?' They said to him, 'Yes, Lord.' Then he touched their eyes and said, 'According to your faith let it be done to you.' And their eyes were opened. Then Jesus sternly ordered them, 'See that no one knows of this.' But they went away and spread the news about him throughout that district. (Matthew 9:27-31)

I wonder what the world and our experience of it would be like if we really trusted that even half of what we say about God is true. It is as though there is a list of magnificent attributes assigned to God, and we go blithely along without ever stopping to ask ourselves if the descriptors we are using are accurate – or even desirable. God is all good, all powerful, all knowing, all loving. But much of what we say about God is very vague and keeps Jesus the Christ at arm's length – close enough to blame, and far enough away to ignore.

That is not the case with the two blind men in this passage. They want Jesus to be close enough to help them, and they trust that he will be able to do so. When Jesus asks them if they believe that he can do what they ask, he is not trying to test their faith. He is insisting that they articulate it. He does not say, "If you believe in me, I will heal you." He says, "Do you agree that I have the power to do this? Then say so!" It is not that their healing is contingent upon or in proportion to their faith; it is that their healing is only possible because they recognize that he is the Messiah. There is a big difference!

This is not to say that those who do not accept the power of Jesus to heal will not be healed – although one might wonder whether such a person would ask Jesus for healing. Nor is it that they believed hard enough. That too, is missing the point. This story is here in the gospel as a witness to the fact that Jesus is the messiah and that as such, he has the inherent ability to provide what they need.

What does Jesus' role as Messiah mean to you? What power do you recognize in him, even if it is not in direct response to one of your own needs? And are you willing to make a public declaration of who he is? That, too, is the work of Advent.

How will we know him? We will know him by those who follow him.

"Then Jesus went about all the cities and villages, teaching in their synagogues, and proclaiming the good news of the kingdom, and curing every disease and every sickness. When he saw the crowds, he had compassion for them, because they were harassed and helpless, like sheep without a shepherd. Then he said to his disciples, 'The harvest is plentiful, but the labourers are few; therefore ask the Lord of the harvest to send out labourers into his harvest.' Then Jesus summoned his twelve disciples and gave them authority over unclean spirits, to cast them out, and to cure every disease and every sickness. These are the names of the twelve apostles: first, Simon, also known as Peter, and his brother Andrew; James son of Zebedee, and his brother John; Philip and Bartholomew; Thomas and Matthew the tax-collector; James son of Alphaeus, and Thaddaeus; Simon the Cananaean, and Judas Iscariot, the one who betrayed him. These twelve Jesus sent out with the following instructions: 'Go nowhere among the Gentiles, and enter no town of the Samaritans, but go rather to the lost sheep of the house of Israel. As you go, proclaim the good news, "The kingdom of heaven has come near." Cure the sick, raise the dead, cleanse the lepers, cast out demons. You received without payment; give without payment." *(Matthew 9:35-10:8)*

What if the fate of the church's work in the world really did rest on what folks think about those who call themselves Christians and follow Jesus? How much of what we do is an accurate reflection of the work to which we are called? Fortunately, the Holy Spirit is able to use us even when we are less than effective. And after all, it is God who builds the church and who calls us into the body of Christ. I also doubt that the disciples were all that worried about what people might think about the church, as their "church" was hardly anything we would recognize as such today. But I do believe that they cared very much about making Jesus and his love and works known in the world.

I also think it is essential to realize just how much Jesus trusted them. Jesus sends them out to do all the things necessary for proclaiming that the kingdom of heaven is at hand. The healings, and the miracles, and the good works are important, but only as vehicles for getting the attention of folks who do not yet recognize that God is with us. Jesus trusted them with everything, including his reputation.

He also trusts us that much. He abides in each one of us, and empowers us to share the Good News with all that we meet. What are you doing with that gift? What kind of stewardship are you exercising over that trust? Make this Advent a time when you do your best to represent the work that Jesus has given you to do.

Healing and Forgiveness of Sin:

When he saw their faith, he said, "Friend, your sins are forgiven you....I say to you, stand up and take your bed and go to your home." (Luke 5:20, 24b)

I do not believe that we get sick because we are sinful. Nor do I believe that healing is contingent on the degree of faith of the sick or injured person. If either of those things were true, healing would be out of the reach of any of us. What I do believe is that if we are burdened with a sense of guilt or unconfessed sin, the weight of that burden may make us feel ill. Notice that I am not saying that sin or guilt creates illness. I am saying that there is an extraordinary connection between spiritual health and a feeling of wholeness; and when our spirits are ill, the best physical health in the world will not make us whole.

When Jesus heals the paralyzed man, he does not ask him how he became injured or what sins he might have committed. Jesus cuts straight to the matter at hand. It is as though he is saying to the man, *"We can all see that you are paralyzed, and that your friends had to carry you here. But I can see that you are also in need of spiritual healing, so before I restore your ability to walk, you need to know that you are free and loved and spiritually whole. Your sins are forgiven."*

We know that the awareness of unconfessed sin can weigh us down; and guilt can create a lifetime of suffering and alienation. Worst of all is what happens when we have been falsely told that we are guilty, shameful or unworthy. We don't know if this is the case with this paralyzed man and we are given no clue as to his spiritual condition. What we do know is that Jesus believed that healing must start from within.

If this seems like a really odd topic for Advent, ask yourself: Am I slogging through Advent with a sense of heaviness in my soul? Am I avoiding entering into the anticipation of the coming of the Christ Child because I don't believe that I deserve to be happy? Is there something weighing on my conscience that makes me feel unworthy to join in the celebration?

If you are answering "yes" to any of these questions, you are being invited to make Advent a time of spiritual healing. You deserve to hear the voice of Jesus as he says to you, "Friend, your sins are forgive. Pray, and you will know what to do, and where to seek and find help for your healing.

All the Sheep in the Manger

"What do you think? If a shepherd has a hundred sheep and one of them has gone astray, does he not leave the ninety-nine on the mountains and go in search of the one that went astray?" (Matthew 18:12)

Some of the best and most endearing family stories are about Christmas Pageants. My siblings recount with great glee the year that I was the Angel Gabriel in the pageant at Goose Creek Baptist Church. I had the 2nd chapter of Luke nailed and was acting as the narrator. When I got to the point "Fear not! For behold I bring you good tidings of great joy, my voice broke and the phrase "fear not" sounded something akin to a slide-whistle. More Harpo Marx than angelic. My mother's family told the tale of her forgetting her lines altogether and yelling into the audience "I forgot it, Aunt Ada!" And of course there was the year that my eldest son was a six month old babe in the manger. The angel had to hold him steady as most of him didn't fit into the trough. That's the best memory of all!

A few years back our pageant at St. Francis was blessed with 20+ toddlers – all dressed as sheep and crawling up the center aisle. Their "ba-ahs" rang out almost as loudly as their giggles and the "oohs and ahs" of their parents. And one or two of them never made it to the manger at all – either standing up and bolting for the nearest set of maternal knees or simply sitting there in the aisle looking terrified until mom or dad swooped down to rescue them.

Lately I have come to wonder if each of these stories is part of the way that Jesus sees us. We always seem to be either flubbing our lines or getting lost on the way to the manger. In terms of Advent, I think that this tale of the lost sheep works really well as an example of how the crèche is not complete until the shepherd has brought all of us to the manger. None of us should be wandering around in the cold and the dark when there is warmth and shelter inside.

So, today, as an Advent meditation, I would like to suggest that you spend some time thinking about the fact that you are of such worth to the shepherd that he will leave the ninety-nine on the mountainside to go and make sure that you are safe. Not because the ninety-nine are not equally precious, but because without you and your great worth, the flock is not whole.

Leaving Your Burdens at the Crèche

"Come unto me all you that are weary and are carrying heavy burdens and I will give you rest." (Matthew 11:28)

Yesterday I suggested that you imagine yourself as the missing lamb from the manger scene and that you remember the lengths to which the Good Shepherd will go to bring you home. Today I invite you to visit the crèche once again...this time as a weary and overburdened traveler who, seeing the light, stumbles into the manger seeking rest and refuge.

Look at the figures gathered there – parents hovering over an infant, assorted livestock finding warmth and shelter huddled against one another, and other visitors who stand in silence observing the scene. The visitors seem to have been invited as witnesses to the event. But you, you are there simply because you are too cold and tired and beaten-down to go any further.

You move toward the light and see the faces of the child and his parents. The parents eyes, though happy, show signs of worry and care. They look at you and with a nod invite you in. But the child, who does not yet know the weight of life, catches you in the freshness and infinite potential of the depth of his eyes. And, suddenly, you remember. You remember that you were not always so tired, or so burdened. You remember when your back was straight and running was a joy. Most of all you remember that the heavy pack upon your back is there by your own choice and filled with things that you have chosen to carry.

And in that moment, you choose to allow the infant's gaze to free you from your self-imposed load of care. You do not go through the pack choosing those things that you ought to continue to carry. You do not ask permission to let go of those things that others have placed upon your shoulders. You do not even walk outside to find a more seemly place to deposit the burdens of a lifetime. You simply shrug the pack off and let it fall.

For it is not only Christ's work at Easter that frees us. It is his very presence in the world that saves us, and the power of the Christ Child's gaze heals us just as surely as does his passion. Go to the manger and be healed. Leave your burdens there and be renewed by his coming.

John and Jesus

"...among those born of women no one has arisen greater than John the Baptist; yet the least in the kingdom of heaven is greater than he." (Matthew 11:11)

According to the Gospel of Luke, John the Baptist is about six months older than his cousin, Jesus. Their mothers Elizabeth and Mary, are cousins, and even in the womb, John recognizes that Jesus is the Messiah.

In Matthew, however, they do not seem to know each other as cousins. In fact, only a few verses before these today, John, who is in prison, has sent messengers to Jesus asking him to confirm that he is the Messiah. Mark gives John the role of the prophet who proclaims the coming of the Messiah and then baptizes him. John the evangelist also portrays John the Baptist as the forerunner prophet, who does not know Jesus personally but who baptizes him and more importantly, is the one who bears witness to Jesus as the "lamb of God who takes away the sin of the world." But, only in Luke are Jesus and John related by family.

What this tells us is that while each of the gospel writers knew of John the Baptist, each of them wrote of John and Jesus in terms of what they considered most important – that Jesus was the Messiah and that John the Baptist was the prophet who recognized and proclaimed that truth.

The season of Advent is an opportunity for us to be prophets as well. We already know that we will find the Messiah as a baby in Bethlehem. But like John, we are also called to prepare the way for him, and to announce his arrival. For that is the foundation of belief. And it is very telling that Jesus himself recognizes and affirms the importance of this prophetic ministry. John is the greatest of the prophets. Yet those who will come to believe, and in believing enter the kingdom of heaven, are even greater than John.

That's a pretty good indication that we can, in our everyday lives, and in our observance of Advent, be folk who announce the coming of the light. We can prepare the way of the Lord by opening our own hearts to his coming and by offering as straight and clear a path as we can.

Today, be alert for any opportunity that God presents for you to proclaim the coming of the Messiah; and when that opportunity comes, speak up!

Feast or Fast in Advent

"But to what will I compare this generation? It is like children sitting in the marketplaces and calling to one another, 'we played the flute for you and you did not dance; we wailed, and you did not mourn.' For John came neither eating nor drinking, and they say, 'He has a demon'; the son of Man came eating and drinking, and they say, 'Look a glutton and a drunkard.'" (Matthew 11:16-19)

Some Christians prefer a quiet and contemplative experience of Advent. Others enter into the season with a growing sense of anticipation and excitement. Which group is doing Advent "right?" As usual, it's not about the right or the wrong way, it's a matter of intention. What are you intending to accomplish in this season? What difference do you hope that it will make in your experience of the miracle of Incarnation?

There is great value in either approach. Quiet reflection and self-examination may open your heart to deep and profound gratitude for the birth of the Messiah. Joyous anticipation may renew your spirit and open your heart to the world around you.

In these verses from Matthew's Gospel, Jesus speaks with irony of the fact that no matter how holiness is expressed someone is likely to be critical and condemning. The same people who judged John the Baptist for being ascetic, condemned Jesus for being undisciplined. The truth is, we human beings have a remarkable ability to find ways to protect ourselves from truths that we do not wish to examine. And one of those truths is that the Holy Spirit speaks to different people in different ways. We might think that it would be easier if all people of faith could share a common vision of how to worship, and how to observe the Holy Days. But that is not how God works. The marvelous diversity of God-given human personalities means that we will not all do things the same way – and that is a gift and a glory.

So open your eyes and your hearts to the wonderful variety of ways in which your brothers and sisters in the family of God are preparing for the coming of Christmas. It's all good, because it is all a gift from God.

Blinded By Anticipation

And the disciples asked him, "Why then, do the scribes say that Elijah must come first?" He replied, "Elijah is indeed coming and will restore all things; but I tell you that Elijah has already come and they did not recognize him." (Matthew 17:10-12a)

Why is it so difficult for us to recognize glory when it is staring us in the face? I think that is because it seldom meets our expectations of what it should look like.

Perhaps the same thing is true of Advent and Christmas. We may become so bound up in our anticipation of what the season is and our expectations of what it will bring to us that we allow it to slip right past us without our noticing. That's why I believe that it is essential for us to set aside time each Advent to simply be in the presence of the Holy. Choose a block of time (as little as 15 minutes) to go apart from the business of your life, to sit quietly and to ask yourself, "What is God doing in my life this year? Right now?" Try not to use the time to remember past Advents and Christmases. Don't compare your expectations to your experiences, and don't fall into the trap of wondering whether this year is the one that will finally be the joyous event that you hope it will be. The past is done, and the future is not yet here. Spend the time quietly looking at what is actually happening now, this year.

And if you discover that you cannot slow down enough to do that, remember that even in that distraction, God is telling you something. Ask, "Why is it that I cannot spare 15 minutes to be present to the Good News that God is coming?" And whatever rises to the surface of your mind as the reason that you simply cannot spare the time – that is the thing that you most need to offer to God in prayer and then (at least for the 15 minutes), step away from. It will be there when you return.

Advent deserves this attention. You deserve this attention. The Christ Child most certainly deserves this attention. It is not about creating perfection in ourselves or in our environments. This is about mindfulness and being present to God here and now. For, it is a very sad thing to expend the time and energy that we do getting ready for the holidays only to discover that when they are past, we have once again avoided really experiencing them.

"By What Authority?"

When he entered the temple, the chief priests and the elders of the people came to him as he was teaching, and said, "By what authority are you doing these things, and who gave you this authority?" Jesus said to them, "I will also ask you one question; if you tell me the answer, then I will also tell you by what authority I do these things. Did the baptism of John come from heaven, or was it of human origin?" And they argued with one another, "If we say, 'From heaven,' he will say to us, 'Why then did you not believe him?' But if we say, 'Of human origin,' we are afraid of the crowd; for all regard John as a prophet." So they answered Jesus, "We do not know." And he said to them, "Neither will I tell you by what authority I am doing these things. Matthew 21:23-27

"By what authority are you doing this?" I don't know about you, but I find this one of the most irritating questions imaginable. I am not saying that it is not a necessary, even prudent question for us all to ask from time to time. It is just that I find it very annoying when it is addressed to me!

To put the best possible spin on it, this question is an honest attempt to ascertain the validity of our actions; it's a sort of "show me your badge, officer" moment. But why are these people in the temple asking Jesus this question, and what does it have to do with Advent? Well, Jesus is behaving in a manner that is challenging some of their bedrock assumptions about their faith, and about how God acts in the world. Besides, no one likes having their spiritual turf invaded. Their incredulity is understandable. But, on the other hand, their appreciation of the fact that they recognize that Jesus has set them a trick question reveals that their questions were not entirely academic.

How about us? Are his words putting us on the defensive? Are our actions congruent with what we are saying? Just as Advent heralds the beginning of the Church Year, this season is the time when God in Christ may be teaching us something new about ourselves and our faith. But one of the greatest challenges to learning something new at this time of year is tradition, and the fact that we want this season to be stable and predictable and to reliably replicate what we expect of it. The problem is that if we rely on tradition as the only valid source of authority, we may miss something.

But there is good news here. The elders and priests even stumble upon it. Sometimes "we don't know" is the best answer. We don't know what this Advent will bring. But if we are open to experiencing what God has for us, we will find out.

Genuine Integrity

"What do you think? A man had two sons; he went to the first and said, 'Son, go and work in the vineyard today.' He answered, 'I will not'; but later he changed his mind and went. The father went to the second and said the same; and he answered, 'I go, sir'; but he did not go. Which of the two did the will of his father?" They said, "The first." Jesus said to them, "Truly I tell you, the tax collectors and the prostitutes are going into the kingdom of God ahead of you. For John came to you in the way of righteousness and you did not believe him, but the tax collectors and the prostitutes believed him; and even after you saw it, you did not change your minds and believe him. Matthew 21: 28-32

My son, once posted on his FB page *"My fellow Episcopalians: Of all the ditches in which to die, is complaining about Christmas trees in Advent really the best choice?"*

Without analyzing this comment beyond what is obvious (and yes, he DID grow up in a house with a Christmas tree in Advent), I do think that this question is very pertinent to this passage in Matthew. What Jesus seems to want us to read, learn, mark and inwardly digest is that it is far more important that in the end we do the correct thing rather just saying what is expected of us and neglecting to act at all.

How many of us talk about keeping Advent and Christmas (with or without a lighted tree in the house) and then behave as though the season doesn't matter at all? Or how many of us harrumph and scrooge our way through the holidays only to be struck dumb by the glory of a starlit night and the singing "Silent Night" by Candlelight?

We don't have to be spiritual descendants of Ebenezer Scrooge to make this mistake. Any time that we judge the way our neighbors, or our communities, or our townships, choose to celebrate (or not) the Christmas season, we are running the risk of behaving like the second brother. And we leave ourselves precious little space in which to be loving or charitable toward those who do not share our particular spiritual practice.

So, when Jesus tells us that the less desirable elements of society may be in line ahead of us at the pearly gates, he is also telling us is that there are ditches, and then there are ditches. And sometimes we can get so busy digging them that we decide to take up residence right there in the dirt and the mud.

Daily Visitation

Purify our conscience, Almighty God, by your daily visitation, that your Son Jesus Christ, at his coming, may find in us a mansion prepared for himself; who lives and reigns with you, in the unity of the Holy Spirit, one God, now and forever. Amen."

Visitation is not a word we use every day. It has a rather formal ring to it, and is most often used to describe grand or solemn religious occasions. When the pregnant Virgin Mary traveled to visit her also pregnant elderly cousin, Elizabeth, that event became known as "The Visitation of Our Lady." When a diocesan bishop comes to a parish for confirmation, baptisms or a regular review of its ministry, that's what's known as an "Episcopal Visitation." And in previous versions of the Book of Common Prayer, the rite for Ministration to Sick was known as the Order for the "Visitation of the Sick".

So it might appear a bit unusual to see the word "visitation" used in this context in the Collect of the Day for this coming Sunday, in which we ask God to visit us daily in order to help us prepare for the visitation of Christ to our souls.

Mary's visitation to Elizabeth was a once in a lifetime event; bishops' visitations are typically once every 18 months or so; and visits to the sick are limited to times of need. But here, as we prepare for Christmas and the coming of the Christ Child, we are reminded that God does not restrict visits to us to Christmas time. They are daily, and they continue throughout our lives – because they are intended to transform our hearts into mansions prepared for the coming of Christ into our lives – which also happens daily.

What a thought! Every day, no matter how well or ill-prepared we are, God is coming to visit us and to make an announcement of ultimate importance. "I am coming to you today. I am here to help you be prepared. I am coming to you tomorrow. And I am here to help you be prepared...always."

Waiting for the Messiah

...and sent them to the Lord to ask, "Are you the one who is to come, or are we to wait for another?" When the men had come to him, they said, "John the Baptist has sent us to you to ask, 'Are you the one who is to come, or are we to wait for another?'" Jesus had just then cured many people of diseases, plagues, and evil spirits, and had given sight to many who were blind. And he answered them, "Go and tell John what you have seen and heard: the blind receive their sight, the lame walk, the lepers are cleansed, the deaf hear, the dead are raised, the poor have good news brought to them. And blessed is anyone who takes no offense at me." Luke 7:19-23

When we look at the life of John the Baptist, it is easy to understand why he might be tired of waiting for the messiah. It's also no wonder that he is losing some confidence in his trust of who Jesus might be. He is in prison awaiting death, so it is no wonder that he wants reassurance that he has not wasted his life proclaiming the wrong message.

But notice how Jesus answers. He does not criticize or judge John for his lack of faith. Instead, he answers the question that John is really asking. What John wants to know is "How will I know that you are the one? How can I trust that I have done the right thing in devoting my life to preparing the way for the messiah?" And Jesus, who seldom directly answers a question, does not say yes or no. He sends them back with a message something like this. "Here is what I am doing. Do you think that I am the one? Am I doing what you expect of the messiah?"

And that is where we come into the story. What does a messiah do? The messiah heals and restores. The messiah redeems that which is lost. The messiah brings hope to those who would otherwise have little or no hope. The question for us becomes "Is Jesus the messiah?" If Jesus is the messiah, doing those things that we would expect a messiah to do, then what are we waiting for? Why are we not proclaiming that he has come and that he is with us? Why do we not act? Is it because we still doubt who he is?

The season of Advent is for us a time of interior waiting. It is a time when we prepare our hearts to receive once again the gift of the Christ Child. This annually renewable gift is one of the things that feeds us for the work we are called to do. But when it comes to doing that work, to actively engaging a ministry that proclaims the reign of Christ, the time of waiting is over. Now is the time.

What Are We Looking For?

When John's messengers had gone, Jesus began to speak to the crowds about John: "What did you go out into the wilderness to look at? A reed shaken by the wind? What then did you go out to see? Someone dressed in soft robes? Look, those who put on fine clothing and live in luxury are in royal palaces. What then did you go out to see? A prophet? Yes, I tell you, and more than a prophet. This is the one about whom it is written, 'See, I am sending my messenger ahead of you, who will prepare your way before you.' I tell you, among those born of women no one is greater than John; yet the least in the kingdom of God is greater than he." (And all the people who heard this, including the tax collectors, acknowledged the justice of God, because they had been baptized with John's baptism. But by refusing to be baptized by him, the Pharisees and the lawyers rejected God's purpose for themselves.) Luke 7: 24-30

Over the years of our marriage, Will and I have come up with a phrase for describing people that we respect or admire – "Let's invite him/her to dinner." I have heard others say things like "That's the sort of guy you'd like to have a beer with."

I rather doubt that John the Baptist would be on either of those guest lists. And if he were, I suspect that he would decline the invitation. He would monopolize the conversation, criticize everyone present, and talk about precisely those things that everyone else would be too polite to mention. As a prophet, John had an opinion, and a message on every topic. And he did not care what others thought of him.

So I have to wonder, just a bit...if Jesus were to send John to speak to us today, would we be willing to listen to him? And I also wonder just how often Jesus sends folks like John the Baptist – folks whose manner of presentation we find offensive or embarrassing – only to have us ignore or laugh them off.

Today, let's all listen to the prophets whose messages disturb us. Bear in mind that some of them may, in fact, be false prophets who are not deserving of being listened to; that sort are fairly easy to spot. But some of them may be bringing us a challenging but essential message. There's a fail-proof method of determining which is which. The way to recognize a real prophet is by the fruit that their message bears. Does it bring love and truth into the world (even if we don't approve of the method)? Does it make us take a closer look at our own lives and suppositions? Does it help us be prepared for the coming of Christ and Christmas?

New Occasions Teach New Duties

Then they said to him, "John's disciples, like the disciples of the Pharisees, frequently fast and pray, but your disciples eat and drink. Jesus said to them, "You cannot make wedding guests fast while the bridegroom is with them, can you? The days will come when the bridegroom will be taken away from them, and then they will fast in those days." He also told them a parable: "No one tears a piece from a new garment and sews it on an old garment; otherwise the new will be torn, and the piece from the new will not match the old. Luke 5:33-36

One of the saddest things in the world for me is seeing the way the world rushes head-long toward Christmas Day, staggers through most of the 24 hours and then immediately packs up, turns off the lights, and leaves the bedraggled tree on the curb. When I see that I want to knock on the door of the house and say, "Please, don't cheat yourself this way, Christmas lasts for 12 days! Laugh, celebrate, feast and party! Lent is coming soon enough."

God coming into the world is cause for the joyous abandon of a hope-fulfilled heart. Don't let it come and go in a flash of exhaustion. Take the time to savor this season. Take the time to look into the faces of the Angels, the Holy Family, the Shepherds, the Magi, and all the cattle and livestock in the manger. God is with us, in human form, in the glory of life.

Yes, it was a new idea when God did it 2000 years ago. And yes, it will be a new idea for many of us today. But that is no excuse for succumbing to the idea that once the presents are opened and exchanged that everyone should run back to the treadmill.

It's neither too early nor too late to let the joy into your heart. Take a deep breath, smile, thank God for the love that surrounds you, and dust off your dancing shoes. You've been invited to a party! It starts in just a few days and it's not too late to R.S.V.P.

And it's not just any party, either. It's a 12 day birthday party for the God of all Creation. Why on earth would we want to miss out on that Celebration?

Hail Mary, Full of Grace

In those days Mary set out and went with haste to a Judean town in the hill country, where she entered the house of Zechariah and greeted Elizabeth. When Elizabeth heard Mary's greeting, the child leaped in her womb. And Elizabeth was filled with the Holy Spirit and exclaimed with a loud cry, "Blessed are you among women, and blessed is the fruit of your womb. And why has this happened to me, that the mother of my Lord comes to me? For as soon as I heard the sound of your greeting, the child in my womb leaped for joy. And blessed is she who believed that there would be a fulfillment of what was spoken to her by the Lord." Luke 1: 39-45

God most assuredly could have accomplished the Incarnation without human assistance. But God did not choose to do so. God choose to become Incarnate by being born into the human family…born of a woman, sheltered by a man, surrounded by brothers and sisters and cousins, and living amid all the grace and grit of human life. God chose to need us, and to invite us to share in making Incarnation possible.

I believe that is why Christmas has the power to reduce all of us to tears of joy. Nearly everyone weeps when the congregation sings "Silent Night" on a candlelit Christmas Eve. The thing that brings tears of joyful astonishment to my eyes is the thought of the divinity of God residing in a human infant. God really does believe that we creatures are good enough!

There is another line in a Christmas hymn that it has taken me decades to come to understand – "Lo, he abhors not the Virgin's womb." (O Come, All Ye Faithful") Throughout most of my adult/childbearing years I had railed against what I was interpreting as some crusty old misogynist's version of "too bad the only way to become human is to be born of a woman!"

But one day I looked at it differently, and it made all the difference in the world. What if "lo, he abhors not the virgin's womb" literally means the same thing as the Ave Maria?

Hail Mary, full of grace. The Lord is with you!
Blessed are you among women, and blessed is the fruit of your womb!"

Bands of Love

And she gave birth to her firstborn son and wrapped him in bands of cloth and laid him in a manger because there was no place for them in the inn. (Luke 2:7)

Although continuously practiced throughout the world, swaddling babies has only very recently returned to popularity in this country. When my first grandchild was born, I was surprised to see how snugly he was wrapped. I was even more surprised to see how much happier a baby he was when he was securely wrapped. My son and his wife are of a generation that has realized the benefit of maintaining some of the security that an infant feels in the closeness of the womb. Aside from the warmth that swaddling provides, it comforts a newborn who has little or no control over its limbs and may be startled or disturbed by its own erratic motion.

Swaddling helps infants learn to live more peaceably in this world. I think that is true throughout life – we humans tend to be better off when we are not flailing about.

We also do much better when we are aware that we are loved. When the arms of a parent, a friend, or a lover surround us, we know that we are being enfolded in love. This awareness is even more intense when we realize that God continually surrounds and enfolds us in bands of love. Just as Mary swaddled Jesus, and Drew and April swaddled their sons until they were old enough to have some control over their muscles, God holds us close.

And even after we have begun to move through life on our own, we all need a good warm embrace every now and then. That is especially true of the times in our lives like the Christmas holidays when we are over-tired, or overwhelmed or feel unequal to the often self-imposed expectations of the season. That's when we are most likely to begin to flail about.

So, today, please, stop and take a deep breath. Feel the warmth of God's swaddling embrace and the security of knowing that you are a precious and beloved child of God. Know, too, that you are not merely an observer at the Christmas Crèche. There is room for you and God loves you just as surely as Mary and Joseph loved Jesus.

CHRISTMAS

December 25th: The True Light

"The true light which enlightens everyone was coming into the world. (John 1:9)

Around the world last night, hundreds of millions of faces were lit by candlelight as Christians knelt in prayer, singing Silent Night. Others may have gathered around candles at a family table or sat in the soft light of fireplace. Still others may have come together around Christmas tree where the light in their faces was not the reflected glow of a candle, but the reflection of the joy and wonder in a child's eyes. Our Holy Night occurs at the darkest time of the year, just days past the winter solstice; and reminds us that no matter how dark it is outside, the light of Christ is now in the world and always will be.

This is the true light – the light of God in Christ among us. And remember, as Charles Dickens wrote, this light does not burn for just one night. It burns all year, and if we just pay attention, we will see that is visible in every action of love and care. It is to our great loss that we so often forget.

It is also a great loss when we do not "keep" Christmas for its full twelve days. What a shame that so many of us allow the light in our faces to flicker and dim as soon as the presents are unwrapped, or as soon as we notice that there are dishes to wash!

Don't do that this year! Resolve, right now while the tree is still up, and the echoes of the angel songs are still in your ears, that you will honor the light in a human face (your own or another's) each day for the next 12 days. Smile at people, wish them a Merry Christmas, remind them of how loved they are. God willing, you may even be the source of their face lighting up!

December 26th: The Feast of St. Stephen ~ 2nd Day of Christmas

Good King Wenceslas looked out, on the Feast of Stephen,
Where the snow lay round about, deep and crisp and even.

Therefore, Christian men, be sure – wealth or rank possessing
Ye who now will bless the poor -- shall yourselves find blessing!

What was it that made King Wenceslas, "good" when he looked out at his realm on the Feast of Stephen? It was the fact that he followed the example of Stephen, who was the first deacon, by attending to the needs of the poor and the lonely in his country.

So strong was this understanding that good sovereigns and leaders care for the poor that the more pious and righteous kings were known to be willing to walk through the snow to bring help to their impoverished subjects.

In Britain, this day is also observed as "Boxing Day" – a time when employers gave gifts to their servants and employees. More recently, it is observed as a day for visiting family and friends with Christmas gifts and greetings.

So, how will you observe the Feast of Stephen? I can think of no better way of observing the Second Day of Christmas than by honoring St. Stephen by helping those who need help. Make a donation to a local charity. Better yet, sign up to make a regular contribution to a local charity. Charities that operate food pantries or soup kitchens or provide assistance with heating costs are especially appropriate on this day.

Or visit someone who is sick, or shut-in, or simply lonely. Or, give a gift to someone who is not expecting it.

And no matter how you observe this day, remember that you take the light of Christ with you. Let it shine in you and on those you meet.

December 27th: The Feast of St. John ~ 3rd Day of Christmas

Shed upon your Church, O Lord, the brightness of your light, that we, being illumined by the teaching of your apostle and evangelist John, may so walk in the light of your truth, that at length we may attain to the fullness of eternal life; through Jesus Christ, our Lord, who lives and reigns with you and the Holy Spirit, one God, for ever and ever. Amen.

Although best known as the "beloved disciple" who was favored by Jesus and entrusted with the care of Jesus' mother after the crucifixion, John is also thought to be the author of the Gospel and the Epistles of John. His symbol is the Eagle and his theme is the Light of Divine Love.

The chalice (cup) is also one of the symbols of St. John. In the Gospel of Matthew James and John send their mother to ask Jesus to grant her sons the privilege of sitting at his right and left hand in heaven. Jesus' response to that request is "no." But he tells her sons that they will surely drink from the same cup as he will. The story is amplified by a legend that John (who was the only of the twelve apostles to die of old age rather than martyrdom) was once handed a cup of poisoned wine, and that when he blessed it, the poison turned to a serpent which rose up out of the cup.

That legend is certainly an evocative one. Many adults have learned the hard way that too much wine definitely carries the serpent's sting the morning after. But because John's blessing rendered the poisoned cup harmless, this day has become associated with the blessing and drinking of wine.

In some places it has become traditional to bring a bottle of wine to Church to be blessed for the evening meal on the Feast of St. John. Of course, you can also bless your own meal, and your own preferred beverage, by sharing it with friends and family.

Wine, in moderation of course (and only for those who can safely and legally consume it), is a good way to celebrate the 3rd day of Christmas. The important thing is to remember the Love of God and to give thanks for the gift of the Christ Child among us.

December 28th: Holy Innocents – 4th Day of Christmas

Almighty God, heavenly Father, you have blessed us with the joy and care of children: Give us calm and patient wisdom as we bring them up, that we may teach them to love whatever is just and true and good, following the example of our Savior Jesus Christ. (Collect For the Care of Children)

How can we possibly "celebrate" the fourth day of Christmas when it commemorates Herod's slaughter of all the male children of Bethlehem under the age of two? We cannot celebrate their death, and so we do not. But we can observe the day by remembering all the "holy innocents" who perish through starvation, illness, violence and neglect.

On this day, we can remember that so long as there is sin in this world, our joy will be dampened by the suffering of others. We can then take that awareness and put it to work by shining the light of the truth into those places of shadow and darkness in which our fellow human beings continue to suffer and die without recourse to help.

You might want to educate yourself today about efforts toward eradicating childhood illnesses, or malaria, or human trafficking, or child slavery. For example, most of us are not aware that much of the chocolate we purchase and consume is farmed and harvested by child slaves. One very simple thing that you can do to force reform in that area is to refuse to purchase chocolate candy unless it is labeled "fair trade."

This does not mean that you should not celebrate the 4th day of Christmas! This is a day for the Light of Christ to shine all the more brightly on the world – as a reminder that we have the ability to protect the weak and vulnerable, and that we are committed to doing so. Celebrate today by acting to help the helpless, and by cherishing and loving the children in your life.

December 29th: 5th Day of Christmas

"Angels from the realms of glory, wing your flight o'er all the earth.
Ye who sang creation's story, now proclaim Messiah's birth:
Come and worship, come and worship, worship Christ the newborn King."
(James Montgomery)

I love this hymn, and am especially fond of the present-tense energy in these lines (above) from the first verse. The same angels that sang Creation's story in the beginning now sing throughout the earth the Good News of the Messiah's birth.

When we sing this hymn, we join the angels in their proclamation and we bring the birth of Christ out of the pages of history and onto the stage of the here and now. For we are surrounded by the angels whose calling it is to sing praises continually before the throne of God, and to lead us in the song.

Everything that God has done is good and is to be praised by all creation, from the angels of heaven to each human heart. And this event, the coming of God into the world, is a sign of God's perfect love for creation. It is also the culmination of God's time-less and time-full intention to be fully present with us. There can be only one response to this Good News – Come and Worship!

December 30th: 6th Day of Christmas

What child is this, who laid to rest on Mary's lap is sleeping?
Whom angels greet with anthems sweet while shepherds watch are keeping.
This, this is Christ the King whom shepherds guard and angels sing;
Haste, haste to bring him laud, the babe the son of Mary. (William Chatterton)

The text of this hymn, set the old English tune "Greensleeves," is from the 19th century, and makes the sort of observations that anyone expecting the messiah might. Why is he here, in a stable? Why is his birth both so ordinary and so spectacular? He is attended by shepherds and by angels and all who would see him must journey to where he is.

Why indeed? In Luke's Gospel Jesus has what Karl Rahner would 2000 years later describe as a "radical orientation to the poor." Luke want us to understand that no matter what we may be expecting of the savior of the world, God chooses to come to us in the humblest, most natural form – a human child.

The gospel of Luke speaks of Anna the Prophet who lived and prayed continually in the temple, looking for the redemption of Israel. She and the Prophet Simeon first saw the infant Jesus when he was brought by Mary and Joseph to the temple. Simeon's response to this meeting is recorded in the Nunc Dimitis (Song of Simeon) but we are not know what Anna said when she met her savior. We only know that she had been praying for years that he would be born, and that with the gift of prophecy, she was able to recognize who Jesus was.

Blessed are those who, like Anna, Simeon, and Luke, can set aside their expectations of pomp, circumstance and majesty in order to see the divine in the face of the Babe in the Manger. That is what makes Anna a Prophet. She had spent a lifetime immersed in prayer while she awaited the redemption of Israel. So when he appears, she knows him.

On this the 6th Day of Christmas, open your heart and your eyes to the unexpected ways in which God seeks, finds, and saves us all – by becoming one of us and living among us.

December 31st: Vigil for New Year's Eve ~ 7th Day of Christmas

"We wish you a Merry Christmas and a Happy New Year!"

As midnight approaches this 7th day of Christmas, many of us will be gathering with friends, sharing a meal and wishing one another a "Happy New Year". Hope is one of the hallmarks of Christmas, and is certainly one of the reasons that New Year's Eve is celebrated with such enthusiasm.

There have certainly been (and still are) folks who see little that is hopeful about this world and who do not believe that anything about it can ultimately be good or wholesome. And yet, we must remember that in the Book of Genesis, God's word to creation and all its components was "And God saw that it was good."

The fact that the celebration of the twelve days of Christmas includes the secular New Year's Eve and New Year's Day, is much more important than its being an occasion for parades, dinners and football games. If we allow it to be, New Year's Eve can become a reminder to us that under the sovereignty of God, life and time are moving forward and are being renewed. If we are able to celebrate New Year's Eve that way, our New Year's Resolutions can produce meaningful, permanent changes in our lives.

So, this year, don't make any resolutions that you are not fully desirous of keeping. And for Heaven's Sake, don't make any that you are almost assured of not keeping. Make your resolutions things that you can offer to God in thanksgiving for the year that is past and as a prayer for help in the year to come. For example, don't resolve that you will not overeat this year. Resolve that you will thank God each day for the gift of your body. Or don't resolve not to argue with your siblings. Resolve that you will pray each day for God's goodness in their lives. That will have a greater impact than you might imagine.

There is a reason that we count down the minutes to the New Year – we believe in the power of hope, and new beginnings. I think that God feels that way about us.

January 1st: Feast of the Holy Name ~ 8th Day of Christmas

"Eternal Father, you gave to your incarnate Son the holy name of Jesus to be the sign of our salvation; Plant in every heart, we pray, the love of him who is the Savior of the world..." (Collect for the Feast of the Holy Name.)

The Feast of the Holy Name (which is also the Eighth Day of Christmas and New Year's Day) is a Feast of Our Lord, and commemorates the naming and circumcision of Jesus on the eighth day of his life.

Sometimes parents might disagree over the name of their child, and be forced to compromise. Not Jesus' parents. Mary and Joseph, in their separate annunciations of the coming birth of Jesus were each instructed to name him Jesus – a name which means "Yahweh is salvation."

The question for us on the 8th Day of Christmas is this – what does the name of Jesus mean to me, today? Is it a word I read and hear and say on Sundays, or when I say my prayers? Or is there more to it? And even more importantly, do I know the One who bears that name? Am I in a relationship with him?

New Year's Day is a very good time to reacquaint ourselves with friends we may have left behind in life. It is also the perfect time to open ourselves to the invitation that Jesus extends to us – to know and be known by God.

Let's start this year on a first name basis with our Savior. And let's resolve to speak to him each day.

January 2nd: John 1:19-28 ~ 9th Day of Christmas

"and he shall reign forever and ever."

In the passage appointed for this day, John the Baptist says that he is only the messenger and is unworthy even to untie the thong of the sandal of the Messiah. That is a very pious statement – and an accurate one as well. But what does it mean to be so aware of the divinity of Jesus that we would be loath even to touch his shoes? Do we even have categories of thought to help us understand the concept? Perhaps not in terms of our intellect or our sense of the rational, but we can experience it through our emotions, and through our senses. Especially through music.

We don't get much opportunity these days to feel the splendor and majesty of a pull-out-all-the-stops worship service. But music can take us there. Have you recently listened to the Messiah? If not, today would be a perfect time to do so. Find a recording of the Messiah and listen to the Halleluiah Chorus. Listen to the words, count the adjectives used to describe Jesus. Feel the pulse of the music, hear the joy and the majesty in the voices of the singers. Play it loud and listen to it several times. And then remember, this is just a little of what John the Baptist must have felt in the presence of Jesus. And it is only one very, very small part of what we will experience in Christ's presence.

And celebrate the 9th day of Christmas!

January 3rd: John 1:29-34 ~ 10th Day of Christmas

"I have seen and have testified that this is the Son of God. (John 1:34)

Happy 10th Day of Christmas! I am willing to bet that if you have been keeping Christmas for 12 days this year that you are loving it. And I suspect that you are more and more comfortable joining John the Baptist in his affirmation that "this is the Son of God." Who else could possibly merit such a celebration?

Think of the last ten days – how many times have you been reminded that Christ is with us? How often have you seen the light of the love of God in the face of another – just because you were willing to believe that it was there? And how willing are you now to carry this sense of witness forward into the New Year?

For that is what we are called to do. Having seen Jesus, and spent so much intentional time in his presence we are now being prepared to testify/bear witness to the fact that we know him to be the Son of God.

But don't panic. You don't have to write a book or travel to the ends of the earth. You don't have to preach or teach or knock on your neighbor's door. Yet. But you do have to be prepared to bear witness to the truth that you have encountered. And when the opportunity presents itself, you do need to be ready to respond. Just consider these twelve days as a sort of discipleship boot-camp in which you have been learning how to recognize the Messiah. You are almost ready to graduate.

January 4th: John 1:35-42 ~ 11th Day of Christmas

"Come and See, Go and Tell"

We have been to the manger. We have seen the Christ Child. We have encountered the response of others to his birth and his presence in the world. And now we are nearing the end of these twelve days. Today, following the example of St. Andrew we are being given our first assignment of the New Year.

"Come and See. Go and Tell." That is the definition of an apostle. Of course the first thing that most of us think when we hear that is "I can't. I don't know enough." And "I don't know what to say." The answer to that series of questions is: "Yes, you can. Yes, you do." and "Tell them what you have seen and heard."

What have you seen and heard as a result of making this journey through the twelve days of Christmas? What you have seen, heard and learned is your apostolic message, and it is your personal response to the experience that will have the most impact on those with whom you share it. People want to know how you feel and what you believe. They want to be able to look at you and know that you are telling them the truth as you have experienced it. They want to know that it is possible for them to have the same experience. They need for you to encourage them in that journey.

Spend a few minutes today writing or remembering what you have experienced. Make a few notes about what was meaningful to you. What was challenging or difficult to understand? What do you wish that you had known before? Then tuck those notes into your wallet and carry them with you. And when the opportunity presents itself, read them to yourself and ask God to help you know what to do next.

January 5th: Twelfth Night

"O God, who wonderfully created and yet more wonderfully restored the dignity of human nature; Grant that we may share the divine life of him who humbled himself to share our humanity, your Son Jesus Christ, who lives and reigns with you, in the unity of the Holy Spirit, one God, for ever and ever. Amen." (Collect for the Second Sunday of Christmas"

Today's lessons are about the visit of the Magi and the flight of the Holy Family into Egypt. Just as Mary and Joseph were directed to name this child Jesus and bring him up in the way of the Lord, they are now instructed to shelter and protect the infant Christ by taking him out of Herod's reach. And just as his ancestor Joseph led Jacob's family into Egypt in a time of famine; Egypt is now a place of refuge for the Messiah. The baby and his family leave quickly, quietly and under the protective wings of the angels are guided to safety.

The twelve days of Christmas are coming to an end. But there is one more thing to be done.

Have a party! At this the close of the season, invite your friends and family to join you for one last celebration of the light and joy and feasting of the holiday. There will be time in a day or two to carefully pack up the decorations and sweep up the pine needles. But today or tonight, give thanks for the love of God in becoming incarnate among us. Gather once more around the table or the tree and remember why this is a time of feasting and abundance.

The collect of the day for this Second Sunday of Christmas is my favorite in the Prayer Book because it is a glorious affirmation of the work of God in creation and in the Incarnation. Read it one more time, and if it seems good to you, read it at your 12th Night Celebration. And give thanks!!

EPIPHANY

January 6, ~ Stumbling Toward the Light

I am the LORD, I have called you in righteousness, I have taken you by the hand and kept you; I have given you as a covenant to the people, a light to the nations, to open the eyes that are blind, to bring out the prisoners from the dungeon, from the prison those who sit in darkness. (Isaiah 42:6-7)

On the winter solstice, just days before Christmas, we in the Northern Hemisphere moved through the shortest and darkest day of the year. With candles lighted in the glow of Christmas Eve, we began the celebration of Light of Christ coming into the world. Throughout the twelve days of Christmas, as we gathered in our homes and in our Churches, the days grew almost imperceptibly longer.

Now we are entering the liturgical season of Epiphany when the light of God is made manifest in Christ Jesus. Even though the days remain short, and the ground is hard and frozen with snow and ice and record-breaking temperatures, it is time to leave the Manger and travel forth into the cold and dark and on to the work at hand. In that work we are invited to bear witness that God in Christ, the Light of the world, comes to us in darkest part of the year and in the darkest hours of our lives.

As Isaiah writes, God's people are not only called forth as a light to the nations with a very specific assignment, they are also led by the hand as they go. What is that assignment? To open the eyes of the blind, and to bring out the prisoners from the darkness of the dungeon. That was, and is, a staggeringly large task; especially when we realize that much of the blindness is spiritual, that many of the dungeons are interior, and that as often as not the prisoners are unaware that they are captive. Not only that, we may find that we ourselves are among the blind prisoners; or that we are only beginning to stumble toward the light of day.

But the light of Epiphany calls us on. Just as the star led the Magi to the Manger, God leads us to the River Jordan and to the One who in his baptism is once again revealed as God among us. And, thanks be to God, we do not travel alone. Just as Yahweh God led the Children of Israel, God in Christ leads us today – and there is a wonderful symmetry in the fact that we are led by the light even as we are called to hold the light for others.

This New Thing

I am the LORD, that is my name; my glory I give to no other, nor my praise to idols. See, the former things have come to pass, and new things I now declare; before they spring forth, I tell you of them. (Isaiah 42: 8-9)

I suspect that for many of us, acknowledging the absolute sovereignty of God would indeed be a new thing! I know that when I become aware that my spiritual life is flagging, it is usually because I have stopped relating to God as God and have demoted the Almighty to the status of a colleague to be consulted when the workload is too heavy for me to handle on my own.

What Isaiah reminds us of is that God alone is God – with knowledge, power and authority over the past, present and future of all of us and of everything. The situation is permanent. There will not come a time when we any of us graduate to spiritual equality with God – and thinking otherwise is idolatrous. It is the idolatry of presuming that God is our "buddy" rather than our Maker.

Of course, there are other idols in our lives to which we are willing to give the attention and devotion which belongs to God alone – wealth, power, ambition, success, even love. But underlying each of those is the human desire to hold onto and attempt to control the world around us. If we understood God to be truly sovereign in our lives, we would not do that. It is as though we are willing to admit that God is in charge of eternity, but that in the meantime, we retain the rights and privileges of being the CEO of our own life – complete with veto power.

There are plenty of times when God gives us free rein to make our own choices; for example, it is probably safe to assume that God wants you to pay your electric bill on time and feed and clothe your family. But what about those things that are not so clear? What about those things that are vying for the honor and attention that are owed to God? We all know them. We all have them. What we all need to do is to remember that it is foolhardy at best, and idolatrous at worst, to simply assume that whatever we want is what God wants.

The Glory Due God's Name

Ascribe to the LORD, you gods, ascribe to the LORD glory and strength.
Ascribe to the LORD the glory due his Name;
worship the LORD in the beauty of holiness.

What does it mean to "ascribe to the Lord the glory due his Name? I have known folks who seem to praise God continually, sometimes even pausing in the middle of a sentence to say "Thank you, Lord" or "Praise God"; and I have no doubt that they are sincerely grateful. I have also known folks who will not even speak the Name of God because they believe it is too holy for use in human speech. Again, I trust that they are utterly sincere. And there have been times in my own life when it seemed to me that the only appropriate prayer was "Thank God!" But I don't think that is what the Psalmist means.

I think that the Psalmist's relationship with God is so real and so compelling, that even the Name of God is worthy of worship. And if that is the case, how much more honor, glory and worship are due the *person* of God?

Living as we do in a world that so values self-confidence and individuality, it is a challenge for us to be quiet, to step back, and to give credit where it is due. It is even more challenging to give praise and worship to God – especially in public. Bending our own will to that of God flies in the face of success and autonomy as they are understood today. Using the Name of God casually does not bother us at all. But, acknowledging the supremacy of God outside of a worship service may seem *"a bit excessive."*

Why is that? I think that is a good question to ponder today. Why is it that we want to make the expression of our faith personal, private, and polite?

No Partiality

Then Peter began to speak to them: "I truly understand that God shows no partiality, but in every nation anyone who fears him and does what is right is acceptable to him." (Acts 10:34)

All of us want to be accepted. We want to belong, to feel that we are worthy, and to feel welcome. And we know that we are constantly being evaluated. The truth is that in just about every encounter in life, we make instant assessments of one another, and that one of those assessments is whether or not someone or something is acceptable. Is her appearance appropriate? Do his manners, breeding, vocation or grades meet expectations? Do they qualify to join us? This concept is so inculcated in our society that one of the most common ways of verbally expressing disapproval is the phrase "That is unacceptable."

The very act of talking or writing about acceptability implies that there are those who are worthy of acceptance and that there are those who are not. In addition we bestow upon some privileged few the authority and the power to decide which is which. (Think about the college admissions process.) And if that is how we choose to order our lives, the whole process leaves us feeling unworthy, unloved, and unwanted.

But, thank God for divine acceptance! For at the heart and soul of the Gospel message is the phrase "You are accepted." (The great 20th century theologian Paul Tillich make a life's work of understanding and explaining that truth.) This verse from the Acts of the Apostles is really, really, Good News. "...in every nation anyone who fears (reverences, respects, honors, obeys) him and does what is right is acceptable to him." It doesn't get much clearer than that!

And let's not get tangled up in the word "right." This is not about being a member of the right Church or sharing the opinions of the right group. This is about doing what is pleasing to God, and God has already spoken about what that is. "Love God with all your heart, and your neighbor as yourself." If we strive to do that, we are acceptable to God.

Baptism of Jesus

Jesus came from Galilee to John at the Jordan, to be baptized by him. John would have prevented him, saying, "I need to be baptized by you, and do you come to me?" But Jesus answered him, "Let it be so now; for it is proper for us in this way to fulfill all righteousness." Then he consented. And when Jesus had been baptized, just as he came up from the water, suddenly the heavens were opened to him and he saw the Spirit of God descending like a dove and alighting on him. And a voice from heaven said, "This is my Son, the Beloved, with whom I am well pleased." (Matthew 3:13-17)

So, why does Jesus, the One without sin, come to John, the one who is preaching a baptism for the repentance of sins, for baptism? More than one teacher and preacher has gotten into serious hot water by trying to answer that question and inadvertently offending the questioner. But the question deserves and demands an answer.

Baptism is the sacrament that makes us Christians – followers of Jesus Christ. We try to follow his example and his instructions. He was baptized; we are baptized. He began the sacrament of Holy Communion at the Last Supper; we eat that meal in remembrance of him.

And there is more. All the texts focus on genuine, heart-felt obedience to God and to the sovereignty of God. They ask us pointed questions about who we believe God to be and how that belief effects our lives. That theme is fully realized in Jesus' actions at his baptism by John in the Jordan River. John knows that Jesus does not need to be baptized for repentance of sins. But Jesus knows that in demonstrating full love of and obedience to God by being baptized, he is doing what is pleasing to God. It is at that point that Jesus' ministry begins. The Holy Spirit comes to him, and the voice of God says, "...I am well pleased."

Jesus shows us what righteousness looks like. It is the willing submission of self to do that which is pleasing in God's sight. And through the grace of God in Christ, righteousness is what we seek. Not simply obeying all the rules (though genuine obedience is a sign of righteousness) and not just being a good person (though righteousness and goodness go hand in hand). Righteousness is loving God with all your heart and your neighbor as yourself.

Beloved Son

Father in heaven, who at the baptism of Jesus in the River Jordan proclaimed him your beloved Son and anointed him with the Holy Spirit: Grant that all who are baptized into his Name may keep the covenant they have made, and boldly confess him as Lord and Savior; who with you and the Holy Spirit lives and reigns, one God, in glory everlasting. Amen.

We are baptized into the Name and Body of Christ. We bear upon our foreheads the seal of Christ. We are nurtured and empowered by the Holy Spirit for the work of God in the world. We are strengthened and accompanied by the Family of Christ in his church. And we have only one task. We are to love God with all our hearts and to love our neighbors as ourselves.

That is the summary of Law.

That is the message of Jesus.

That is why we were baptized and that is the work we are called to do.

May God grant us the will and the grace to do this.

Named by God

Listen to me, O coastlands, pay attention, you peoples from far away! The LORD called me before I was born, while I was in my mother's womb he named me. He made my mouth like a sharp sword, in the shadow of his hand he hid me; he made me a polished arrow, in his quiver he hid me away. (Isaiah 49:1-2)

The Prophet has found his calling. He knows this so fully that he is able to describe his vocation as a part of himself from the moment of his conception. Even in the womb he was known by God, and formed and shaped for the work that God would ask him to do. Because he understands that his calling is to speak a prophetic (and often unpopular) word to the people of Israel, he describes his voice as a sharp sword, and his words like polished arrows. He knows who he is and what he is called to do.

Do you believe that God has a purpose for you and for your life? I am not asking if you believe that there is only one thing in this world that you are called to do. Nor am I asking if you believe that God has your ideal life all mapped out. I am asking if you believe, as Isaiah did, that God has given you gifts and talents and interests that are part of God's love and concern for creation. In other words, do you believe that your being alive matters in the scheme of things. And if you do believe that, what are you doing in order to discern and respond to God's call in your life?

A spiritual inventory is a good place to start.

In prayer, open your heart to the leading of the Holy Spirit.
Make a list of the things you are good at, and the things you love to do.
Ask God to help you discern what to do with those skills and talents.
Share your thoughts with someone you trust and pray about what to do next.

And remember, God has entrusted us with the task of making the love and presence of God known in our lives and in our world. Each of us has something to contribute to that work.

Personal Epiphanies

"It is too light a thing that you should be my servant to raise up the tribes of Jacob and to restore the survivors of Israel; I will give you as a light to the nations, that my salvation may reach to the end of the earth." (Isaiah 49:6)

In Epiphany, we expect that our Sunday lessons will show us the ways in which the light and presence of the God of all creation are made manifest in the world in the person of Jesus the Christ. We remember that Israel was chosen not for privilege, but to be a light to the nations. That is the theology of Epiphany.

But, sometimes Epiphanies are personal. Sometimes, we learn and discover things about God that seem to relate to us personally and individually – and such epiphanies often arrive when we least expect them. We cannot control epiphanies, but we can certainly open ourselves to receive them. One of the best ways to do that is to pray our way into Scripture, reading it as though it were addressed to us, personally.

So, imagine that the words of this passage from Isaiah are addressed to you, specifically. You are not just a servant of God bidden to do God's will. You are also invited to be a living example of a life lived in relationship to God – an example for the benefit of those who have not yet understood or accepted such a relationship. God has chosen you to shine with the light of salvation and to live a life that draws others to the light.

This is a sign that God values you and trusts your ability to do the work. And it is also intimidating. Most of us would feel quite inadequate if given such a challenge. But note that God is not calling you to create the light, or produce the effect. "I will give you as a light to the nations, that my salvation may reach to the end of the earth." God is providing the light – and the light is in you. All you need to do is allow it to shine. And you don't need to produce the salvation either. It is God's salvation that you will be demonstrating by the light of your life.

Jesus is the light of the world. Epiphany is the season of God's manifestation of that light. But we are all a part of it. First we recognize its presence. Then we allow it to transform us. Then we let it shine through us so that all may see it.

Behold, I Come

Great things are they that you have done, O LORD my God!
how great your wonders and your plans for us!
there is none who can be compared with you.
Oh, that I could make them known and tell them!
but they are more than I can count.
In sacrifice and offering you take no pleasure
(you have given me ears to hear you);
Burnt-offering and sin-offering you have not required,
and so I said, "Behold, I come. (Psalm 40:5-8)

Imagine what it would feel like to suddenly discover that you have been totally wrong about your greatest fears – and that your mistaken belief had cost you a great deal of happiness in your life. Would you feel embarrassed? Maybe. Would you feel a sense of regret for what you had missed? Probably. But wouldn't you also feel wonderfully freed and liberated?

There have been many instances in my life in which I have made such a discovery. I felt really silly when I actually enjoyed Statistics and Analysis in graduate school. I have often wished that I had gotten to know someone years earlier than I finally did. But the most wonderful and liberating truth I have ever learned is that God is not an ogre.

So much of Scripture, written by human beings through the filters of their own life situations and personalities, focuses on the fear of offending God – which makes passages like this one shine like the sun on a cloudless day. We need not live shackled by the idea that God is angry and must be appeased. We need not cower before our Creator. God is love, and God desires but one thing – our loving hearts.

I will say that again. God desires but one thing – our loving hearts. We are all worthy of the love of God because God has made us that way. And when our behavior is less than loving, God does not require a sin-offering or a sacrifice. It is at those times that God desires our loving hearts even more. For, to have a loving heart is to be able to recognize when we have sinned, when we need to repent, and when we require amendment of life.

Great indeed are the wonders, plans and gifts of God – far more than we can ask or imagine – and there are no strings attached. We are called to love and to be loved. How could we say anything other than "Behold, I come."

Enriched in Christ

I give thanks to my God always for you because of the grace of God that has been given you in Christ Jesus, for in every way you have been enriched in him, in speech and knowledge of every kind-- just as the testimony of Christ has been strengthened among you-- so that you are not lacking in any spiritual gift as you wait for the revealing of our Lord Jesus Christ. He will also strengthen you to the end, so that you may be blameless on the day of our Lord Jesus Christ. God is faithful; by him you were called into the fellowship of his Son, Jesus Christ our Lord. (1 Corinthians 1:4-9)

Do you ever stop to think about how being a Christian enriches your life? And if you do think about it, do you also share what it means to you? St. Paul, in this letter to the church at Corinth believes that being part of the Body of Christ is a blessing that genuinely changes us giving us the spiritual gifts necessary to become evangelists (proclaimers of the Good News that God is with us).

All of us are called to be witnesses to the love of God in the world and to the presence of Christ in our lives. All of us are necessary to that work, and we all receive the gifts needed to do our part. None of us has all the gifts, and none of us is expected to do all the work. It is a shared ministry, but few of us are aware of the gifts that we have been given, and even fewer have the confidence to exercise them. And very often, we cannot see or recognize our own gifts but can readily discern the gifts of others. That is why prayer and community and Christian education are so important. That is also why pastors are thrilled when people come to them and ask for help in discerning God's calling in their lives.

During this season of Epiphany, try to pay closer attention to the opportunities that God places before you. Look for ways to affirm the gifts that you see in others and to trust that God will use others to help you discern your own gifts.

God has called us to be a light to the nations – don't forget that you are part of that light.

Finding the Messiah

The next day John again was standing with two of his disciples, and as he watched Jesus walk by, he exclaimed, "Look, here is the Lamb of God!" The two disciples heard him say this, and they followed Jesus. When Jesus turned and saw them following, he said to them, "What are you looking for?" They said to him, "Rabbi" (which translated means Teacher), "where are you staying?" He said to them, "Come and see." They came and saw where he was staying, and they remained with him that day. It was about four o'clock in the afternoon. One of the two who heard John speak and followed him was Andrew, Simon Peter's brother. He first found his brother Simon and said to him, "We have found the Messiah" (which is translated Anointed). He brought Simon to Jesus, who looked at him and said, "You are Simon son of John. You are to be called Cephas" (which is translated Peter). (John 1:35-42)

"I sought the Lord" is a hymn which provides the perfect description of the way that Christ encourages us to seek him by first seeking us:

"I sought the Lord and afterward I knew
he moved my soul to seek him seeking me.
It was not I that found, O Savior true; no I was found of thee."

It is absolutely true that the people of Israel were waiting and watching for the Messiah. It is also true that John the Baptist recognized Jesus and pointed him out to James and Andrew and that Andrew returned and brought Peter back. But it was God who placed that yearning and seeking for the Messiah within their hearts; it was God who prompted them to know and proclaim "we have found the Messiah" and it was God in Christ who called them all to a life of discipleship.

Such Epiphanies are by no means limited to folks who lived two thousand years ago. God continually seeks each one of us. We are that special, that precious, and that beloved. We are also that necessary to the work of the gospel. God needs us to be willing and able to say, by word and example "We have found the Messiah!" and then to go and bring our own brothers and sisters, and all those others that God seeks to find. But until we are convinced ourselves that we have found and been found by God, we will not be convincing messengers to others.

The question is this: Are you aware of how much God loves you? In another place, Jesus says, "Seek and ye shall find." When you do, you will also find that God is and always has been seeking you.

Mirroring the Light of the World

Almighty God, whose Son our Savior Jesus Christ is the light of the world: Grant that your people, illumined by your Word and Sacraments, may shine with the radiance of Christ's glory, that he may be known, worshipped, and obeyed to the ends of the earth; through Jesus Christ our Lord, who with you and the Holy Spirit lives and reigns, one God, now and for ever. Amen. (Collect for Second Sunday in Epiphany)

The message of Epiphany is not going to get much clearer or more specific than this. Christ is the light of the world, and we are the mirrors whose lives reflect that light to everyone around us.

What is amazing is that anyone would ever utter such a prayer without being willing to be aglow with the radiance of Christ's glory. But often, it is as though we view these words as a petition for some far distant event that won't happen in time to really include us.

But guess what? When we read or hear these words, we should fully expect to shine – not for our own edification or as some sort of reward for believing, but because we are part of God's Epiphany to the world. Our faces and our lives should shine so radiantly that everyone we meet will be compelled to ask us why. Then, when we tell them, their faces will also shine, and so on, until the light has truly come to all the nations.

Be prepared to glow! Remember this Saturday night collect from the Evening Prayer: *"O God, the source of eternal light; Shed forth your unending day upon us who watch for you, that our lips may praise you, our lives may bless you, and our worship on the morrow give you glory. Amen"*

Breaking the Yoke

The people who walked in darkness have seen a great light; those who lived in a land of deep darkness-- on them light has shined. You have multiplied the nation, you have increased its joy; they rejoice before you as with joy at the harvest, as people exult when dividing plunder. For the yoke of their burden, and the bar across their shoulders, the rod of their oppressor, you have broken as on the day of Midian. (Isaiah 9:2-4)

The purpose of Scripture from the first page to the last, is to proclaim a message of liberation. The power of whatever holds the people of God captive – oppression, violence, sin or illness – is subject to the power and presence of God. In the end, all those things are overcome by the work of God in the world and in our lives, for God desires that we all be freed from the "yoke of burden and the rod of oppression."

Liberation is conversion. It is also a form of repentance, in that it creates within us the desire to change the world and to allow ourselves to be changed as well. Liberation and conversion are accomplished by the light of God's truth when it is proclaimed, received and acted upon by those who are willing to be instruments of God's peace.

We are all called to take part in this work, but it is not an easy calling. Pointing out those things that hold us captive is a tricky business, for we all like to think of ourselves as free and independent. But calling attention to the ways in which we oppress or hold others captive can be downright dangerous. Those who would speak God's truth by proclaiming liberation, especially when it challenges the status quo, must be willing to risk losing comfort, security, reputation, and at times even their lives in its service.

The Power of Fear

*The LORD is my light and my salvation; whom then shall I fear? **
the LORD is the strength of my life; of whom then shall I be afraid? (Psalm 27:1)

Sometimes I wonder if fear isn't the greatest challenge to human existence. There are so many things we fear, and those fears, even the less than rational and reasonable ones, have such great power over us!

Fear is a normal response of the human body and nervous system to a perceived threat. Like anger, it is not something we summon, it just happens. Sometimes the autonomic nervous system takes over and we respond in a fight or flight manner.

But often, fears are much less powerful than we give them credit for being; because like anger, fear is something over which we do have some degree of control. The greatest control we have is in our decision of whether and how to respond to our fears. For example, do I really need to let my fear that I might make a mistake if I sing solos, keep me from singing at all? Or is it reasonable to let my fear of being emotionally injured if I love someone prevent me from getting close to others?

Those fears, while real enough to those who experience them are nothing compared to the damage done by our fears that we are unworthy, shameful, or unacceptable to God. Those are the ones that cripple us spiritually and keep us from knowing the joy of life and the security of love.

Overcoming such fears is the work of spiritual growth. And the Psalmist knows that the foundation of such growth is the realization that in God's presence fear is destroyed. There is no room for fear when we understand that God is our light and salvation, and our strength.

Granted, trust is required if we are to live these words with confidence, but if we do not learn to trust God, we will never learn to trust anyone else.

Unity in Mind and in Purpose (Part 1)

I appeal to you, brothers and sisters, by the name of our Lord Jesus Christ, that all of you be in agreement and that there be no divisions among you, but that you be united in the same mind and the same purpose. (1 Corinthians 1:10)

After six decades on the planet with three-quarters of those years spent in leadership roles, the one thing I know is that it is rare for even two people to truly agree about something and that the odds of agreement between three or more people become exponentially lower – unless the object of agreement is experienced as equally essential by all parties concerned. That is why the debates about things like climate change and gun control are so volatile – different groups value different "goods." But when there is a common and undeniable "good" at stake, groups of people can come together in new and spontaneous communities of common interest, as when communities are devastated by natural disasters. The scope of agreement and participation is larger when war and conflict threaten regions of cultural similarity. But there has not yet been a threat or a blessing large enough to bring together all the peoples of the earth. In my somewhat jaded opinion, only the imminent threat of a hostile interstellar invasion would do it! And even then, I doubt it would work if it required folks of various religions and denominations to find common ground and accept the worth and truth of the other's position.

So while I know the unity to which St. Paul is referring -- God is incarnate with us in Christ Jesus and that changes everything -- I find myself wondering just what he hoped to accomplish with this appeal to the church at Corinth. Just what is this "same mind and same purpose" and why is it so difficult that it has always been a huge problem for the church? He is not telling them that they must all behave the same way. He's not telling them that they must all believe the same way. He is telling them that they, as a part of the Body of Christ, must have a common proclamation of what God has done and is doing in the world. That is unity.

Unity in Mind and in Purpose (Part 2)

I appeal to you, brothers and sisters, by the name of our Lord Jesus Christ, that all of you be in agreement and that there be no divisions among you, but that you be united in the same mind and the same purpose. (1 Corinthians 1:10)

So, what prevents unity?

I think that the problem the church has always had is that it mistakes dogma for doctrine and doctrine for God. We seem to start at the outer edges with what we want everyone to think and do, and then work our way back to the center, all the while forcing the increasingly deeper truths we encounter into the framework of the surface rules. In the end, even the concept of unity becomes superficial, and the product of seeking the lowest common denominator.

But what if we were to start at the center? God is love and God is with us. It doesn't get more fundamental than that. And most people of most faiths can come together around that statement. So if God is the center, what is the doctrine by/through which that idea is expressed? *Love God with all your heart, and your neighbor as yourself.* That, too, is easily recognized as the doctrine of our faith. And, then, finally, we come to the dogma/rules of the faith. What do we do in order to love God and Neighbor? What do our lives look like?

That is where the Christians of Corinth and of planet earth usually get into trouble. We start making up rules about church governance and liturgy that are almost entirely functional and then promote those rules to the status of divine law. And it is even worse when we gradually transfer personal opinion (or prejudice) from the realm of behavior to the precincts of the throne of God.

Why do we do that? Because it is easier and because it requires little or no self-examination and virtually ensures that we will not need to change.

But it doesn't have to be that way. And the reformation begins with you. What is it that you know to be true about God? What do you think that God wants you to do? What difference will that make in how you live?

Message of the Cross

For the message about the cross is foolishness to those who are perishing, but to us who are being saved it is the power of God. (1 Corinthians 1:18)

The message of the cross is not just about the death of Christ, it is also about his resurrection. Nor is it merely his death that saves us. We are saved by the love of God whose works are unified and seamless – from creation to the end of all things. But we seldom tell the whole story – focusing instead on crucifixion.

And so long as we limit our teaching about the cross to the doctrine of substitutionary atonement -- i.e. even though we deserve death for our sins, Jesus takes the punishment for us and makes things right with God -- the message of the cross may indeed seem "foolish". Upon hearing that description, most people would wonder, "Why would God require God to be a blood sacrifice to appease God?"

Of course, it all depends on your frame of reference. If you believe that wrongs must be made right and that the greater the offense the greater the penalty, then a sacrificial system makes a great deal of sense. Sin is an offense against the honor and righteousness of God. But only a perfect sacrifice will perfectly satisfy the righteousness of God, so only God can pay the price. This system works very well for very many people.

Others believe that the message of the cross concerns not only the righteousness of God but also the love of God. What if God is saying to us – "Can you see how much I love you? I will die for you." Punishment is still merited, but God loves us enough to take the punishment for us.

Still others believe that the message of the cross is only about love. God does not demand a blood sacrifice. God only loves, and there are no limits to that love. It is as though God is saying to us, "Nothing you can do will make me stop loving you." For the people who understand the message of the cross this way, the crucifixion is the work of humanity, not the work of God -- just one more example of the enormity of human sin. We would rather try to kill God than to accept that God really does love us.

God always prevails, and the work of God is revealed in the resurrection. For the final message of the cross is that it is empty. Through the Resurrection, God shows us that the love of God overcomes death.

Fishing for People

"From that time Jesus began to proclaim, "Repent, for the kingdom of heaven has come near." As he walked by the Sea of Galilee, he saw two brothers, Simon, who is called Peter, and Andrew his brother, casting a net into the sea-- for they were fishermen. And he said to them, "Follow me, and I will make you fish for people." Immediately they left their nets and followed him. As he went from there, he saw two other brothers, James son of Zebedee and his brother John, in the boat with their father Zebedee, mending their nets, and he called them. Immediately they left the boat and their father, and followed him."

There is no getting around it, "fishers of men" does sound better than "fish for people". As the phrase is rendered in the King James Version of the Bible, it is poetic and evocative and even sounds more spiritual. On the other hand, "fish for people" is a more direct translation of the original text. But in either case, it is not worth fighting over.

Fights over translations, unless they change the meaning of the text, are often just a very convenient way of avoiding taking the text to heart. Be honest, now. Wouldn't you rather lament the loss of a lovely 16th century phrase than seriously consider dropping everything and following Jesus?

Besides, Jesus only mentions fishing because the guys he's recruiting are all fishermen! What he is really doing is letting them know that if they decide to go with him, they may not be coming home any time soon. If he had been talking to a group of teachers he might have said, "Follow me and I will teach you enlighten to the world." Or if his words had been addressed to the financial advisors of the day, he would most likely have said, "Come with me and you will learn about real savings."

The call to follow Jesus is particular and specific to those being called. So, what would Jesus say to you? Whatever it is, I am certain that it would be just the right thing to get your attention. The question is, what would you do? If you had been in the boat with Peter, Andrew, James or John, would you have allowed his call to change you and your life and your future?

Well, that point is moot. Jesus is no longer recruiting for his original mission, and most of us do not need to leave home in order to follow him. But he is asking each of us to remember that the kingdom of heaven is near and that there are lots of folks in this world who are dying to hear about it. And whether we fish or teach or manage portfolios, Jesus is still inviting us to use our gifts and talents to spread the Good News.

Marvelous Works

Give us grace, O Lord, to answer readily the call of our Savior Jesus Christ and proclaim to all people the Good News of his salvation, that we and the whole world may perceive the glory of his marvelous works; who lives and reigns with you and the Holy Spirit, one God, for ever and ever. Amen.

"Works" is an interesting word. Most of the time we use it to describe some sort of task, as in a public-works project. Sometimes it carries the connotation of energy as in fire-works. We've even made it into a verb showing agreement, as in "works for me!"

But in the context of today's collect, works is much closer to "opus" or a complete life's work. Jesus' marvelous works are the sum of his presence among us as God incarnate. And they encompass much more than his healing and teaching ministry, because they are contained within a larger word and concept – the WORK of Christ.

The work of Christ in the world is salvation and that work is accomplished when God Incarnate is made visible to us in Christ. That means that everything he said or did from his birth to his ascension is intended to point us toward God, and is an expression of God's love. And, that is what makes the Good News such good news!

What we sometimes overlook is that God has chosen to include us and our efforts in that work as well. When we answer his call, we are empowered by the Holy Spirit to celebrate the love of God with other believers and to share that Good News with those who do not yet know about it. We need the grace of God to hear and to answer that call, of course, but that grace is always abundantly available to us. We need only receive and act upon it.

A Refiner's Fire

"But who can endure the day of his coming, and who can stand when he appears? For he is like a refiner's fire and like fullers' soap; he will sit as a refiner and purifier of silver, and he will purify the descendants of Levi and refine them like gold and silver, until they present offerings to the LORD in righteousness." (Malachi 3:2-3)

One of the greatest challenges to authentic spirituality in our day and age is our deep and largely private belief that whatever we offer to God will be enthusiastically received and gratefully acknowledged. But I wonder, does it ever occur to most of us that what we think is generous and meaningful does not seem so to God?

This is especially a problem when we believe that God is just one more charity on our list of causes to support. I have "x" number of dollars and hours of time to give to a worthy cause. Surely each of them will be appreciative of my efforts and my generosity. It would be rude of them to feel otherwise, right?

Well, that is probably true when we are figuring out how best to distribute gifts from our abundance. But God expects sacrifices and offerings from our substance, not our abundance. And anytime that our sacrifices do not reach down to draw from our substance, we are simply acting as administrators of a fund.

In other words, if we treat God like just one more demand on our time and treasure, how can we expect that our offerings will be considered righteous? For until our lives and our sacrifices and offerings are based on what really, truly matters to us, we are not offering true or genuine worship. It would be like saying to your beloved. "I'll see where I can work you into my life with the least possible inconvenience." Such a statement betrays the need for some radical refining!

When God melts us down and purifies us, we lose the dross – but we also learn to recognize when we are lying to ourselves about what really matters. God does not want our left-overs. God wants our first-fruits of soul, mind, talent and treasure; and just like the descendants of Levi, every once in a while we require the sort of attitude adjustment referred to in this passage.

The King of Glory

Lift up your heads, O gates; lift them high, O everlasting doors;
and the King of glory shall come in.
"Who is this King of glory?" "The LORD, strong and mighty,
the LORD, mighty in battle."
Lift up your heads, O gates; lift them high, O everlasting doors;
and the King of glory shall come in.
"Who is he, this King of glory?" "The LORD of hosts,
he is the King of glory." Psalm 24:7-10

Who is this king of glory? What are we looking for and would we know him if we saw him? Imagine the splendor of a royal christening, the opulence of the coronation of the heir to the throne of the richest kingdom on earth, or the pageantry of a parade in honor of the return of a conquering emperor.

That is what the citizens of Jerusalem were expecting with the arrival of the Messiah. But here is the paradox. Everyone expected that when the Messiah, the King of Glory, entered Jerusalem and the Temple for the first time, he would do so in splendor and majesty, and that the very gates of the city would recognize and welcome him. Instead, our Scriptures tell us that Mary and Joseph quietly brought Jesus to the temple to offer the sacrifice required by the law upon the birth of a first-born child. The Messiah comes, not as a mighty king but as a 40 day old infant.

But that is not all. The offering made for the redemption of this first-born is the offering of impoverished parents. The offering would normally have been a lamb and a pigeon or turtledove. But Luke tells us that Mary and Joseph did not offer a lamb, presumably because they could not afford such a sacrifice. Their offering was made via an exception in the law that allowed families who could not afford a lamb to substitute either a pair of turtle doves or two young pigeons. Thus, rather than being presented in the temple accompanied by all the wealth and riches of royalty, this Messiah comes in both humility and poverty.

Who are we expecting? If we are bound to the idea that the Messiah will be an earthly king of great power and military might, then why do our Scriptures present us with a baby born into poverty? What if the glory, power and might of God are revealed in our humanity? What if the gates of the kingdom swing open to welcome the One who comes enfolded in the love of his parents and appareled in the robes of humility?

Company in Suffering

Because he himself was tested by what he suffered, he is able to help those who are being tested. Hebrews 2:18

For many people, the worst part about suffering is the feeling of isolation or loneliness that so often accompanies pain or distress. In fact, studies have demonstrated how feelings of loneliness actually interfere with the healing process. Human contact is a very necessary component of health and wholeness; and people who are in regular contact with others are much likely to be healthy, or to recover when they are ill or injured.

The power of companionship is especially evident in situations of mental or spiritual suffering. The knowledge that someone loves us, cares about us, and is willing to be present with us in our pain has great therapeutic value. Most people know this intuitively and are led to seek out a sympathetic person or agency in such situations. But do we remember that Jesus also knows what it is to be human, to be tempted and tested, to suffer and die?

The blessing and blessedness of Incarnation lies precisely in the fact that in his humanity, Jesus experienced all that we experience; and even though he overcome and conquered, he knows what we are going through. Our suffering can never surprise him. Instead, our suffering can be an opportunity for us to remember that he not only walks alongside us, but that he has also walked this path himself.

How does he help us? When we are united to him in prayer, our hearts are reassured that we are not alone. And when we are in a community of faith, we are reminded by the presence and ministry of others that we are surrounded by those who participate in the work of Incarnation by embodying the love of God for us.

Does this always work? Yes and no. Heartfelt prayer in which we ask for the comfort and reassurance of Christ's presence is a prayer which will be answered, perhaps not with immediate physical or mental healing, but with the faith and confidence to persevere. And no, communities do not always respond as promptly or as lovingly as they might, and individuals who are suffering do not always make their needs known. But the work of the Church is to be the Body of Christ in the world, and an agent of healing. We are not called to judge. We are called to the work of love, empathy and compassion, and we are led by the One who has gone there before us, and who is always with us. We are not alone.

Feast of the Presentation ~ February 2nd

Almighty and everliving God, we humbly pray that, as your only-begotten Son was this day presented in the temple, so we may be presented to you with pure and clean hearts by Jesus Christ our Lord; who lives and reigns with you and the Holy Spirit, one God, now and for ever. Amen. (Collect for the Feast of the Presentation)

This prayer is a reminder that we, too, are presented to God for dedication and for redemption.

Just as it is the work of Christ to redeem the world, it is the work of the Church to bear the Light to the world; and in order to take our place for the work of the Church, it is the work of the individual Christian to allow the truth of God as revealed in the Light of Christ, to cleanse and purify our hearts.

When you are next in a church, sit in silence for a time. Look at the candles and know them to be metaphors for the light of Christ. Feel their light shining into your life. Let it illumine your mind. Bask in the light for a time before you ask God what light you are being called to bear. Do not be in a rush to know the answer, but be awake and alert for the answer when it comes – in an hour, a day, or a year. And in the meantime, make your life an offering.

Discernment

"Now there was a man in Jerusalem whose name was Simeon; this man was righteous and devout, looking forward to the consolation of Israel, and the Holy Spirit rested on him. It had been revealed to him by the Holy Spirit that he would not see death before he had seen the Lord's Messiah. Guided by the Spirit, Simeon came into the temple; and when the parents brought in the child Jesus, to do for him what was customary under the law, Simeon took him in his arms and praised God, saying, "Master, now you are dismissing your servant in peace, according to your word; for my eyes have seen your salvation, which you have prepared in the presence of all peoples, a light for revelation to the Gentiles and for glory to your people Israel." (Luke 2:25-32)

Sometimes we call it intuition, but we all know how on certain occasions we just "know" things. Scripture refers to this knowledge as the spiritual gift of discernment. Like intuition, or any other gift of the Spirit, exercising a spiritual gift requires practice, patience and humility and may be stronger in some folk than in others. But discernment is one of those gifts which is so essential to the life of faith that it seems to be available to everyone.

Spiritual Discernment involves the Spirit-led ability to see God at work, and to recognize and respond to the presence of God in others. It is what assists us in knowing what we are being called to do (or to avoid), and to proclaim the work of God when we encounter it.

And discernment works best when we are focused on what it is that we are looking for. Simeon looked forward to the coming of the Messiah. He had spent his life in reverent and watchful anticipation. So, when he encountered Jesus, he was able to recognize him.

Are you looking for the Messiah? Are you open to the leading of the Spirit? Are you prepared by prayer, study and participation in community to discern God's work in this world? And when you encounter it, are you willing to give God praise and glory?

Prophecy

There was also a prophet, Anna the daughter of Phanuel, of the tribe of Asher. She was of a great age, having lived with her husband seven years after her marriage, then as a widow to the age of eighty-four. She never left the temple but worshiped there with fasting and prayer night and day. At that moment she came, and began to praise God and to speak about the child to all who were looking for the redemption of Jerusalem. (Luke 2:36-38)

Anna has the spiritual gift of prophecy. She is able to look at something taking place in the present and interpret its importance for the future. It is important to remember this because prophecy is not fortune-telling. It is much more than that. To be a prophet is to say, "If this – then that." And so she is able to see the infant Jesus and affirm what had been said about him by the prophets and by Simeon.

But she also shows us the cost of being a prophetic voice. She is a widow, and as such is without family support or income. She survives, physically, by living in the temple. She prays and fasts continually. She offers up all that she is to the service of God. And her offering is accepted. When Jesus is presented in the temple, her gift and her piety allow her to see what he will become and to give voice to her praise to God.

I cannot help but wonder what our world would be like if those among us with the gift of prophecy were more willing to exercise it. Granted, most prophets are not perceived as being as benevolent (or harmless) as Anna. Prophets are more often called to deliver a message of warning. So, being a prophet can be a challenging, if not dangerous, occupation. Prophets often encounter ostracism, and become the object of the anger and defensiveness they may provoke.

But what if we had the courage to speak up anyway? What if we were to let the Spirit guide us in speaking the truth? Because, speaking the truth is also the work of Epiphany. The truth sheds light on whatever it touches. And when the truth is spoken in love, without the intention to harm, to embarrass or to even a score, it has extraordinary power to lead us to health and wholeness.

Fasting for Justice

Is not this the fast that I choose: to loose the bonds of injustice, to undo the thongs of the yoke, to let the oppressed go free, and to break every yoke?

Fasting is not just an act of self-denial. In order to effective, a fast must be undertaken with the idea that we are refusing one thing in order to make room to receive something else. For example, if I choose to fast on Ash Wednesday by not eating during the daylight hours, I will certainly be hungry and will have the opportunity to take those feelings of hunger and turn them toward an awareness of how many people are hungry all the time. Or if I give up eating chocolate on the weekdays of Lent, I am free to take the money I would have spent on chocolate and give it to a worthy cause. (Not to mention that I will really appreciate the taste of chocolate if I eat any on Sundays.)

In short, fasting is a spiritual discipline which focuses on honoring God by self-denial accompanied by action.

Fasting is an internal action intended to help us turn outward. It is not simply for our benefit, it is an act of worship. Fasting unaccompanied by action runs the risk of becoming rote or mechanical, or worse yet, self-serving.

That is the point of this lesson from Isaiah. The people are quite adept at offering the sacrifices with which they are comfortable. But they have forgotten how to fast from selfishness and comfort. The prophet reminds them that they are be actively engaged in seeking justice and peace for the world. And, just as Jesus tells us that when we neglect the least among us we are in fact neglecting him; Isaiah tells the people that God is not pleased with or satisfied by worship that merely follows the formulas.

God desires freedom for God's people. In fasting, accompanied by action, we are liberated from bondage to self, and freed to join in the work of freeing others.

Light in the Darkness

*Light shines in the darkness for the upright; **
the righteous are merciful and full of compassion. (Psalm 112:4)

I am not afraid of the dark; probably because I had a severe case of measles when I was six that required me to stay in a darkened room for three weeks. Even with that precaution, I was very ill, and have been shockingly near-sighted ever since. And though I do manage to get around quite well in my own home in the dark, I am very uncomfortable navigating in unfamiliar surroundings, especially outdoors.

So I can really resonate with this verse from the Psalms. I need a light shining in the darkness! I would really prefer to see the tree roots, holes and rocks in my path before I run into them. The moral and spiritual life is like that as well. So long as we are still in the "darkness" of selfishness or indifference (both of which can cause us to be inordinately focused on picking our own solitary way through life), we are far more prone to stumbling.

The season of Epiphany reminds us that there is a light in the darkness. It is a light which is especially evident to those who are "upright" or at least seeking to be so. When we are focused on following the light of Christ, the darkness we encounter along the way is lessened by the righteousness we strive to embody. And because we know the dangers of stumbling over a tree-root in the dark, we are more likely to be merciful to and compassionate toward those who do stumble.

Most of all, as we learn to walk in the light, we also learn to shed that light upon others. We become light-bearers, and the light we share serves to light the way for those who need it.

The Power of a Personal Witness

When I came to you, brothers and sisters, I did not come proclaiming the mystery of God to you in lofty words or wisdom. For I decided to know nothing among you except Jesus Christ, and him crucified. And I came to you in weakness and in fear and in much trembling. My speech and my proclamation were not with plausible words of wisdom, but with a demonstration of the Spirit and of power, so that your faith might rest not on human wisdom but on the power of God. (1 Corinthians 2:1-5)

For those of us who live primarily "in our heads", life is often one long journey of trying to make things make sense. We want to know the how, why and wherefore of our experiences and we expect our experiences to conform to our expectations. I imagine that's why I loved the study of systematic theology. But as essential as that study was, and gratifying as it was to be able to fit the pieces of Scripture, Tradition and Reason together into a coherent and internally consistent whole, there was little in the process that could touch or move my heart. And any argument I might make to convince another would be heavy on detail and very light on conviction. In other words, largely academic.

It was only when I was able to combine the "facts" of my beliefs with the "witness" of my faith that I was able to begin to preach.

That is what makes the writings of St. Paul so effective. To be sure, he knows his material! But he does not try to persuade with logic and argument. He tells the story of his own relationship to the risen Christ, and he dares to let others see that until he had a personal encounter with Him, he was unable to bear witness to the saving love of God in Christ.

That should be good news for all of us. We don't need to win a debate. We just need to share what we know from personal experience, allowing the Holy Spirit to guide us in what we say and do. God does most of the heavy lifting. We are simply allowing the message to be translated into the language of our own hearts.

Salt of the Earth – Light of the World

*Jesus said, "You are the salt of the earth; but if salt has lost its taste, how can its saltiness be restored? It is no longer good for anything, but is thrown out and trampled underfoot. You are the light of the world. A city built on a hill cannot be hid. No one after lighting a lamp puts it under the bushel basket, but on the lampstand, and it gives light to all in the house. In the same way, let your light shine before others, so that they may see your good works and give glory to your Father in heaven. (*Matthew 5:13-16)

After having seen one too many crude and insulting bumper stickers, my husband, Will, decided to design his own. The difference was that his sticker would quote Jesus and communicate a blessing rather than invite a curse. Now anyone stopped in traffic behind either of our cars reads:

"You are the salt of the earth. You are the light of the world."

As this lesson from Matthew's Gospel reminds us, Jesus blesses us freely, but not casually. Being the light of the world or the salt of the earth is serious business. Light reveals the truth. Salt is a preservative. This quote is both an admonition and a blessing. It is as though Jesus is saying to us "Remember who and what you are!" We are blessed with the responsibility of bringing light and salt to an often chaotic and decaying world. Yes, it requires work, but it is also an indication of how much God depends upon us for the proclamation of the Good News. It is also a reminder that others are watching and that what we do matters.

But being salt and light is not an individual blessing intended for our personal edification. It is the task of the Body of Christ to embody this work. We, collectively, need one another and the benefits of worship in community to help us keep our saltiness and our light – not so that our worship community can be the best kept secret in town – but so we can give light to others and so that God gets the glory.

The Law Fulfilled

"Do not think that I have come to abolish the law or the prophets; I have come not to abolish but to fulfill. For truly I tell you, until heaven and earth pass away, not one letter, not one stroke of a letter, will pass from the law until all is accomplished. Therefore, whoever breaks one of the least of these commandments, and teaches others to do the same, will be called least in the kingdom of heaven; but whoever does them and teaches them will be called great in the kingdom of heaven. For I tell you, unless your righteousness exceeds that of the scribes and Pharisees, you will never enter the kingdom of heaven." (Matthew 5:17-20)

Jesus the Christ is the fulfillment of the Law. He is the sum total of righteousness. And he accomplishes this through his unflinching obedience to the summary of the law. "Love God with all your heart, and your neighbor as yourself." Everything that he said, taught or did was an enacted sermon on what it means to love God and neighbor.

When we are considering whether to ignore or discard any part of the Law, it is incumbent upon us to ask and answer this question, "How does this Law/Commandment help or hinder me in loving God and neighbor?" That is the only permissible standard by which to make a decision. It is also the only way to tell which of those laws are inspired by God and which may reflect the desires of lesser entities. Some are pretty obvious – killing another person in order to get their land does not demonstrate love for God or for your neighbor. Thus "thou shalt not covet" and "thou shalt not kill" are ratified by the words and actions of Jesus. But when Jesus meets people intending to stone a woman for adultery, he fulfills the law by pointing out that only those who are without sin are morally competent to cast the first stone. In this case, loving God and neighbor is fulfilled by an act of mercy and compassionate confrontation.

It may seem easier to follow the letter of the law and then rest on our "righteousness", but such a path is not worthy of the gifts of faith and reason which God has given us. The truth of the law endures, of course, and serves to point us toward the will of God. But the law is only fulfilled when we follow Jesus' example in interpreting the law through the filter of the Great Commandment.

Abundant Living

Set us free, O God, from the bondage of our sins, and give us the liberty of that abundant life which you have made known to us in your Son our Savior Jesus Christ; who lives and reigns with you, in the unity of the Holy Spirit, one God, now and forever. Amen. (Collect for the Fifth Sunday of Epiphany)

How easy it is for us to be weighed down by the awareness of our own failings! And how tempting it can become to believe that God has given up on us or that we can never possibly be worthy of God's love and forgiveness. But such thinking is simply wrong.

If we feel weighed down, that awareness is an invitation to repentance, forgiveness and healing. God has already forgiven us – that was accomplished by God in the Work of Christ. But the only way that we can know and receive that forgiveness is to acknowledge our need for it and open our hearts to receive it.

And while it is true that we cannot, in and of ourselves, ever be good enough or worthy enough, we don't have to be! The liberty of abundant life is a free gift from God, revealed to us through Christ.

So if we already have these things, what are we asking for when we say this prayer? We are asking God to open our hearts and our minds to an understanding of what already is. We are asking for the strength and courage to confess, repent/turn around, and move on.

Ignorance is a burden. Self-delusion holds us captive. The sin of believing that we are beyond help is a terrible form of bondage. But each of those misconceptions can be instantly and totally dispelled. We need only remember that God sees us as precious and beloved and worthy of the status of daughters and sons; and that God has done the work of making this so. Once having remembered that, we are free to accept it as truth and begin to live an abundant life.

Fire and Water – Life and Death

If you choose, you can keep the commandments, and to act faithfully is a matter of your own choice. He has placed before you fire and water; stretch out your hand for whichever you choose. Before each person are life and death, and whichever one chooses will be given. For great is the wisdom of the Lord; he is mighty in power and sees everything; his eyes are on those who fear him, and he knows every human action. He has not commanded anyone to be wicked, and he has not given anyone permission to sin. (Ecclesiasticus 15:15-20

When Scripture speaks of life and death, the reference is too much more than physical existence. Life means abiding in the presence of God, while death means being cut off from a relationship with God and God's people.

As in everything else, God allows us to choose whether or not we will dwell in love and righteousness. Each of us bears the image of God in our souls because we are created that way. And each baptized person is a member of the Body of Christ. But that does not mean that we are compelled to participate in the fullness of life offered to us.

The writer of Ecclesiasticus reminds us that while God has given us all we need, God has also left us free to choose our own path. For God does not desire that we be slaves or puppets. God desires that we enter freely into a relationship that will form and shape us throughout our lives.

That choice is both an opportunity and a challenge. But no matter what we choose, God will love us none the less. God does not write us off. God waits.
May we all respond to the invitation!

Blessedness

*Happy are they whose way is blameless, **
who walk in the law of the LORD!
*Happy are they who observe his decrees **
and seek him with all their hearts!
*Who never do any wrong, **
but always walk in his ways.
(Psalm 119:1-3)

In Greek, "happy" and "blessed" are both expressed in the same word – "makarios." It is a good and blessed and happy thing to be in a right relationship with God. In fact, righteousness is best described as "being in a right relationship". But that does not mean that merely keeping the letter of the law brings happiness. An angry, fearful or evil person is perfectly capable of keeping the rules while having no concern about the people involved or the state of one's own heart.

A happy, blessed and righteous person walks in the way of the Lord, but walking in the way of the Lord is much more than just obeying the law. It means allowing the law to transform us, and to redirect our hearts toward God and others. Such a manner of life and of keeping the law is based on our wanting it to become natural to us, because we understand it to be what God desires for us and has provided for our welfare. Indeed, over time, it does become second nature to us – not because we are afraid of punishment, but because we are desirous of wholeness and righteousness.

And while none of us is ever going to be able to say that we "never do any wrong", all of us are on a journey of sanctification. Throughout our lives, God is working on us so that we may grow in the goodness for which we were created. That growth enables us to recognize when we are on the path, and when we are straying away from it, and each time we choose to return we are stronger and happier.

May God grant us the grace to see the path and the desire to walk it.

Mature Faith

Brothers and sisters, I could not speak to you as spiritual people, but rather as people of the flesh, as infants in Christ. I fed you with milk, not solid food, for you were not ready for solid food. Even now you are still not ready, for you are still of the flesh. For as long as there is jealousy and quarreling among you, are you not of the flesh, and behaving according to human inclinations (1 Corinthians 3:1-3)

I have often marveled at the manner in which the Church has treated its members as infants. We have been reluctant to examine and teach the difficult parts of Scripture, we have systematically lowered our expectations for faithful participation, and we have talked down to those willing to listen to us. So, while St. Paul may have been absolutely correct in his comments to the 1st century church at Corinth, it seems to me that the contemporary church is determined to keep the Body of Christ on a lifelong diet of milk.

The Good News of God in Christ is easily understood. God is with us. But living the Good News requires effort, discernment, courage and perseverance – as well as the willingness to change and to grow. We must be fed a diet on which our faith can thrive.

Surely we are capable of moving on to solid food. We navigate each day through an extraordinarily complex world of science, technology, and interpersonal relationships. We deserve an experience of church which demands the full engagement of our hearts, minds and spirits. We need to be chewing on and digesting Scripture and Tradition as the solid food of an adult faith. And we need training in thinking through and articulating our beliefs.

I believe that we are ready.

First be Reconciled:

Jesus said, "You have heard that it was said to those of ancient times, `You shall not murder'; and `whoever murders shall be liable to judgment.' But I say to you that if you are angry with a brother or sister, you will be liable to judgment; and if you insult a brother or sister, you will be liable to the council; and if you say, `You fool,' you will be liable to the hell of fire. So when you are offering your gift at the altar, if you remember that your brother or sister has something against you, leave your gift there before the altar and go; first be reconciled to your brother or sister, and then come and offer your gift. (Matthew 5:21-24)

When the Episcopal Book of Common Prayer was last revised in 1979, an ancient liturgical practice –exchanging the Peace – was re-introduced to our Sunday worship. At first, the response of many congregations was less than enthusiastic. ("Why should we interrupt the service to say hello to people? What is this – intermission???") But within a few years, "passing the Peace" had become not only normal but quite popular. It builds community, encourages us to actually look at one another, and makes visitors feel welcome.

Unfortunately, it had also lost a good bit of its meaning.

As Matthew makes clear in this passage, being at peace with one's neighbors is a prerequisite to right worship. The fact that this event takes place just before Holy Communion begins demonstrates that the folks who revised our prayer book had made the connection as well. Before we offer ourselves, our gifts of bread and wine, and our tithes to the Lord, we should offer peace and reconciliation to our brothers and sisters with whom we are in conflict. In other words, it's pretty difficult to worship the God of all Creation when we are angry at one of God's creatures.

Of course, we don't have to wait until Sunday morning to make peace with one another. And the sooner we reach out, the easier it will be. So, if you are in conflict with a brother or sister, consider how the conflict affects your ability to worship God, and to see God in that person. Then do what you can to do reconciled, and give thanks to God.

Ordering Our Lives and Desires

"You have heard that it was said, `You shall not commit adultery.' But I say to you that everyone who looks at a woman with lust has already committed adultery with her in his heart. If your right eye causes you to sin, tear it out and throw it away; it is better for you to lose one of your members than for your whole body to be thrown into hell. And if your right hand causes you to sin, cut it off and throw it away; it is better for you to lose one of your members than for your whole body to go into hell. "It was also said, `Whoever divorces his wife, let him give her a certificate of divorce.' But I say to you that anyone who divorces his wife, except on the ground of unchastity, causes her to commit adultery; and whoever marries a divorced woman commits adultery. (Matthew 5:26-32)

Human sexuality has always been a hot topic. The order (or disorder) of what we euphemistically refer to as our "personal lives" speaks volumes about our values, and when in disarray may provide an endless source for gossip or speculation. In our culture, sexuality also sells. Many celebrities and most contemporary entertainment could not survive financially without the marketing of sex.

Chastity, however, is not so hot a topic. Chastity means recognizing that our sexuality is a gift which greatly enhances our lives, but which also has the power to ruin and destroy. Chastity requires that we respect the other person and that we refrain from using, abusing or manipulating others for the sake of our own gratification.

As in most spiritual situations, sin a question of intention as well as action. It is sinful to take that which does not belong to us. But it is also sinful to look at another person as an object. It is demeaning to that person, and even if they are unaware of your thoughts toward them, it is harmful to your own spirit.

Jesus was quite fond of "pushing the envelope" when it came to interpreting the law. He was not content to have us think that so long as we obeyed the letter of the law, we were practicing righteousness. He wanted us to know that entertaining the desire to sin (even if we do not follow through physically) is dangerous. It allows us to build the habit of fantasy and the stronger the fantasy, the easier it becomes to act upon.

Besides, lust is a form of greed, and greed is a soul-killer.

Balance in Life

O God, the strength of all who put their trust in you: Mercifully accept our prayers; and because in our weakness we can do nothing good without you, give us the help of your grace, that in keeping your commandments we may please you both in will and deed; through Jesus Christ our Lord, who lives and reigns with you and the Holy Spirit, one God, for ever and ever. Amen. (Collect for Epiphany 6)

Seeking righteousness, and walking in the way of the Lord is a matter of intention and of action. Both need to work together in harmony with the grace of God in order to find balance in our lives.

Through grace we are able to desire to please God, and by grace we are empowered to act. When we keep the commandments in our hearts, it is easier to obey the law, and when we act with obedience, we strengthen our intentional will.

Neither will be perfect. But with the grace of God working in and through us, we are sheltered and nurtured as we walk the journey toward the righteousness to which God calls us. Grace is God's free gift to us to help us on the way. We need only reach out to receive it.

Holiness

The LORD spoke to Moses, saying: Speak to all the congregation of the people of Israel and say to them: You shall be holy, for I the LORD your God am holy. When you reap the harvest of your land, you shall not reap to the very edges of your field, or gather the gleanings of your harvest. You shall not strip your vineyard bare, or gather the fallen grapes of your vineyard; you shall leave them for the poor and the alien: I am the LORD your God. You shall not steal; you shall not deal falsely; and you shall not lie to one another. And you shall not swear falsely by my name, profaning the name of your God: I am the LORD. You shall not defraud your neighbor; you shall not steal; and you shall not keep for yourself the wages of a laborer until morning. You shall not revile the deaf or put a stumbling block before the blind; you shall fear your God: I am the LORD. You shall not render an unjust judgment; you shall not be partial to the poor or defer to the great: with justice you shall judge your neighbor. You shall not go around as a slanderer among your people, and you shall not profit by the blood of your neighbor: I am the LORD. You shall not hate in your heart anyone of your kin; you shall reprove your neighbor, or you will incur guilt yourself. You shall not take vengeance or bear a grudge against any of your people, but you shall love your neighbor as yourself: (Leviticus 19:1-2, 9-18)

To be holy is to be set apart for God. Holiness is not perfection, but it is very intentional. When we are engaged in a life of holiness we are engaged in a life of seeking the will and the presence of God. And how do we do that? In this passage from the Holiness Code of the Hebrew Scriptures we see that there is only one standard by which God judges holiness: Love your neighbor as yourself. And this is not just a model for an ethical life. This is an order from God. Be holy, God says, because I, your God, am holy.

Each of these admonitions is predicated on treating others with respect, dignity, justice and compassion. The people are to provide for the poor and the alien, to be honest in trade, business, employment practices and conversation. They are to care for the disabled, treat everyone equally, and avoid gossip, holding everyone, especially themselves, to a standard of love and forgiveness.

Even when societies do not regard them as religious or spiritual obligations, these values provide a foundation for safety and mutual growth. But as people of faith, we also practice these behaviors because we are in a covenanted relationship with God who has created us with the potential for holiness. When you love your neighbor you are also loving God.

Law and Structure

Teach me, O LORD, the way of your statutes, and I shall keep it to the end.
Give me understanding, and I shall keep your law; I shall keep it with all my heart.
Make me go in the path of your commandments, for that is my desire.
Incline my heart to your decrees and not to unjust gain.
Turn my eyes from watching what is worthless; give me life in your ways.
Fulfill your promise to your servant, which you make to those who fear you.
Turn away the reproach which I dread, because your judgments are good.
Behold, I long for your commandments; in your righteousness preserve my life.
(Psalm 119:33-40)

Do you remember how in grade school your teacher would start each year by writing the rules for proper behavior on the blackboard? As a child I found it comforting when I knew what the rules were. Even if I thought they were silly or if I decided to disobey them, the rules provided a structure for the classroom. The rules also told me a good bit about the teacher and what she valued. They helped me understand the process, and know the limits.

The law and statutes of the LORD are intended to provide a similar structure for us. When we study them, we are seeking to learn what pleases God and what will preserve our lives. The problem arises, of course, when we focus on the individual laws at the expense of the "way", "path" and "inclination" resulting from adherence to the law. All of the law, taken together, leads us along the way and helps us to grow in righteousness. Unthinking obedience to the letter of the law does not.

Because what is the point of all the law? Life. "Give me life in your ways", the Psalmist prays. That is why it is so important for us to always examine rules, laws, or commandments in terms of whether they are life-producing. And that is why it is essential for us to be able to re-interpret or even discard individual laws when they do not bring us to life. That is what Jesus was doing every time he taught using the phrase *"you have heard it said...but I say to you..."*

A life of walking in the path of God's commandments will be a life of spiritual growth which makes us think about what we are doing, why we are doing it, and what fruit it is producing.

You are God's Temple

According to the grace of God given to me, like a skilled master builder I laid a foundation, and someone else is building on it. Each builder must choose with care how to build on it. For no one can lay any foundation other than the one that has been laid; that foundation is Jesus Christ. Do you not know that you are God's temple and that God's Spirit dwells in you? If anyone destroys God's temple, God will destroy that person. For God's temple is holy, and you are that temple. (I Cor. 3:10-11)

This was one of my mother's favorite bible passages, which she used to great effect when teaching me proper behavior. "Your body is God's temple. Do not take it anywhere or do anything with it that would embarrass Jesus." Believe me, those instructions gave me more than a little pause over the years. If my body was temple then it had to be clean, beautiful, and meticulously maintained. And it had to be located at all times in wholesome and proper surroundings. It was probably a good thing that I did not know how much time Jesus himself spent hanging out with the wrong people. My youth would have been a great deal more entertaining than it was!

Yes, I believed her. It took me decades, though, to believe that Jesus would actually visit this temple. Nor did I understand that I was expected to be "at home" if he did drop by. In fact, I was so busy doing my best not to neglect the exterior of the premises that it never occurred to me that there was an interior spiritual component to the stewardship of my life, my health, and my personhood.

But if the Holy Spirit dwells in the temple of our individual selves, then that is where we will most surely encounter the holy. God is not some distant, transcendent force. The Spirit of God dwells in each of us, and in all of us together. But do we dwell there as well?

Finding balance and wholeness – being a home in our own lives – is one of the greatest challenges of contemporary life. Many of us are so fractured that we are never fully present to ourselves or to anyone else. But if God is willing to dwell with us, to abide with us, then shouldn't we feel at home in our own selves?

Fools for Christ

Do not deceive yourselves. If you think that you are wise in this age, you should become fools so that you may become wise. For the wisdom of this world is foolishness with God. For it is written, "He catches the wise in their craftiness," and again, "The Lord knows the thoughts of the wise, that they are futile." So let no one boast about human leaders. For all things are yours, whether Paul or Apollos or Cephas or the world or life or death or the present or the future-- all belong to you, and you belong to Christ, and Christ belongs to God. (I Corinthians 3: 16-23)

Christianity is a powerfully counter-intuitive faith. Is wisdom futile? Didn't Solomon ask for and receive the gift of wisdom? Didn't Jesus instruct his disciples to be wise as serpents and gentle as doves? Yet St. Paul, in this passage, seems to believe otherwise.

Not really. The wisdom which St. Paul challenges is the tendency toward self-aggrandizement that is often associated with power, success, and celebrity. We might even call it personal charisma with the ability to manipulate. But such wisdom of the world, as powerful and persuasive as it may be is foolishness to God.

The power of the proclamation of the Good News does not depend on how smart, eloquent or articulate the speaker may be. The Good News is easily understood, and easily proclaimed. God in Christ is with us. There is no need to make it any more complicated. Theologians may delight in studying and expounding on the Good News, but no amount of embellishment or explanation can improve on the message.

We have that truth and we are called to proclaim it. May our lives be our sermons.

Love Your Enemies

Jesus said, "You have heard that it was said, `An eye for an eye and a tooth for a tooth.' But I say to you, Do not resist an evildoer. But if anyone strikes you on the right cheek, turn the other also; and if anyone wants to sue you and take your coat, give your cloak as well; and if anyone forces you to go one mile, go also the second mile. Give to everyone who begs from you, and do not refuse anyone who wants to borrow from you. "You have heard that it was said, `You shall love your neighbor and hate your enemy.' But I say to you, Love your enemies and pray for those who persecute you, so that you may be children of your Father in heaven; for he makes his sun rise on the evil and on the good, and sends rain on the righteous and on the unrighteous. For if you love those who love you, what reward do you have? Do not even the tax collectors do the same? And if you greet only your brothers and sisters, what more are you doing than others? Do not even the Gentiles do the same? Be perfect, therefore, as your heavenly Father is perfect." (Matthew 5:38-48)

Life would be so much easier if Jesus did not have such high expectations for us! He delights in expanding our awareness and challenging our comfortable faith. "It is not good enough just to do what is required of you" he says, "Go on, do more, search for and explore the outer limits of what it means to love." In other words, "Be Perfect."

Now, perfection in this sense does not mean that we are to be without flaws, but it does mean that we are to be full, whole and complete. If we are doing the least possible amount of work, or showing the smallest allowable amount of cooperation, then we are far from complete. We haven't done all that we can do.

Please remember: this is not a prescription for exhausting ourselves and our lives in the pursuit of holiness or perfection. Christ does not require that we die in his service. But this is a reminder that we are far more likely to under-perform our duties of love and charity than we are to overdo them.

And as always, this is a question of intention. What are we expecting to achieve by acts of love, charity and obedience? Are we responding in hope of reward? Or are we learning to be motivated by compassion for others, and by love of God?

Jesus wants us to grow beyond the ideas of balance and equality, even beyond the ideas of justice and fairness. He wants us to glimpse the larger possibilities of the life of faith, and to pursue them.

The Gift of Love

O Lord, you have taught us that without love whatever we do is worth nothing: Send your Holy Spirit and pour into our hearts your greatest gift, which is love, the true bond of peace and of all virtue, without which whoever lives is accounted dead before you. Grant this for the sake of your only Son Jesus Christ, who lives and reigns with you and the Holy Spirit, one God, now and forever. Amen. (Collect Epiphany 7)

Sometimes we Christians are very glib with our comments about the Holy Spirit. We tend to soften and domesticate the "breath of God", the One who moved over creation in the beginning. But the Holy Spirit is the keeper of spiritual gifts and presence of God which gives life to the Church. And love is the greatest of the gifts of the Spirit. Without love, all that we do is without worth. And without love, we are as good as dead.

But, do we dare to ask for the gift of love? Do we know what it will require of us?

The spiritual gift of love requires us to open the doors of our hearts to life, to one another and to God. Once opened, everything flows in upon us; and as with any flood, closing the doors again may not be possible. We will be confronted with the hopes, dreams and needs of others. We will see the truth about our own lives. And we will find ourselves in the all-embracing and eternally demanding presence of God.

And yet, we do ask for this, the greatest of gifts. It is as though we know that without it we cannot be fully human, and the prize of being fully human is worth the price that love will exact from us. For we know that we do not walk alone and that the same God who bestows the gift of love, is the One who embodied Love in human form, and who has created us with the capacity to receive and to share it.

Actively Seeking God

The LORD said to Moses, "Come up to me on the mountain, and wait there; and I will give you the tablets of stone, with the law and the commandment, which I have written for their instruction." So Moses set out with his assistant Joshua, and Moses went up into the mountain of God. To the elders he had said, "Wait here for us, until we come to you again; for Aaron and Hur are with you; whoever has a dispute may go to them." Then Moses went up on the mountain, and the cloud covered the mountain. The glory of the LORD settled on Mount Sinai, and the cloud covered it for six days; on the seventh day he called to Moses out of the cloud. Now the appearance of the glory of the LORD was like a devouring fire on the top of the mountain in the sight of the people of Israel. Moses entered the cloud, and went up on the mountain. Moses was on the mountain for forty days and forty nights. (Exodus 24:12-18)

Moses must have been one of the bravest and most patient men ever to have lived. I can understand how he might have stopped to look at a burning bush, but I am not at all certain that I would be able to sit waiting on a mountain top for six days, let alone walk into a cloud. But from what we know of him, Moses lived the sort of adult life that would certainly have taught him patience and courage. And his relationship with Yahweh God meant that when God spoke, Moses obeyed. Because of that, Moses was one of the few people to experience firsthand the glory of God.

Scripture often speaks of how mere human beings must be sheltered from such a direct experience of the Holiness of God. We are told that we would be overcome if not killed by such glory. And I suspect that most of us are perfectly happy not to have to find out. We rather like keeping God at a safe and respectful distance.

But I wonder about what we miss by not actively seeking the presence of God? What do we lose when we don't sit waiting for God? And when God calls out our name, why not step into the cloud?

If you are willing to try, silence is an excellent way to wait for God. It is also the first step in learning how to enter the cloud. As the psalmist writes: "Be still and know that I am God." That is really all that is required – even patience and courage to be still.

He Is the Holy One

Proclaim the greatness of the LORD our God and fall down before his footstool; he is the Holy One. (Psalm 99:5)

There seems to be plenty of fear and trembling in the world these days, but not so much awe and wonder. The lines of demarcation in our society put people and things in one of two camps – good, friendly and helpful, or bad, hostile and dangerous. This seems to be true even of our experience of God. Faith systems tend to depict God either as wrathful or innocuous, but seldom as Holy and Other. We can wrap our minds around anger, especially righteous indignation, and we are quite adept at softening the ferocious love of God into something softer, friendlier, and more accessible. But we are at a loss when we come to the area of whole-hearted worship.

This was not true of the Psalmist. He understands God as the Maker and Doer of all things. He understands that God makes and maintains all of creation and that he, the Psalmist, is a creature. He knows God to be utterly Holy and totally Other, which is what makes it possible for him to write of falling down before God's footstool. In fact, his being on his knees before the throne of God is an appropriate response, and is actually an image of trust and intimacy.

The thing is – it is not necessary to make God either angry or accessible. God is what God is, and does not need our assistance with any descriptions. But, I do believe that we would all benefit from a greater appreciation of the Holiness of God and a response of awe and wonder.

The One who made us is also the One who loves and keeps us and the One who calls us to a life of holiness. What an awesome and wonderful thing.

Telling the Story

We did not follow cleverly devised myths when we made known to you the power and coming of our Lord Jesus Christ, but we had been eyewitnesses of his majesty. For he received honor and glory from God the Father when that voice was conveyed to him by the Majestic Glory, saying, "This is my Son, my Beloved, with whom I am well pleased." We ourselves heard this voice come from heaven, while we were with him on the holy mountain. (2 Peter 1:16-18)

St. Peter was a plain-spoken man telling the story of his own experience. He had known Jesus as a human teacher and friend. He had witnessed Jesus' transfiguration on the mountain-top. He had heard the voice of God announcing that Jesus was God's Son, the Beloved. And he wants his readers to remember what he has said.

Those living in the Near Middle East in time of Jesus were well acquainted with stories of gods and demi-gods, most of whom had one human and one divine parent. Peter wants to make certain that no one thinks his witness to Jesus is such a myth. Peter has seen and heard and is convinced that Jesus is the Son of God. It is a conviction that he is about to die for, and there is an urgency to his message. "We had been eyewitnesses of his majesty" he tells them.

As we come to the end of the season of Epiphany and prepare for Lent, let us remember the light that we have experienced through the witness of Jesus' disciples, through our own experience of following Him, and through living in his body the church. And may God grant us all the grace to tell the story of how we know and follow Jesus. Along with Peter, we, too, have been eye-witnesses of his glory in this world. We have been fed at his table and we have seen the light of his love in the faces of those around us.

Being Transfigured

Six days after Peter had acknowledged Jesus as the Christ, the Son of the Living God, Jesus took with him Peter and James and his brother John and led them up a high mountain, by themselves. And he was transfigured before them, and his face shone like the sun, and his clothes became dazzling white. Suddenly there appeared to them Moses and Elijah, talking with him. Then Peter said to Jesus, "Lord, it is good for us to be here; if you wish, I will make three dwellings here, one for you, one for Moses, and one for Elijah." (Matthew 17:1-4)

Human beings are really attracted to liminal places – those spots where earth and sky and water seem to meet. That is probably why so many cultures believed that God lived on a mountaintop, or that the oceans were the womb of the world. When I was a child, I could not wait each year for our trip to visit my grandparents. I loved them, of course, but I also loved the hills and mountains where they lived. And once we got there my sisters and I would collect sticks and pebbles and rocks and build little houses. We also loved the ocean and the wonderful things that we could build with wet sand.

So, I can completely understand St. Peter's desire to build dwellings for Moses, Elijah and Jesus. Here he was, on a holy mountain top with three of the holiest of all people. The natural thing to do was to mark the occasion by offering hospitality and shelter. He no doubt wanted to create something that would be a permanent reminder of what he, James and John had experienced there.

Something wonderful had happened on the mountain. Jesus had been transfigured in face and apparel and fully revealed to human eyes as one on equal footing with Moses and Elijah. It was an affirmation of who and what Jesus was, and a moment of extraordinary importance for Peter, James and John.

Remember all the ways in which we have witnessed the light of the world been made manifest in Christ, and in our lives. From the arrival of the Magi to the arrival of Moses and Elijah, we have been repeatedly reminded that this is the Son of God, the Light of the World, and that God is well pleased with him. We bear witness to that light.

Hearing the Voice of God

While he was still speaking, suddenly a bright cloud overshadowed them, and from the cloud a voice said, "This is my Son, the Beloved; with him I am well pleased; listen to him!" When the disciples heard this, they fell to the ground and were overcome by fear. But Jesus came and touched them, saying, "Get up and do not be afraid." And when they looked up, they saw no one except Jesus himself alone. As they were coming down the mountain, Jesus ordered them, "Tell no one about the vision until after the Son of Man has been raised from the dead." (Matthew 17:5-9)

Peter, James and John love Jesus, and were in the process of coming to know him as the Christ. But there was obviously something about the familiarity of Jesus as a fellow human being that allowed the disciples to be in his presence without fear. The disembodied voice of God, however, knocked them to the ground. This experience of the Holy was totally “Other” and completely beyond their comfort zone.

It is only when Jesus touches them and reassures them that they need not fear that they are able to get up and go on. Jesus, the immanence of God, bridges the gap between their humanity and the terrifyingly transcendent majesty of God.

That is what Incarnation does for us. It mediates the utterly unknowable by making it accessible to our understanding. God was not content to be separate from us. And God wanted us to know and experience God’s presence in a form that we could comprehend. That presence is God, and the light of the world, and the manifestation of God’s own self to creation.

In the Transfiguration of Jesus, his disciples learned who he was. In our life together in the Body of Christ he is revealed to us as well.

How Much Is This Going to Cost?

O God, who before the passion of your only begotten Son revealed his glory upon the holy mountain: Grant to us that we, beholding by faith the light of his countenance, may be strengthened to bear our cross, and be changed into his likeness from glory to glory; through Jesus Christ our Lord, who lives and reigns with you and the Holy Spirit, one God, for ever and ever, Amen. (Collect for the Last Sunday after the Epiphany)

I do wish that so many of the prayers of the Church did not immediately jump to an assumption that those who follow Jesus will be called to a life of suffering. We are called to participate in the proclamation of the Good News of God in Christ, and make him known to the world. While that may at time be a difficult calling, I am not at all convinced that discipleship and bearing a cross are the same thing.

Suffering comes to us all in this life. Sometimes that suffering is associated with choices we make about how we will order our lives, and who we will follow. But we do not bear the cross as Christ did, and it is far too easy to mistake the ordinary, inevitable challenges of life for something similar to passion of Christ.

What we bear is the weight of glory, but we do not bear it alone. All of us together in the Body of Christ share the weight. And the Body of Christ is led and supported by Christ himself, so that if we are willing to receive the transfiguring power of his Light, we are transfigured as well and are strengthened to be disciples.

That is good news indeed.

The Upward Fall

The LORD God took the man and put him in the Garden of Eden to till it and keep it. And the LORD God commanded the man, "You may freely eat of every tree of the garden; but of the tree of the knowledge of good and evil you shall not eat, for in the day that you eat of it you shall die." So when the woman saw that the tree was good for food, and that it was a delight to the eyes, and that the tree was to be desired to make one wise, she took of its fruit and ate; and she also gave some to her husband, who was with her, and he ate. Then the eyes of both were opened, and they knew that they were naked; and they sewed fig leaves together and made loincloths for themselves. (Genesis 2: 15-17, 3; 6-7)

We human beings instinctively dislike limits – especially when they seem to be arbitrary. Tell any two year old "no" and chances are the next words out of his mouth will be "Why???" Knowing that about human nature, I have often wondered by the writer of Genesis did not have Adam ask why. Linking our tendency to question things to the serpent seems to be a way of passing the blame. It also seems to turn our God-given curiosity (which is necessary for survival) into a liability.

That is why this passage is sometimes described as the "upward fall". There is a price to be paid for knowledge, but in this case the price of knowledge is self-awareness, which is also a blessing. If Adam and Eve had not been curious, they would not have sinned. And had they not sinned, they would have remained in the moral innocence of the garden. But God placed the tree in the middle of the garden, and then said "no." Was that merely to test Adam's obedience, or was it perhaps part of God's plan that the first humans should have the opportunity to purchase (albeit at a great price) autonomy? And, had they not reached for the forbidden fruit, would we recognize them as human?

As we enter Lent, we exercise the self-awareness so dearly purchased for us by our ancestors. Lent is a time for prayer and reflection on the choices that we have made. But Lent is not a time for self-denigration. When Adam and Eve recognized that they were naked, they did not pretend that they had not noticed. They clothed themselves. We ought to do the same.

When we become aware that we are in need of healing or forgiveness, no purpose is served by denying the need, or engaging in self-loathing. Instead, we are given the opportunity to clothe ourselves by seeking what we need.

Shrove Tuesday

Happy are they whose transgressions are forgiven, and whose sin is put away!
Happy are they to whom the LORD imputes no guilt,
and in whose spirit there is no guile! (Psalm 32: 1-2)

Shrove means confess, and in the past it was traditional to go to confession on this day is preparation for beginning the fast of Lent. More recently, however, especially for those who will be observing a period of fasting during Lent, the day before Ash Wednesday is known as Mardi Gras or Fat Tuesday. Because the Lenten fast was a very strict one, during which no sugar, meat or dairy was consumed, it was necessary to remove those foods from the larder. A good way to use sugar, butter, milk and eggs was to make pancakes. And thus was born the Annual Parish Shrove Tuesday Pancake Supper.

But there is also a profound theology truth to the observance. Lent will remind us of our sins, but for the moment we are still basking in the light of Epiphany. God Incarnate, the Light of the World, dwells among us. That, like Christmas Day, is an occasion for feasting, and we are happy. "Happy are they whose transgressions are forgiven and whose sin is put away!" The work of God in Christ frees us from our bondage to sin and reminds us that God forgives us. Celebrate!

Tomorrow we will begin the season of reflection. We will walk with Christ through the final stages of his earthly ministry, and we will be invited to understand the consequences of sin, and the enormity of suffering which accompanies the failure to love.

We will do that tomorrow. Today and tonight, let us remember the coming of the Christ Child and be happy.

LENT

Ash Wednesday

Almighty and everlasting God, you hate nothing you have made and forgive the sins of all who are penitent: Create and make in us new and contrite hearts, that we, worthily lamenting our sins and acknowledging our wretchedness, may obtain of you, the God of all mercy, perfect remission and forgiveness; through Jesus Christ our Lord, who lives and reigns with you and the Holy Spirit, one God, for ever and ever. Amen. (Collect for Ash Wednesday)

The Church embraces ambiguity on this day. We describe ourselves as both wretched and beloved. We begin Lent by acknowledging our sins and by being reminded that God does not hate us. Our foreheads are marked with the ashes of mourning but we remember that we are made of the dust of creation.

Ash Wednesday is a day which fully recognizes the paradox of being human. We have the ability to know and follow God, and we very seldom manage to do so. But Ash Wednesday also includes the invitation to keep a Holy Lent. It is as though God says to us, "Stop. Slow Down. Think about your life, your relationships, and your spiritual health. Think about who you are and where you are going. And if you are going in the wrong direction, turn around."

So, on this day, be mindful of your humanity and of God's love and grace. But most of all, remember that God hates nothing that God has made, and that you were made by God. God does not hate you. God loves and forgives you. All you need to do is accept the love and the forgiveness with a new and humble heart.

Thanks be to God.

Made Righteous

But the free gift is not like the trespass. For if the many died through the one man's trespass, much more surely have the grace of God and the free gift in the grace of the one man, Jesus Christ, abounded for the many. Therefore just as one man's trespass led to condemnation for all, so one man's act of righteousness leads to justification and life for all. For just as by the one man's disobedience the many were made sinners, so by the one man's obedience the many will be made righteous. (Romans 5:15, 18-19)

Language changes over time. The meanings of words change. But often, we mistakenly apply the newer definition of a word to an older text. Take the word, "righteousness". In contemporary usage, we equate righteousness with the achievement of good and observable religious attitudes and behaviors. But that is not what the word means in this passage from Romans. The theological meaning of righteousness is "to be in a right relationship with God." Now, while good behaviors are to be expected from people who are in a right relationship with God, those behaviors do not create the state of righteousness. God determines and declares what constitutes being righteous; and thanks be to God, righteousness is not the absence of sin. In fact, the righteous person is far more likely to be aware of the sin in her own life and be grateful to God for the ability to recognize it.

Jesus Christ, in the fullness of his humanity and his divinity, has achieved the obedience to the will of God which we can never achieve. In his perfect, whole, and complete obedience Jesus restored humanity's right relationship to God. We do not have to restore it, but we do have to engage it.

The season of Lent encourages us to reflect upon the condition of our relationship to God. Do we earnestly love God? Do we strive to be faithful in prayer? Do we seek out ways in which to serve God by serving others? Are we mindful of our own need for amendment of life? None of those things will make us righteous, but each of them is an indication that we are seeking to live our lives in a right relationship with God.

Possible Does Not Mean Inevitable

After Jesus was baptized, he was led up by the Spirit into the wilderness to be tempted by the devil. He fasted forty days and forty nights, and afterwards he was famished. The tempter came and said to him, "If you are the Son of God, command these stones to become loaves of bread." But he answered, "It is written, 'One does not live by bread alone, but by every word that comes from the mouth of God.'" Then the devil took him to the holy city and placed him on the pinnacle of the temple, saying to him, "If you are the Son of God, throw yourself down; for it is written, 'He will command his angels concerning you,' and 'On their hands they will bear you up, so that you will not dash your foot against a stone.'" Jesus said to him, "Again it is written, 'Do not put the Lord your God to the test.'" Again, the devil took him to a very high mountain and showed him all the kingdoms of the world and their splendor; and he said to him, "All these I will give you, if you will fall down and worship me." Jesus said to him, "Away with you, Satan! For it is written, 'Worship the Lord your God, and serve only him.'" Then the devil left him, and suddenly angels came and waited on him. (Matthew 14:1-11)

It would have been so easy for Jesus to demonstrate his power by doing all the things that Satan tempted him to do. He could have accomplished all that most people would ever have expected of the messiah simply by following the tempter's lead. But he chose to do things the hard way. He suffered hunger, endured anonymity and refused power because he would not take short cuts in learning who he was and what his work was to be.

We may be tempted to think, "Well, he was Jesus, and Satan had no real power over him." That is true. But what we forget is that the tempter has no real power over us either. So when we choose to take the easy way out, we cannot blame Satan.

In Lent we are invited to take the time – the leisure – to determine who we are and what God is calling us to be. Are we willing to be hungry for the truth about our real needs? Are we ready to do the challenging work of finding and occupying our appointed place in God's world – even if it is less visible or less lucrative than we might wish? And are we prepared to notice and remedy the places in our lives where we worship something other than God?

This, too, is the work of Lent.

Mighty to Save

Almighty God, whose blessed Son was led by the Spirit to be tempted by Satan: Come quickly to help us who are assaulted by many temptations; and, as you know the weaknesses of each of us, let each one find you mighty to save; through Jesus Christ your Son our Lord, who lives and reigns with you and the Holy Spirit, one God, now and for ever. Amen. (Collect for First Sunday in Lent)

Temptation is inevitable. In fact, I believe that there is a direct correlation between our desire to follow Jesus and the degree of temptation we encounter. And if nothing else, temptation is an excellent means of clarifying what it is that we really want. But being tempted is not a sign of weakness, succumbing to temptation is a sign of weakness. Resisting temptation requires strength and that is why we pray that Jesus will quickly come and help us.

Because Jesus shares our humanity, he knows our need. Because he was himself tempted, he knows the power of temptation. And because he endured, his is mighty to save.

Portions of the Great Litany will be recited in many churches on the First Sunday in Lent. In this powerful prayer, we are reminded of all the ways in which we are tempted to abandon our walk with Christ. But in each case, we are also reminded of the grace and power of God that will sustain and carry us through the temptation. Be present in Church and bathe yourself in the strength of God who is mighty to save, and who will not abandon you to temptation.

Radical Trust

The Lord said to Abram, "Go from your country and your kindred and your father's house to the land that I will show you. I will make of you a great nation, and I will bless you, and make your name great, so that you will be a blessing. I will bless those who bless you, and the one who curses you I will curse; and in you all the families of the earth shall be blessed." So Abram went, as the Lord had told him; and Lot went with him. (Genesis 12:1-4a)

Contemporary Americans are highly mobile. We go away to school. We relocate throughout our years of employment. We take vacations to distant lands. And when we retire, we move to places with the best climates and the lowest taxes. But all that is a very recent development in human life. Our ancestors might live their entire lives within a radius to 10-15 miles, and unless they were pioneers, even our grandparents tended to remain close to the families and neighborhoods of their youth. So, while this passage may not strike us as especially unusual, what God required of Abram and Sarai was extraordinary.

This is radical trust. "Leave your country, your kindred, and your father's house. Be separated from all that you know and all that you expect to experience. Trust me" says God. And Abram packs up and goes.

And although the promise of blessings and prosperity no doubt make Abram's obedience easier, I do not think that Abram makes this journey simply because he wants to be the patriarch of a great nation. He could have done that in Ur. Abram's choice to obey God is also a matter of faith. He discerns God's call, and he trusts that God will keep the promises.

Can you imagine having such faith? We live in an age of contracts and guarantees. We trust in that which we can see, touch, and document. And unless driven by desperation we are loathe to risk our security, not to mention the health and safety of our families and children to something as uncertain as the promise of a new beginning.

That spirit of trust is precisely what God requires of us. Lent is the time for the sort of self-examination that allows us to test the measure of our trust. To what adventure is God calling you? It is unlikely to be as grand as that of Abram and Sarai, but it may well be as important to you as it was to them.

Quiet Trust

I lift up my eyes to the hills; from where is my help to come?
My help comes from the LORD, the maker of heaven and earth.
He will not let your foot be moved and he who watches over you will not fall asleep.
Behold, he who keeps watch over Israel shall neither slumber nor sleep;
The LORD himself watches over you; the LORD is your shade at your right hand,
So that the sun shall not strike you by day, nor the moon by night.
The LORD shall preserve you from all evil; it is he who shall keep you safe.
The LORD shall watch over your going out and your coming in,
from this time forth for evermore. (Psalm 121)

What do we do when our Faith tells us one thing and our gut insists on another? We know that we are to trust in God for our protection. We are continually told that God watches over us and preserves us from evil. And yet, we read the papers, and watch the news, and have our own personal experiences of pain, sorrow and loss. Even if we manage to train our minds to trust that God is in charge, our bodies still sweat and hurt and tremble.

That is because our bodies are responding to the physical realities in which we live. But we are more than just our bodies. We are body and spirit. The problem of course, lies in taking these passages literally and specifically. These Psalms and the teaching of the Church itself are as often as not poetic and metaphorical. They promise us that we are not alone. They do not promise us that we will be literally sheltered from harm.

A closer reading of this passage reminds us that what we are being called to do is to trust that God is the source of our help, our comfort, our endurance and the preservation of our spirits in times of trial. Even when we are standing in the scorching noonday heat, God watches over us. Even when surrounded by evil, our souls are preserved by God. Wherever we go and whatever we do, God precedes, follows and travels alongside us.

Julian of Norwich expresses this idea simply and beautifully:

He did not say "You shall not be tempest tossed,
you shall not be discomforted."
But He said, "You shall not be overcome."

Nothing, not even death, overcomes the love and presence of God.

All Shall Be Well

"All Shall Be Well and All Shall Be Well, and All Manner of Thing Shall Be Well."

God continually watches over us, and even when our intellect may tell us that something is impossible, our hearts and our souls tell us that with God all things are possible. Perhaps our prayers may not be answered as we would like, but God does hear and answer us. Sometimes the answers come through the love, care and actions of others. Sometimes the answers come in the form of a sense of peace or confidence that in the end "All shall be well."

The important thing is that we continue to pray, and that we hold one another in our hearts before the throne of God, trusting that God has more in store for us than we can ask or imagine. Yes, I know that such trust is enormously counter-intuitive in the face of what we perceive to be real about the universe and our place in it, but prayer, confidence and trust are not empirically demonstrable. God answers us as God wills. And what God wills for us will always be the love and presence of God in our lives.

When we cling to that truth we join countless others who have trusted in the power of intercessory prayer and in the abiding presence of God. Like Nicodemus, we may wonder whether an adult can re-enter the womb and be born again, but like the Psalmist we may trust that God, who watches over us, neither slumbers not sleeps.

Reckoned as Righteousness

For if Abraham was justified by works, he has something to boast about, but not before God. For what does the scripture say? "Abraham believed God, and it was reckoned to him as righteousness." Now to one who works, wages are not reckoned as a gift but as something due. But to one who without works trusts him who justifies the ungodly, such faith is reckoned as righteousness." (Romans 4:2-5)

Rudy, our Schnoodle is one righteous dog! Like the rest of his breed, he is very loyal and very demonstrative of his love for Will and me. He especially likes sharing upholstered furniture, easily insinuating himself into the smallest space between us, where he will happily sleep for hours or until (heaven forbid!) someone rings the doorbell. When that happens, Rudy goes from zero to sixty in a heartbeat, racing over and through all obstacles while barking loud enough to wake the dead. We think he is trying to impress us with his skills as a watchdog. What he doesn't realize, of course, is that he doesn't have to prove his worth, or earn our love. In fact, we might love him even more if he did not respond to the doorbell as if it were signaling the start of Armageddon.

I think that some of the passages in Romans might have been a bit easier to read and understand if St. Paul had shared his home with a dog. Dogs are not concerned with theories of justification or righteousness. They just want to love and be loved. In fact, dogs are living sermons on the topic of unconditional love. It is we human beings who put conditions on love and who seek to purchase, deserve, or earn everything.

But even without Rudy to inspire him, St. Paul knew a lot about human nature; and based on his own self-awareness, he knew that we can never earn God's love or purchase our salvation. He understood that God loves us, no matter what. Even more importantly, he realized that our attempts at righteousness will not persuade God to love us any more than we are already loved – because we are already perfectly and completely loved.

What if we could all just accept that and instead of responding to every door-bell as if it were judgment day, we just learned to love God back? Abraham knew that. He didn't earn "righteousness." It was "reckoned" to him because he trusted and believed God. What is to keep us from doing the same?

Trusting the Impossible

There was a Pharisee named Nicodemus, a leader of the Jews. He came to Jesus by night and said to him, "Rabbi, we know that you are a teacher who has come from God; for no one can do these signs that you do apart from the presence of God." Jesus answered him, "Very truly, I tell you, no one can see the kingdom of God without being born from above." Nicodemus said to him, "How can anyone be born after having grown old? Can one enter a second time into the mother's womb and be born?" Jesus answered, "Very truly, I tell you, no one can enter the kingdom of God without being born of water and Spirit. (John 3:1-5)

When confronted with a really challenging idea, many folks will relieve their tension by reducing the argument to the ridiculous. At first reading, it may seem that this is what Nicodemus is doing when he says "how can anyone be born after having grown old?"

But Nicodemus is a much more complex person than that. After all, he has come to Jesus after dark, so clearly he is not trying to trap Jesus into saying something damaging in front of witnesses. And even though he tries to keep his meeting with Jesus a private matter, Nicodemus does recognize and is drawn to the power and presence of God in Jesus.

We might think, then, that Jesus would treat him a bit more gently than he does. Instead, as usual, Jesus cuts straight to the chase. It is as though he says, "Don't try to flatter me, Nick. If you want to see the kingdom of heaven, repent and be born again." Just like that. No wonder Nicodemus tries to change the subject by pointing out the physical impossibility of re-entering his mother's womb! He doesn't want to deal with the challenge of spiritual rebirth. Perhaps like Charles Dickens' Scrooge, he believes himself too old for the new way of life that Jesus is offering him.

But Jesus is adamant. "No one can enter the kingdom of God without being born of water and Spirit." This is not an argument over what form of baptism is required or how many times it may be administered. Jesus is pointing out that we are both physical and spiritual beings and that while being born from the amniotic waters of the womb makes us human, it is our birth from above (or anew, or again) that makes us able to see and enter the kingdom of God.

We face the same challenge. Are we willing to be born from above?

Understanding Salvation:

"For God so loved the world that he gave his only Son, so that everyone who believes in him may not perish but may have eternal life. Indeed, God did not send the Son into the world to condemn the world, but in order that the world might be saved through him. (John3:16-17)

I seldom watch sports on TV. But it seems that every time I do, I see a bare-chested football fan with John 3:16 painted across his abdomen. That's when I want to say "Right! But what comes after that? Can you recite John 3:17?" Of course, I started out my adult life as a teacher and I love to give pop-quizzes. But, thanks be to God, there are no trick questions or pop-quizzes in the Kingdom of Heaven! Besides I know that the aforementioned football fan is engaging in his particular form of evangelism; and as the saying goes, "it couldn't hurt."

In fact, "not hurting" is the point of the entire Doctrine of Incarnation. God does not want to hurt us. God wants to help us.

That's why God becomes one of us in the person of Jesus Christ. God does that out of love – pure and simple. God does not want any of us to perish, languish, drift or fall away from full and eternal life. So, to make sure that the world is saved from itself, God the Father sends us God the Son. Not to condemn the world, but to save it.

When we learn to understand salvation in those terms, we are freed to step away from the idea that heaven is only for those who ace the test. But sadly, many of us are stuck in the fear which casts God as an ogre just waiting for us to mess up.

No, the truth is that God is doing absolutely everything possible to get our attention. Jesus is the light of the world, the Word of God, and the demonstration that God intends each of us to enter into the realms of blessedness in the Reign of God.

The Word is a Person

O God, whose glory it is always to have mercy: Be gracious to all who have gone astray from your ways, and bring them again with penitent hearts and steadfast faith to embrace and hold fast the unchangeable truth of your Word, Jesus Christ your Son; who with you and the Holy Spirit lives and reigns, one God, for ever and ever, Amen. (Collect for the Second Sunday in Lent)

We humans are pretty fickle. But God is constant. We slip and fall into sin as often as we stand and walk the straight and narrow. Thank Heaven, then that part of God's constancy is always to have mercy, and to extend grace. As often as we go astray, Christ calls and leads us home. As often as we forget God, the Light of Christ reminds us of God's eternal presence.

Because Jesus Christ is the Word of God, and that Word is Truth. Steadfast and unchanging, God is present with us in Word and in Sacrament, but most of all in the person of Jesus the Christ.

There is a wonderful 19th century hymn by William Washam How which begins,

"O Christ, the Word Incarnate,
O Wisdom from on high.
O Truth unchanged, unchanging,
O Light of our dark sky."

Obviously Mr. How was familiar with the Prologue to the Gospel of John. But I think that he was even more acquainted with the challenges of life and that he knew just how much we need the Word, Wisdom, Truth and Light of God.

As we end this second week of Lent, and as we face our own challenges in navigating our way through life, may we always remember that Christ is the light of our dark sky, and may we remember to embrace and hold fast to the unchangeable truth of the Word of God.

"Give Us Water to Drink"

From the wilderness of Sin the whole congregation of the Israelites journeyed by stages, as the Lord commanded. They camped at Rephidim, but there was no water for the people to drink. The people quarreled with Moses, and said, "Give us water to drink." Moses said to them, "Why do you quarrel with me? Why do you test the Lord?" But the people thirsted there for water; and the people complained against Moses and said, "Why did you bring us out of Egypt, to kill us and our children and livestock with thirst?" Exodus 17:1-3

This is neither the first nor the last time that the Children of Israel will rise up in complaint against Moses and his leadership of their exodus from Egypt. In the previous chapter they complained of hunger and were given manna and quail to eat. Now they are camped in the desert and are thirsty.

But, we dare not spiritualize this lesson. The people are in the desert, exhausted and dehydrated. There are in real, imminent danger of dying of thirst; and they are suffering from a serious lack of trust in Moses. But at least they have the meager consolation of knowing that it is God who has called them forth and put them in this position, and that it will be God and his prophet Moses who will bring what help is to be had. But what about all those people alive today without access to potable water? Has God placed them in the desert, or in areas of drought or pollution? And if so, where is their Moses? Who will find water for them?

Stewardship of the natural world is an act of faith. Without water, human beings die. Depending on an individual's environment, death from dehydration can occur in a matter of hours. Children can and do die from dysentery from contaminated water and the younger and weaker they are, the more quickly they die. Cholera from sewage infected water kills people of all ages. And we do not yet know the full consequences on our water tables of the toxins and chemicals produced by mining and industry.

Think about water in terms of stewardship and of Lent. When you make your coffee, brew your tea, or get a drink from the tap, stop and experience what it feels like to drink water. Feel it in your mouth, in your throat, and as it moves through your body. Imagine what your life would be like if you were not able to bathe, or wash? How would you feel if you could not trust that your children were brushing their teeth with clean water? Then bring your awareness into your Lenten discipline and act.

"He's Got the Whole World in His Hands"

In his hand are the caverns of the earth, and the heights of the hills are his also. The sea is his, for he made it, and his hands have molded the dry land. (Psalm 95)

In Revelations of Divine Love, Dame Julian of Norwich describes the world as a hazelnut in the palm of God's hand. Creation, she writes, exists because God made it, loves it, and keeps it. As is evidenced in this Psalm (also known as the Venite from the Morning Prayer Service) our ancestors in the faith had a healthy appreciation for the fact that God is the maker, lover and keeper of the universe and that we are called to be stewards of creation.

When we forget our task and responsibility, assuming that we are privileged to exercise power and dominion over the world, we are prone not only to damaging the world but to committing the sin of arrogance. When we neglect to thank God for the beauty of the earth, our lack of gratitude encourages us to waste and squander the very things that sustain our lives. When we fail to preserve natural places of rest and refreshment, we ignore the fact that we are God's guests on the planet. And when we construct our cities in a manner that isolates us from one another, we deny ourselves the awareness that we are all part of creation.

Stewardship of creation requires respectful and self-less behavior. We are called to respect the fact that we do not own the earth, we merely inhabit it. God is the owner of this property, and we are expected to keep it in good repair. And because we are neither the first nor the last inhabitants of the world, we must think of those who will come after us. As our Mennonite brothers and sisters say, "We must live simply that others may simply live."

Today, give God thanks for this world and for the blessing of being alive. Think about and be grateful for the manner in which God's providence provides all that is necessary to sustain our physical lives and to nurture our spirits. And remember that you, too are part of the world that God holds in the palm of his hand.

All Good Gifts around Us

And not only that, but we also boast in our sufferings, knowing that suffering produces endurance, and endurance produces character, and character produces hope, and hope does not disappoint us, because God's love has been poured into our hearts through the Holy Spirit that has been given to us. (Romans 5:3-5)

This passage has always reminded me of my father, who when I was a student in college and complaining about how difficult it was to have to work full time while going to school, said to me, "Poverty builds character." I remember thinking, "Maybe – but only if you survive it."

Sometimes it is very difficult to see blessings when they come to us in the form of challenges. But sometimes it is very easy to get things turned around. That's why I disagreed with Dad, and why I challenge what St. Paul has written. It is not the suffering that produces endurance and therefore character. It is the choice to endure suffering that strengthens and reveals character.

But it is truly a sign of character to be a hopeful person, and to recognize that even in our suffering we are enfolded by the love of God and surrounded by gifts. In fact, it is often in the lives of those who are suffering that hope is most evident. Folks with that sort of character have learned that the goodness of God and the glory of life are even more precious when we stop to give thanks in the midst of suffering. It is in the moments when I feel the most lousy or angry or frightened that I most need to see the health and exuberance in others, observe the silent depths of a river, or rest against the solid comfort of a sun-warmed boulder.

It is also in those times that God invites me to respond to those around me who are also suffering, not because misery loves company, but because company eases misery.

Being stewards of creation keeps us in touch with life, the earth, and one another. It calls us out of isolation and into community. It reminds us that while suffering is a part of life, it is not all of life. And in making us aware of the good things that continually surround us, we come to know the power of the love of God which the Holy Spirit pours into our hearts.

Mountains and Hilltops

The woman said to him, "Sir, I see that you are a prophet. Our ancestors worshiped on this mountain, but you say that the place where people must worship is in Jerusalem." Jesus said to her, "Woman, believe me, the hour is coming when you will worship the Father neither on this mountain nor in Jerusalem." (John 4:19-21)

Human beings are spiritually attracted to hillsides and mountain tops. They are liminal places in which air and land meet. So, it is no surprise that hilltops and mountains so often become holy sites. Around the world, monasteries are reached by steep climbs over precarious paths.

But the significance of hills and mountains is even more basic than that. We all appreciate the exhilaration of standing on a windy hillside, or the challenge of a steep climb up a mountainside. We may even consider such climbs to be pilgrimages after which we feel closer to God. That is why there are so many cairns (piles of rocks and stones) on hilltops and mountains.

Imagine a world without parks and hiking trails. Imagine a world without mountains and mountain climbers. Imagine a world in which no one would have been inspired to write "Climb every mountain." And don't forget that many of these hills are forested and that the oxygen produced by those trees is essential for life on earth.

The conservation and stewardship of the natural world serves a far more than aesthetic purpose. And important as the spiritual is, even that is secondary to the fact that hills and mountains are an essential part of our eco-system. Weather, rivers, water-tables, arable land, and air-quality are all dependent upon the topography of our planet. And God has entrusted us with the responsibility of being good stewards of this planet. That means we are to be actively engaged in conservation, reforestation, and green space preservation. They are physical necessities, and they are spiritual obligations.

Fields Ripe For Harvesting

Meanwhile the disciples were urging him, "Rabbi, eat something." But he said to them, "I have food to eat that you do not know about." So the disciples said to one another, "Surely no one has brought him something to eat?" Jesus said to them, "My food is to do the will of him who sent me and to complete his work. Do you not say, `Four months more, then comes the harvest'? But I tell you, look around you, and see how the fields are ripe for harvesting. The reaper is already receiving wages and is gathering fruit for eternal life, so that sower and reaper may rejoice together. For here the saying holds true, `One sows and another reaps.' I sent you to reap that for which you did not labor. Others have labored, and you have entered into their labor." (John 4:31-38)

Yes, when he speaks of the sowing, reaping, harvesting and eating in this passage, Jesus is speaking metaphorically. But meals and table fellowship were also very important to him and there are numerous other places in the gospels from the feeding of the five thousand (Luke 9, Matthew 14, Mark 6, and John 6) to the breakfast on the shore (John 21), where Jesus is concerned with actual food.

As are we. Hunger is perhaps the most obvious sign of our mortality. An infant is born hungry. And table fellowship is a universal practice. All cultures celebrate life with food. But out of the 57 million deaths reported on the planet last year, more than 36 million were associated with malnutrition and hunger.

Stewardship of the natural world means figuring out how to feed everyone. Ours is a problem of stewardship and allocation of resources. No one should go hungry, especially in a nation that produces far more food than is needed; and in which mountains of food are thrown out each day. But until we accept that stewardship of the natural world includes feeding the hungry, and that feeding the hungry is a spiritual matter, we are not likely to do so.

Pray for the hungry. Pray that God will open our hearts and minds to respond to their need. And then act. Demand Fair-Trade products. Limit your intake of resource wasting foods. Support educational nutrition programs and agencies that feed the world's poor. The process begins with us – with what we eat and with what we purchase. So long as we support poor stewardship by purchasing and consuming foods that ultimately deprive others of the necessities of life, nothing will change.

Minimizing Our Footprints

Almighty God, you know that we have no power in ourselves to help ourselves: Keep us both outwardly in our bodies and inwardly in our souls, that we may be defended from all adversities which may happen to the body, and from all evil thoughts which may assault and hurt the soul; through Jesus Christ our Lord, who lives and reigns with you and the Holy Spirit, one God, for ever and ever. Amen. (Collect for the Third Sunday in Lent)

We hear a great deal these days about our "carbon footprint" or the impact of our consumption of fossil fuels. But there are all sorts of footprints, and there is a correlation between our spiritual health and the footprints we leave behind. There is also a correlation between our footprints and our awareness, our footprints and our abundance.

We are so blessed. We have so many options and so many choices. We are blessed with affluence and relative safety. And we give thanks to God for those blessings.

But when those blessings are taken for granted, or when we assume that we are entitled to the comforts that they bring, then even those things we consider blessings can become "adversities which may happen to the body...and...evil thoughts which may assault and hurt the soul."

Blessings are not evil. Being blessed does not make us evil. It is what we do that determines our character. When we are poor stewards of our bounty, we leave a far bigger footprint on the world than is either necessary or faithful.

When I take more than I need, my footprint increases. So does my tendency to take even more the next time. When I am too fearful to share or too anxious to trust, I may be tempted to protect myself by hoarding rather than sharing God's blessings.

We are creatures of Spirit and of Flesh. Good stewardship requires our seeking balance in our lives. May God challenge us with understanding this, and strengthen us to respond as the good stewards we are called to be.

Health and the Body

"Do not look on his appearance or on the height of his stature, because I have rejected him; for the Lord does not see as mortals see; they look on the outward appearance, but the Lord looks on the heart... Now he was ruddy, and had beautiful eyes, and was handsome. The Lord said, "Rise and anoint him; for this is the one." (1 Samuel 16: 7, 12b)

These lines from the anointing of David as Saul's replacement as King over Israel are somewhat confusing. In the first part of the passage, the prophet is told to ignore physical appearances when choosing a successor (after all Saul was tall and handsome - though not the most intelligent of men). Just a few verses later, however, The Lord instructs Samuel to choose David, who is ruddy and handsome with beautiful eyes. What are we to make of this?

Perhaps what is happening is that Samuel is learning about a connection between the condition of one's heart and the appearance of one's face and eyes. Our eyes reveal a great deal about the health of our bodies and our spirits. Is our gaze direct? Are our eyes bloodshot or yellow? It is certainly not fair to judge someone's character on so slight a sign, but it is true that (especially for sighted individuals), our faces and our eyes can be very indicative of our overall health. Some folks even believe that it is possible to read an individual's honesty and sincerity by their eye movement. And poetry, music and maternal wisdom abound with examples ~ "You have the cool, clear eyes of a seeker of wisdom and truth." "Nancy with the laughing eyes." Or as my mother would say, "I can tell if you are lying by looking at your eyes." It still works. Take a look at your eyes.

Are they wrinkled? Great, you've earned those wrinkles by living!
Are they puffy? Maybe you need to get some more sleep.
Do they reflect pain or sorrow in your life? Seek and accept help.
Do they light up when you smile? Smiling eyes reflect light and love.

We are fully incarnate spirit, and fully spiritual physical beings. It's a wonderfully interdependent combination - but in the end the health of our spirits trumps the health of our bodies. Illness cannot mar the beauty of a loving spirit. But neither can a beautiful body create a lovely spirit. The stewardship of health means paying appropriate attention to both.

Health and the Soul

The LORD is my shepherd; I shall not be in want.
He makes me lie down in green pastures and leads me beside still waters.
He revives my soul and guides me along right pathways for his Name's sake.
Though I walk through the valley of the shadow of death, I shall fear no evil;
for you are with me; your rod and your staff, they comfort me.
You spread a table before me in the presence of those who trouble me;
you ha [illegible] with oil, and my cup is running over.
Surely your [illegible] my life,
and [illegible] 23)

What does a he [illegible]

A healthy soul [illegible] t mean that the owner of s [illegible] y in life; such a person is as [illegible] temptations that life can [illegible] pects to be accompanied [illegible] allow it to be overcome.

It is no accide [illegible] d of Psalms. It is a glorious [illegible] tained by the Good Sheph [illegible] faith that will endure – not [illegible] satisfied, but because it is grounded in an unshakeable trust.

Try praying this Psalm and monitor how you feel as you do. Then ask yourself. How healthy is my soul? What am I doing to keep it healthy? Do I believe that God is with me? Do I believe that God is reliable and trustworthy? If not, why not?

And remember that health does not take place in a vacuum. Take the time to pray, but also take the time to talk to someone you trust. Share what you are experiencing and support one another in love.

Health and Morality

Once you were darkness, but now in the Lord you are light. Live as children of light-- for the fruit of the light is found in all that is good and right and true. Try to find out what is pleasing to the Lord. Take no part in the unfruitful works of darkness, but instead expose them. For it is shameful even to mention what such people do secretly; but everything exposed by the light becomes visible, for everything that becomes visible is light. Therefore it says, "Sleeper, awake! Rise from the dead, and Christ will shine on you." (Ephesians 5:8-14)

I have often recoiled from what seems to be our obsession with equating light with goodness and dark with evil. The negative consequences of that obsession have been particularly evident in terms of racial difference. So when looking at this passage it is important to place light and dark in the correct context. There are many good things in the world for which both light and dark are necessary – the circadian rhythms of the human body and the art of photography are only two examples.

The writer of Ephesians, however, is speaking psychologically and constructing a dichotomy between the desire to hide or obscure one's actions, and the willingness to have those actions revealed for all to see. Light reveals and illuminates the object upon which it shines. Darkness hides and obscures. To use contemporary language, a healthy morality requires transparency. Our behavior should be able to withstand the scrutiny of public knowledge. Just think of how many news sources and investigative reporters would be out of work if no one needed or tried to hide anything!

The meaning of this passage is contained in the phrase, "Try to find out what is pleasing to the Lord." God will not be pleased by those things of which we are ashamed. Nor does God want us to compartmentalize our lives, placing some things in the light of day, and keeping others in hidden shadowy depths.

It is pleasing to God when our lives are and our moral actions are in sync with our stated beliefs for which we can gladly and openly take responsibility. And not only is such transparency pleasing to God, it is good for our health. Living with guilt, shame and secrets is both spiritually and physically debilitating; and a life of secrets (whether by choice or necessity) consumes a great deal of energy which might be far better spent on something more productive.

Health and Reason

As he walked along, Jesus saw a man blind from birth. His disciples asked him, "Rabbi, who sinned, this man or his parents, that he was born blind?" Jesus answered, "Neither this man nor his parents sinned; he was born blind so that God's works might be revealed in him. (John 9:1-3)

Sometimes our religious beliefs seem to be on a collision course with our rational minds. When that happens, our internal alarms tend to go off. We think, "Wait a minute. What did they just say? That doesn't make sense!"

The Evangelist's narrative description of the healing of the man born blind provides two examples of that collision. First, St. John presents us with the disciples' assumption that the man's blindness is the result of human sin – either his or his parents'. The second is how John writes Jesus' response to their assumption. The man is blind so that Jesus can demonstrate God's power by healing him. In the first instance I can choose to explain away the conflict by thinking, "Well, that's a cultural assumption. They thought illness was a symptom of and punishment for sin". But there is no way that I can silence the alarm bells that go off when I hear that this man is blind so that his being healed will reveal God's glory.

The study of Scripture, belief in God, and the ability to reason tell us that something is wrong. We do not believe that God punishes sin by injuring someone. Nor, do we believe that God allows suffering to exist for the sake of spectacular healing. We are left conflicted, and there are two ways forward: change what we believe about God; or confront the conflict, acknowledge the contradictions and work through it.

Obviously the latter is more challenging, but exercising good stewardship of our reason and rationality means that we must be willing to confront inconsistencies. The idea that God is just and loving, and that God would punish a child for its parents' sins is inconsistent. The notion that God would impose and maintain decades of blindness so that the healing would become an object lesson is not only inconsistent, it is offensive.

But we cannot stop there. The appropriate us of human reason involves prayer, study and humility. Hard work, indeed, and the willingness to be changed by what we find. That's stewardship of reason.

Health and Humility

Jesus said, "I came into this world for judgment so that those who do not see may see, and those who do see may become blind." Some of the Pharisees near him heard this and said to him, "Surely we are not blind, are we?" Jesus said to them, "If you were blind, you would not have sin. But now that you say, `We see,' your sin remains." (John 9:39-41)

This passage always reminds me of Robert De Niro in "Taxi Driver". "You talkin' to me???" The Pharisees are more than ready for a confrontation, and sound as though they have been waiting forever to deliver their line. "Are you talking about US, Jesus? Are you saying we're ***blind***?!?"

What a shame then, that when they finally get to say it, Jesus ignores them. He just continues. "No, I'm not saying you are blind. If you were blind you would have an excuse for not seeing. Your problem is that you are too proud to see anything differently."

Now, they know that they are proud. They believe that their pride is justified. They have worked hard and they know their material. So who is this Jesus to question their authority? In fact, given their position in life, they would rather risk being wrong than attempt to be humble.

And isn't that the case with all of us? We pride ourselves on having found a niche in life and a way in which to stay there. And we really don't like being told that we may be wrong. But the stewardship of life includes having a healthy approach to humility. It is enormously freeing to admit that we don't have to have all the answers. We are not too old or too important to learn, to be challenged, or to change.

Humility is healthy because humility means knowing who you are and being comfortable with it. Humility relieves us of the burden of defensiveness and self-promotion. And it makes a physical difference, too. Humility makes for deeper sleeping, easier breathing and more natural laughter.

And that is pretty good.

Health and Wholeness

Gracious Father, whose blessed Son Jesus Christ came down from heaven to be the true bread which gives life to the world: Evermore give us this bread; that he may live in us, and we in him; who lives and reigns with you and the Holy Spirit, one God, now and forever. Amen. (Collect: Fourth Sunday in Lent)

Jesus Christ is the bread of life. We receive that bread spiritually and physically in the Eucharist each Sunday, and we receive it metaphorically each day in our life of prayer and our relationships with others in the Body of Christ.

It is what sustains us and what empowers us to do the work of Christ's Body in the world. That is why it is essential that we be part of a community and we be regular and faithful in participation. We need to be fed the bread of life in order to be whole and healthy. We need the love and support of a community fed with true bread in order to engage a life of wholeness. Without it, we will starve.

It is certainly true that we can do good works without being part of the Church, but we cannot do the work of the Body of Christ unless we are part of his Church.

So, be a good steward of your health and your wholeness by coming to the table of the Lord to be fed the true bread. You will be filled and renewed not just for your own health but for the work of the church and for the good of the world.

Being Part of a Community

Then he said to me, "Mortal, these bones are the whole house of Israel. They say, `Our bones are dried up, and our hope is lost; we are cut off completely.' Therefore prophesy, and say to them, Thus says the Lord GOD: I am going to open your graves, and bring you up from your graves, O my people; and I will bring you back to the land of Israel. And you shall know that I am the Lord, when I open your graves, and bring you up from your graves, O my people. I will put my spirit within you, and you shall live, and I will place you on your own soil; then you shall know that I, the Lord, have spoken and will act," says the Lord. (Ezekiel 37:11-14)

When asked why they join a group, participate in an alumni organization, or affiliate with a parish the first reason most folks will give is "for the sense of community and connection." Human beings are "wired" for relationships, and all but the most reclusive of people need human companionship. In fact, when we find ourselves removed from community, by illness, retirement, or relocation, we grieve. The loss is a bit like a death.

So when Ezekiel receives his vision of the dry bones, he is immediately able to recognize that it is a metaphor for the condition of the house of Israel. It is as though they are dead. "We are cut off completely," they lament. But they are not left that way. Their health will be restored and they will be made whole when they are returned to their own land, and when they are restored to their relationship with God. Notice that because community lies at the center of their nation, all this is phrased in the plural. They are ALL dried up, ALL without hope, and ALL cut off. But, just as their illness has been collective, their healing will be collective as well.

The same is often true of our own lives. When we try to live as "lone wolves" we cut ourselves off from the love, support and benefits of community. When we only look to others when we are at our most desperate, we deny ourselves the continual benefit of living and growing in community. And when we only come to church when we are in need of help or healing, we starve ourselves of the continual nurture and support of the family of faith.

Think of those times in your life when you felt like a bundle of dry bones. Most likely you were also estranged from community. And even more likely, returning to community was part of your rebirth. Give thanks to God for the gift of community; and prayerfully resolve that you will cherish that gift and that that you will offer it to others.

Being with God

I wait for the LORD, my soul waits for him; in his word is my hope.
My soul waits for the LORD, more than watchmen for the morning;
more than watchmen for the morning.
O Israel, wait for the LORD, for with the LORD there is mercy;
With him there is plenteous redemption,
and he shall redeem Israel from all their sins. (Psalm 130:4-7)

Think of all the ways that we use the word "wait." We wait for a bus. Servers in restaurants wait on tables. That job will have to wait. The children can't wait for Christmas. Wait for me! It's a multipurpose word, but unless we are waiting for the answer to a prayer, we seldom use it in thinking about God.

And yet, waiting upon God is the perfect description of the most intimate relationship we will ever know. Because waiting is more than pausing, or being detained; to wait means to give full and patient attention and service to another. It means to yearn for the presence of the beloved. Such waiting is what the Psalmist calls Israel to do. It is the definition of prayer and the linchpin of faith.

It is also what we are called to do. Our lives are to be ordered with time and space set aside to wait upon the LORD. Not just in terms of service and worship, but in a state of prayerful attention and heartfelt devotion. To be in the presence of God is to enter into a sacred relationship of trust, hope, forgiveness, redemption and love; and the language of that relationship is prayer – especially "still" or silent prayer.

In such prayer we surrender our expectations. We refrain from making requests, confessions or intercessions. Those are good and worthy things for other times and types of prayer. But in still prayer, we simply wait upon the LORD, devoting our full attention to being in the presence of God while remaining open to whatever God chooses to do or not to do.

Today, honor this most important of relationships by intentionally waiting upon the LORD. Start with five minutes, and consider that time your gift of self to God.

Being Incarnate

To set the mind on the flesh is death, but to set the mind on the Spirit is life and peace. For this reason the mind that is set on the flesh is hostile to God; it does not submit to God's law-- indeed it cannot, and those who are in the flesh cannot please God. But you are not in the flesh; you are in the Spirit, since the Spirit of God dwells in you. Anyone who does not have the Spirit of Christ does not belong to him. But if Christ is in you, though the body is dead because of sin, the Spirit is life because of righteousness. If the Spirit of him who raised Jesus from the dead dwells in you, he who raised Christ from the dead will give life to your mortal bodies also through his Spirit that dwells in you. (Romans 8:6-11)

Of all our relationships, the one most often neglected or unbalanced is that between our own spirit and flesh. The problem is exacerbated by western ambivalence toward physicality. We seem to have a great deal of trouble seeing ourselves as "incarnate spirit", so we tend either to focus solely on the flesh, discounting the spiritual; or to consider the flesh a burden to be cast aside in favor of the spirit.

And it doesn't help that while the Greek word "sarx" (flesh) conveys a variety of meanings, it is usually translated only as "flesh". Sarx can mean flesh as in skin and bones, or as in alive, or as carnal, or animal, or as "the two become one flesh." Unfortunately, most translations make it all too easy to read St. Paul as being squeamish about the physical nature of human life.

Refusing to separate the spirit from the flesh puts the two into a balanced and wholesome relationship. We are simultaneously both spirit and flesh; and to set them at odds with one another is to deny the goodness of the gift which God has given us. As verse 11 shows, St. Paul understood that. If the Spirit of Christ dwells in us, then the same Spirit gives life to our mortal bodies. It's a question of balance.

Both Spirit and Flesh are able to witness to the glory of God. Both are required to make us whole; and both are the subject of the stewardship of our lives. Reflect upon the balance of spirit and flesh in your life. Do you separate the two? Do you deny one at the expense of the other? Are you ashamed of your body? Do you ignore the needs of your spirit?

God has made us whole – a union of spirit and flesh. Cherish that gift.

Friendships

Now a certain man was ill, Lazarus of Bethany, the village of Mary and her sister Martha. Mary was the one who anointed the Lord with perfume and wiped his feet with her hair; her brother Lazarus was ill. So the sisters sent a message to Jesus, "Lord, he whom you love is ill." But when Jesus heard it, he said, "This illness does not lead to death; rather it is for God's glory, so that the Son of God may be glorified through it." Accordingly, though Jesus loved Martha and her sister and Lazarus, after having heard that Lazarus was ill, he stayed two days longer in the place where he was. (John 11:1-6)

Jesus, Mary, Martha and Lazarus were good friends. They lived in Bethany some two miles from Jerusalem and when Jesus' ministry took him near the city, he often stayed with Lazarus and his sisters. That is why when Lazarus fell ill, Mary and Martha quickly sent word to him. That is also why Jesus' delay in going to his friend's bedside seems so odd.

At least it seems odd until we remember that friends are people we can trust. In fact, trust is the basis of friendship. In sending word to Jesus, Mary and Martha trust that he will do what he can to help their brother. When he does not come at once, they must also trust that Jesus is still their friend and that he has their brother's best interest at heart.

As the rest of the story tells us, even though the two sisters did not understand Jesus' delay, they continued to believe that if he wanted to, Jesus would be able to revive Lazarus. What a testimony to the power of friendship that even in the midst of their grief, and their anger ("Lord, if you had been here, my brother would not have died"), their relationship endures.

And how weak and pale our own friendships may appear when compared to this one! How often do we fail to be good stewards of the gift of friends? How often are our friendships matters of convenience? How often do we fail to trust, or refuse to forgive? How willing are we to be honest with our friends, even when the truth is uncomfortable?

The stewardship of our relationships requires attention, care and vulnerability; and genuine friendship deserves nurturing. Today, give thanks for the friends in your life. Tell them of your love, trust them with your joys and your sorrows, and remember that these relationships are icons of Christ's love for us.

Family Relationships

Martha said to Jesus, "Lord, if you had been here, my brother would not have died. But even now I know that God will give you whatever you ask of him." Jesus said to her, "Your brother will rise again." Martha said to him, "I know that he will rise again in the resurrection on the last day." Jesus said to her, "I am the resurrection and the life. Those who believe in me, even though they die, will live, and everyone who lives and believes in me will never die. Do you believe this?" She said to him, "Yes, Lord, I believe that you are the Messiah, the Son of God, the one coming into the world." (John 11:21-27)

Mary and Martha clearly loved their brother, Lazarus. Aside from the fact that Jesus raises Lazarus from the tomb, Scripture tells us very little about him, and does not record his having said anything at all. But he was the head of the household and presumably was the sole support of his sisters. As no spouses or children are mentioned in the references to the three, it appears that they were unmarried adult siblings sharing a home. That sounds like a rather challenging arrangement.

Mary and Martha give us a perfect example of the cost and the blessing of family relationships. Family life is sometimes difficult, requiring patience, compromise and a healthy sense of humor. But, living together in families can also be a source of comfort, safety, and happiness. It is also a wonderful reminder of how much more manageable those relationships are when the individuals concerned recognize the authority of Jesus Christ in their lives.

It is also very interesting that in this chapter of John, the Evangelist has both Martha and Mary make the same statement – "Lord if you have been here my brother would not have died." When Martha speaks (11:21), it is in the context of action. She goes to meet and confront him on the road; but she ends by affirming her faith in the resurrection and in Jesus as Messiah and the Son of God. She speaks as a witness to the power and authority of Jesus. When Mary speaks the same words (11:32), it is in the context of devotion. She goes to Jesus weeping in grief and kneels at his feet. She makes a statement not of faith but of love; and her unabashed demonstration of love moves Jesus to tears.

Two different women bound in love to their brother and to each other and by Jesus. He is the tie that binds.

Ordering the Unruly

Almighty God, you alone can bring into order the unruly wills and affections of sinners: Grant your people grace to love what you command and desire what you promise; that, among the swift and varied changes of the world, our hearts may surely there be fixed where true joys are to be found; through Jesus Christ our Lord, who lives and reigns with you and the Holy Spirit, one God, now and forever. Amen. (Collect 5th Sunday in Lent)

For most of us, bringing order into our lives and affections is a bit like herding cats. We may know exactly where we want them to go, but each of them has a mind of its own and a nearly complete indifference to our intentions. In fact, it was only after having spent decades attempting to bring order to my own unruliness that I finally acknowledged that I could not do so, and understood that it was only by the grace of God that anyone could.

That is why this prayer is such a blessing. We know that we cannot do this by will alone – we will surely wander off into some new adventure, or be hopelessly distracted by the nearest dangled string or shining object. So, we are driven by our own weakness to pray for the grace to embrace God's commandments and promises as the anchor of our lives, and as the guiding star of our actions.

Yes, the prayer probably casts us in a better light than we deserve since most of us are fully capable of walking away from the grace of God. But grace, like any other gift from God, is continually offered to us. And perhaps if we pray for it every day, we will form the intention of receiving it; and eventually that intention will become habit.

I like to think about it this way. I only hang up my clothes, wash the dishes, and make the bed because my mother forced me to do so until I had formed the habit. In large part, it is only by the grace of my mother's efforts to instill those habits in me that I am a reasonably good or consistent housekeeper.

God's commandment and promises work the same way. We are not likely to love and embrace them on our own. But by repetition and the grace of God we may learn to.

Knowing Your History

When Jesus and his disciples had come near Jerusalem and had reached Bethphage, at the Mount of Olives, Jesus sent two disciples, saying to them, "Go into the village ahead of you, and immediately you will find a donkey tied, and a colt with her; untie them and bring them to me. If anyone says anything to you, just say this, `The Lord needs them.' And he will send them immediately." The disciples went and did as Jesus had directed them; they brought the donkey and the colt, and put their cloaks on them, and he sat on them. A very large crowd spread their cloaks on the road, and others cut branches from the trees and spread them on the road.

For me, the most amazing thing about this passage is that the owner of the donkey is presumed to know enough about Israel's history to recognize the honor he is being shown when the disciples take it away. Anyone without such knowledge could only assume that someone was stealing his livestock. But this person, along with any others who might wonder what was going on, is expected to remember the tradition of the anointed king *"gentle and riding on a donkey, on a colt, the foal of a donkey" (Zechariah 9:9)* and understand that the Messiah is about to enter the city.

Only slightly less amazing is the manner in which the people of the city respond. Even if only a few of them knew to offer the king their cloaks and to scatter branches along his path, everyone else appears to catch on immediately. These people were immersed in their own history. They had a national identity which was rooted in their faith, and which informed their understanding of themselves as a people, even when under foreign occupation. In keeping that history alive, and passing it on to their children, they were not only citizens of Israel, they were stewards of their history.

We recognize the dangers of theocracy in the modern world, and we have separated Church and State, but in doing so, we have often abdicated our responsibility to be stewards of our own citizenship. When we do not know our own religious history we are left at the mercy of the loudest voice, the richest lobby, or the most charismatic personality.

Being good and honest stewards of our history is a birthright and a responsibility. When history is misrepresented, we have a spiritual obligation to speak the truth. When heroic effort is not acknowledged and celebrated, or when egregious wrong is ignored rather than rectified, we are all shamed and diminished.

Encouragement

The Lord GOD has given me the tongue of a teacher, that I may know how to sustain the weary with a word. (Isaiah 50:4)

I am blessed in my life to have known many people with the gift of encouragement. These friends, teachers, and mentors have been almost unfailingly attentive to and supportive of the best interest of all concerned; and they have not hesitated to speak the truth, even when it is difficult to hear. They have been living examples of the sort of faith and trust Isaiah is describing – people with the tongue of a teacher and the ability to sustain the weary with a word.

Sometimes the sustaining word has been an affirmation of what I am doing. And sometimes that word has presented me with a caution or a challenge. In either case, it was offered in love and without subterfuge. That word was delivered as the gift that it is.

We all hunger for encouragement and for a sense of purpose and direction. We want to know that we are part of a shared vision and that our actions have meaning. Responding to God's call in life can be lonely and disheartening. That is why we need others along the way to keep us going. And if we are in danger of wandering off the path, we need someone who will expend the time and energy to bring us back. Those who lack such faithful companions carry a double burden.

Imagine the weight of the burden that Jesus bore as he traveled to Jerusalem to face his destiny. His disciples could share neither his burden nor his vision. They could only tell him what they wanted him to do. The crowds along the way on Palm Sunday cheered him on without beginning to understand who he was or what he was doing. And in the last days of his earthly life, even the voice of God grew quiet. But Jesus was sustained and encouraged none the less. His life of prayer and humble service, along with his immersion in and trust of his relationship with his "Abba/Father" gave him the strength and courage to stand firm in his commitment to seeing his work through to the end. And weary as he was and broken as he became, he was sustained.

Let us all give thanks for those who offer us faithful encouragement. And let us pray that God will continue to raise up people that calling.

Compassion

I have become a reproach to all my enemies and even to my neighbors,
*a dismay to those of my acquaintance; **
when they see me in the street they avoid me.
*I am forgotten like a dead man, out of mind; *I am as useless as a broken pot.*
(Psalm 31:11-12)

Some religious communities use "shunning" as a form of internal discipline. Until an individual acknowledges sin and repents, they are socially excluded. Harsh as that sounds, and painful as it is, shunning is usually applied as a motivation toward reconciliation. But that is not what the Psalmist refers to here. This Psalm concerns intentional shaming, gossip, and exclusion. This is intended to damage and to kill the spirit.

If you have ever been treated with scorn, humiliation, or ostracism, you know how devastating it can be. For many people, being the object of shame and derision is so pervasive that it becomes a way of life. Think of those who are bullied or harassed on a daily basis. Remember those whose lives have been reduced to a constant search for food, shelter or medicine. Watch the evening news and look into the faces of those who know themselves to be outcast, but do not know how or why.

And do not forget how adept we human beings are at turning each other into objects of reproach and dismay to family, friends and neighbors – how easy it is to cross the street to avoid someone – and how intrinsic gossip has become to daily conversation. All this flies in the face of the Great Commandment to "Love God with all your heart, and your neighbor as yourself." A lack of compassion is a failure to honor our baptismal promise to "seek and serve Christ in all persons, loving your neighbor as yourself."

The stewardship of our lives demands that we be compassionate people and that we stand in opposition to ideas, actions, or attitudes which debase the human spirit. There is a vast difference between holding someone accountable for their actions and intentionally demeaning them. Compassion requires us to preserve an individual's dignity and humanity. Compassion sees and honors the image of God in all people.

Selflessness

Let the same mind be in you that was in Christ Jesus, who, though he was in the form of God, did not regard equality with God as something to be exploited, but emptied himself, taking the form of a slave, being born in human likeness. And being found in human form, he humbled himself and became obedient to the point of death--even death on a cross. (Philippians 2:5-8)

The self-emptying love of God in Christ is known as "kenosis." Kenosis is not self-abnegation. Nor is it passive. Christ Jesus intentionally and actively stepped away from the power and privilege to which he was entitled so that he could be open and obedient to the work before him.

Notice how active he was in being the steward of his life. Jesus was not humbled – he chose humility. He was not coerced – he embraced obedience. He was not emptied – he emptied himself.

Jesus never "pulled rank" on anyone, and he quietly slipped away when others tried to make him a king or impose authority that he did not want.

How different our lives might be if we were able to imitate him in the stewardship of our lives. Instead of fiercely striving to protect our interests and our status, we might learn to move through the day with grace and quiet confidence. We might learn to replace cynicism and distrust with the honesty and openness. We might even learn to think more highly of others, and of ourselves – for our assessments of others and our own self-esteem would be based on reality rather than fear.

And in this imitation of Christ's selflessness, we would become more fully human and far more authentically loving.

Leadership

Now Jesus stood before the governor; and the governor asked him, "Are you the King of the Jews?" Jesus said, "You say so." But when he was accused by the chief priests and elders, he did not answer. Then Pilate said to him, "Do you not hear how many accusations they make against you?" But he gave him no answer, not even to a single charge, so that the governor was greatly amazed. (Matthew 27:11-14)

Leadership is a spiritual gift. Along with personal integrity, genuine leaders have the ability to inspire others to follow. They engender hope, trust, and the willingness to work for the greater good. They do not exploit or manipulate others, perhaps because real leaders do not need to do so. Guided by the strong core of their personal integrity, they know when to speak and when to remain silent – when to command, when to encourage – and when to get out of the way. They lead by their example.

Pontius Pilate was not gifted as a leader. Throughout his encounter with Jesus he appears totally reactive, moving from belligerence to cajoling to indifference, but never seeming to know just what to do. In fairness, being Governor of Judea was an awful job and was fraught with professional and personal dangers. Caught between Rome, Herod, and a nearly ungovernable province, he was clearly in over his head.

Jesus was a leader. He was able to challenge Pilate, the chief priests and the elders even while standing silent before them. He knew who he was and what he trusted and believed. He did not ask others to do what he was not willing to do himself. And the focus of his life and ministry pointed not to himself, but through him and on to God.

Competent and faithful leadership remains a challenge. Few people understand what leadership actually is, with the result that it may be confused with ambition, organizational skill, or personal charisma. That confusion is evident throughout public life. Because it is a spiritual gift, intended for the building up of the body, leadership must be understood in terms of the stewardship of life; especially when we recognize it in others and wish to encourage it. Identifying leaders is not the difficult part. We know leaders when we encounter them. And despite any reluctance to draw attention to themselves, leaders know who they are. The difficult part lies in helping leaders develop and manage their gift.

HOLY WEEK

Empathy

Almighty and everliving God, in your tender love for the human race you sent your Son our Savior Jesus Christ to take upon him our nature, and to suffer death upon the cross, giving us the example of his great humility: Mercifully grant that we may walk in the way of his suffering, and also share in his resurrection; through Jesus Christ our Lord, who lives and reigns with you and the Holy Spirit, one God, for ever and ever. Amen. (Collect for Palm Sunday)

Jesus Christ, in perfect empathy with us, lived a fully human life. He was born, lived, loved, suffered, and died as one of us. As God Incarnate there was nothing to prevent his accomplishing our salvation and redemption through any manner of his choosing. But he chose to become one of us and to know all that we know about being incarnate spirit.

Empathy is expensive. It requires full feeling, experiencing, and knowing on a meaningful, and visceral level. We cannot empathize by remote control. And so, God chose the costly route in finding and saving us from ourselves and our sin. But lest we be content to say "Thank You, God. We appreciate that" and move away, God also invites us to walk the way of the cross, the path of Christ's suffering, and fact of his resurrection. We are meant to know the motive, the method and the meaning of the work of Christ.

Holy Week is our annual opportunity to walk with Jesus through the last week of his life, it is God's eternal invitation to know the meaning of it all.

In the last Chapter of Julian of Norwich's Revelations of Divine Love, she writes:

"Would you learn our Lord's meaning in this (Incarnation)? Learn it well. Love was his meaning. Who showed it to you? Love. What were you shown? Love. Why were you shown? For Love. Hold yourself in that love and you will learn and know more of the same. But you will never know or learn anything greater than that. Thus did I learn that Love was our Lord's meaning."(paraphrased)

Only through the total empathy of God in Christ could such love be made known.

Walking in the Way

Almighty God, whose most dear Son went not up to joy but first he suffered pain, and entered not into glory before he was crucified: Mercifully grant that we, walking in the way of the cross, may find it none other than the way of life and peace; through Jesus Christ your Son our Lord, who lives and reigns with you and the Holy Spirit, one God, for ever and ever. Amen.

We are all familiar with the phrase, "no pain, no gain". Unfortunately, we tend to misunderstand it. That phrase does not condone suffering, nor does in indicate that suffering is inevitable. It simply means that achieving our goals requires commitment and significant expenditure of energy and effort. That is not to say that the work will not be difficult or challenging, or that we are guaranteed a life without pain or suffering. But it is a serious mistake to say that suffering in and of itself is good for us.

Jesus walks the way of the cross because he loves us enough to do so. He dies because he is committed to the path that he has chosen and is single-minded in his devotion to God. He enters into joy and glory after he suffers, not because he suffers. He is glorified because he endured. There is a big difference!

If that were not the case, it would make no sense for us to use this collect. This prayer reminds us that following Jesus, walking in his way, is the Way of Life and Peace. He has done the work of Redemption – we do not have to complete it on his behalf. Ordinary daily life will present us with plenty of challenges which may or may not lead to happy outcomes. But the Way of Life in Christ leads to eternal/full Life and Peace. And it begins here and now. We imitate Christ because we are joined to him in Baptism and because we understand that following him means spiritual and spiritual participation in the work of making God's love real in this world. Sometimes that work is glorious, sometimes it is deeply painful, but it is through enduring and persevering that we see Glory.

In The Cross of Christ We Glory

O God, by the passion of your blessed Son you made an instrument of shameful death to be for us the means of life: Grant us so to glory in the cross of Christ, that we may gladly suffer shame and loss for the sake of your Son our Savior Jesus Christ; who lives and reigns with you and the Holy Spirit, one God, for ever and ever. Amen.

Human beings can be demonically creative in finding ways to destroy one another. It is as though we are afflicted by a lust for violence and a voyeuristic need to see its consequences. Crucifixion is a Roman example – intended not only to kill but to inflict maximum pain while doing so. Recent accounts of genocide, mutilations and terrorism throughout the world show us that humanity has not lost its taste for blood -- especially when that suffering is inflicted in the name of religious faith.

How then, are we to see and appreciate glory in the cross of Christ? We do so by remembering that God is in the business of transformation. There is nothing beyond the reach of God's saving embrace and there is nothing beyond God's intention to redeem. The worst that humanity could do to God Incarnate was in no way sufficient to overcome God's purpose. Viewed in that manner, the cross becomes the symbol of invincible love.

We glory in that symbol. And should shame or loss come to us as a result of the exercise of our faith and trust in Christ, we are empowered to suffer/endure it gladly. Not because shame and loss are enjoyable, but because we understand that we merely follow in the footsteps of one who gladly suffered and died.

And we remember that God, through love, is able to transform the results of even the most gruesome and hateful of humanity's efforts.

Trusting God's Future

Lord God, whose blessed Son our Savior gave his body to be whipped and his face to be spit upon: Give us grace to accept joyfully the sufferings of the present time, confident of the glory that shall be revealed; through Jesus Christ your Son our Lord, who lives and reigns with you and the Holy Spirit, one God, for ever and ever. Amen.

The Passion of Christ was not merely physical. And if we focus entirely on physical suffering and death of Jesus on Good Friday, we may overlook the full price of God's love for us in the Passion of Christ.

Because Christ's suffering was also spiritual. After having poured his life, his energy and his love into a ministry of healing and reconciliation, he is betrayed by his own disciples. He dies tormented not just by physical pain but by an awareness that he has not been heard. His teaching has not been effective, his example has been entertaining for some but it has not had the power to convert. In the end, he feels abandoned even by God.

But Christ's Passion was also an emotional assault on his dignity and his humanity. Yes, he was beaten and nailed to a cross. But he was also spit upon, scorned as a lunatic, ridiculed as a failure and false prophet, and stripped and humiliated as less than human. He was utterly discounted.

And in his humanity, he had no guarantee of the glory that would follow. He was called upon to make the sacrifice of his life in total obedience but without the confidence that it would make any difference.

That is the price of Divine Love – to offer everything for the sake of the Other – and to do so without thought of reward. The totality of his offering is what makes it possible for us to accept the trials we may encounter, trusting in the glory to be revealed. But Christ Jesus make that offering from Love alone.

"Oh love how deep, how broad, how high, how passing thought and fantasy,
That God the Son of God should take our mortal form for mortal sake."
"For us to wicked hands betrayed, scourged, mocked in purple robe arrayed,
He bore the shameful cross and death; for us gave up his dying breath."

Bread of Heaven, Cup of Salvation ~ Maundy Thursday,

Almighty Father, whose dear Son, on the night before he suffered, instituted the Sacrament of his Body and Blood: Mercifully grant that we may receive it thankfully in remembrance of Jesus Christ our Lord, who in these holy mysteries gives us a pledge of eternal life; and who now lives and reigns with you and the Holy Spirit, one God, for ever and ever. Amen.

The Sacrament of Holy Communion is Jesus's "Last Will and Testament" to us. With death imminent, he takes the time to insure that we will receive the fullest blessings of his presence among us. From this moment on, every time that we share table fellowship, breaking the bread and sharing the cup, we receive our full and inexhaustible inheritance as his sons and daughters – the pledge of eternal life.

"Take, eat. This is my body which is given for you. Do this for the remembrance of me. Drink this, all of you; this is my Blood of the new Covenant, which is shed for you and for many for the forgiveness of sins. Whenever you drink it, do this for the remembrance of me."

"Eucharist" literally means thanksgiving – and in this meal, we give thanks for the work of God in salvation. In Holy Communion, we are united to Christ through the mystery of his gift to us, and through the physical actions of breaking bread and drinking wine. We physical and spiritual beings share a common meal – one loaf, one cup shared among many – binding us together in his Body as one family. It is a meal celebrated through the millennia, grounded in the promises he made on the night before he died.

On Maundy Thursday we remember that even though we may stand at the foot of the cross tomorrow, tonight we are at table with our friend, Jesus, who is leaving us not only with memories, but with the physical and tangible proof of his gift and of our inheritance.

No Greater Love~ Good Friday

Almighty God, we pray you graciously to behold this your family, for whom our Lord Jesus Christ was willing to be betrayed, and given into the hands of sinners, and to suffer death upon the cross; who now lives and reigns with you and the Holy Spirit, one God, for ever and ever. Amen.

More words are spoken in one hour in the liturgy on this day than in any other throughout the year.

Because this is the day on which all words fail us. We seem to lurch and lunge through the prayers, the psalms, the readings and Gospel, searching for something that will explain what is happening and help us make sense of it. But nothing can explain it. This day is visceral. A man is dying and we are compelled to watch. God hangs before us, and we have no remedy for his pain, and no excuse for his suffering.

That is why, as the service begins, we acknowledge our helplessness in the face of what is happening. "Almighty God, we pray you graciously to behold this, your family." Confronted with the enormity of what has happened it is as though all we can is fall to our knees, remind ourselves and the Almighty that we are God's children, and plead for mercy.

And that is why, at the end of all the words of the liturgy, we pray, "Lord Jesus Christ, Son of the living God, we pray you to set your passion, cross and death between your judgment and our souls, now and in the hour of our death."

We have said all that we can say, and done all that we can do. Everything is in God's hands.

Waiting and Watching ~ Holy Saturday

O God, Creator of heaven and earth: Grant that, as the crucified body of your dear Son was laid in the tomb and rested on this holy Sabbath, so we may await with him the coming of the third day, and rise with him to newness of life; who now lives and reigns with you and the Holy Spirit, one God, for ever and ever. Amen.

Every year I ask myself, "What would this day be like if I did not know about tomorrow? What if I had been there at the foot of the cross, had watched the dying Jesus, had seen his body removed and hastily buried. What if I saw my life in ruins at my feet, cowering in terror at what might happen next?"

And every year I give thanks that I do know how the story ends.

But because I know how it ends, I find it all too easy to float through the day, thinking of tomorrow's services, planning Easter dinner, helping to decorate the church, managing to close the book on suffering while avoiding any real experience of what is happening in the meantime.

For those who know how the story ends, this day should be pregnant with the weight of glory. We cannot know what happened in the time between Jesus' death and resurrection. Our theology can imagine the joy in heaven, his triumph in the harrowing of hell, the revelation of his resurrected body. But we cannot know what it felt like to those who were there – those who have loved and followed him, and must now endure the Sabbath day of rest as a quiet day of mourning. They can only bear, and we can only imagine, the weight of glory.

God the Creator finished his work and rested on the seventh day of creation. God the Son rests on the seventh day when his work of redemption is complete. Can we learn to wait as well? Can we abide in the quiet unknown, trusting, waiting and watching?

EASTER

Easter Monday

Suddenly Jesus met Mary Magdalene and the other Mary and said, "Greetings!" (Matthew 28:9)

What a master of understatement! In Matthew's account of Jesus' first post-Resurrection appearance, the risen Christ's first words are the first century equivalent of "Hello!" It is almost as if he is demonstrating that his being back with them is the most normal and ordinary thing in the world. "What's with the surprised faces? I told you I'd be here, and here I am."

And he had told them, repeatedly, that he would return. In fact, these women had just left the empty tomb where the angels had told them that Jesus was risen from the dead.

But they were surprised and terrified as well. And who wouldn't be? Resurrection is just about the most profound reversal of human life and expectation that any of us can imagine. If death is truly overcome, then life is truly affirmed. And if life is truly affirmed, then we must experience life differently. It is no longer something that has a beginning, middle and end. Life is eternal. It is abundant, full, and forever. And while we may find it interesting to think or talk about, actually being physically, viscerally confronted by the reality of eternal life is a mind-blowing experience.

It's also about the best possible news that we could ever receive. And it is true.

So believe it, celebrate it! Rejoice with the abandon of King David dancing before the Ark of the Covenant. Sing with the hosts of heaven. Feast with the Saints of God.

Jesus says to us, "Hello! Greetings!" And we say in response, "Wow! Alleluia!!!"

Tuesday in Easter Week

Mary Magdalene went and announced to the disciples "I have seen the Lord." (John 20:18)

Mary Magdalene was the first Apostle. She was, in fact, the apostle to the apostles. Her message was clear, honest and world-changing. "I have seen the Lord."

Did they believe her? Not at first. But then, they did see Jesus and they came to believe. We too, though separated by two thousand years, are also given the opportunity to see Jesus and having seen him, to bear witness to the truth by asking others, "Have you seen Jesus my Lord?"

"Have you seen Jesus my Lord" is a song included in the nearly every Cursillo, Faith Alive or Happening event. The words and music and words are catchy and the theology is dead-on right. Jesus is all around us. Our resurrected Lord remains present to us in the world in myriad ways. His glory is reflected throughout creation, and it resides in each of God's children. Incarnation is eradicable.

I don't remember all the verses, but there are two that are indelibly printed on my heart and brain.

Have you seen Jesus my Lord? He's here in plain view.
Take a look, open your eyes. He'll show life to you.
Have you ever looked at the sunset? With the sky mellowing red
And the clouds suspended like feather?
Then, I say....You've seen Jesus my Lord.

Have you seen Jesus my Lord? He's here in plain view.
Take a look, open your eyes. He'll show life to you.
Have you ever stood in the family with the Lord there in your midst?
Seen the face of Christ on each other?
Then I say...You've seen Jesus my Lord.

This is the message of the Gospel on the third day of Easter and on every day of our lives. To be an evangelist is to see Jesus and to go and show him to others.

Wednesday in Easter Week

"When he was at table with them he took bread, blessed and broke it and gave it to them. Then their eyes were opened and they recognized him....Then they told what had happened on the road, and how he had been made known to them in the breaking of the bread. (Luke 24:31-31a, 35)

Holy Communion is Jesus gift to us so that we will know, not just intellectually or spiritually, but physically and viscerally that he is still with us. Throughout our history, the Church has recognized this sacrament, this family meal, as the reminder that Jesus Christ is the host at our table, and that the food with which he feeds us in his body and blood are the food and drink of eternity which sustains us now for the work he has called us to do.

What we have often forgotten is that every opportunity for table fellowship may also become a sacramental moment when those who share food and drink do so in the spirit of Christian community. Quite literally, that means that Christ is present in our homes, our lunch rooms, and our restaurants, and that by remembering him there, we also bear witness to his resurrection.

The Eucharist, as celebrated in our Church's is the primary and fundamental form of our worship. But let us not leave the spirit of Eucharist at the altar when we leave the church building. Take it forward to the rest of your life. Remember Jesus whenever you gather for meals. Acknowledge his presence whenever you gather in fellowship, and like the couple on the road to Emmaus, let your eyes be opened and your heart's set to burning when you encounter him in the breaking of the bread.

Thursday in Easter Week

"Thus it is written, that the Messiah is to suffer and to rise from the dead the third day, and that repentance and forgiveness of sins is to be proclaimed in his name to all nations, beginning from Jerusalem. You are witnesses of these things." (Luke 24:36-38)

Have you ever received a subpoena to testify before a judge? Most of us haven't but all of us have probably seen one delivered on television. Based on that limited sample, it seems to me that most of recipients of subpoenas go out of their way to avoid being served.

I wonder if maybe that is not also how the apostles and disciples felt when Jesus appeared to them and told them that they were being sent forth as witnesses to his resurrection. Even if they were thrilled and energized by his return to them after the resurrection, they were probably also glad for the opportunity to let things in their lives return to some semblance of the normal. That, of course, did not happen. The subpoena was served, and they set out to testify. And thus, the Church was born.

We, too, may be tempted to let the excitement of Easter begin to wane in our hearts as the hours and days of the season pass. But we dare not. The message of Easter is not confined to one hour, day, or season. It is a permanent reality in the world, and we are witnesses. From the moment of Jesus' resurrection, Easter is the new "normal".

Let your life, today and always, be a testimony to the saving love and grace of God in Christ. Go forth to all the "nations" of your life proclaiming and rejoicing in the Good News.

Friday in Easter Week

Jesus said to them, "Come and have breakfast." (John 21:12a)

This is my favorite verse in the Bible. Can you imagine anything more wonderfully welcoming and honoring than having Jesus himself stand before you saying, "Come and have breakfast."

So much of the language of "church" concerns judgment, repentance, and unworthiness. We are admonished to remember our sins, and to amend our lives. And that is fitting. But while that is clearly the message of John the Baptist, it is not the message of Jesus Christ. Yes, Jesus does speak of judgment, repentance and confession. But he always does so in the context of new life, of sustenance, and of grace.

In fact, when Jesus invites us to the table, it is the light of his love and his outstretched hand that shines judgment/truth upon us. We do well, even as we stand in that light to remember that we are always in need of turning and returning to Him and to the light. But we must also remember that the light in which we stand at his invitation is a light which makes us whole and worthy.

"Come, have breakfast," he says to us. "I know that you are weary, and hungry, and I have food for your bodies and your souls." It is this food that sustains us in the work we do. It is this food that gladdens our hearts and makes us able to proclaim the Good News. It is this food that reminds us that the post-resurrection appearances of Jesus Christ continue and are made manifest every time we accept his invitation to come to the table and to go forth to the world.

Saturday in Easter Week

After Jesus rose early on the first day of the week, he appeared first to Mary Magdalene, from whom he had cast out seven demons. She went out and told those who had been with him, while they were mourning and weeping. But when they heard that he was alive and had been seen by her, they would not believe it. After this he appeared in another form to two of them, as they were walking into the country. And they went back and told the rest, but they did not believe them. Later he appeared to the eleven themselves as they were sitting at the table; and he upbraided them for their lack of faith and stubbornness, because they had not believed those who saw him after he had risen. And he said to them, "Go into all the world and proclaim the good news to the whole creation." And they went out and proclaimed the good news everywhere, while the Lord worked with them and confirmed the message by the signs that accompanied it. (Mark 16:9-15,20)

Mark's Gospel recounts that when Mary Magdalene brought the Good News to the Apostles in the midst of their grief and mourning, they did not believe her. When the couple on the road to Emmaus encountered Jesus and raced back to tell the eleven, they did not believe them. It was not until Jesus himself appeared to them at table, and basically bawled them out for being stubborn and faithless, that they accepted the reality of Jesus' resurrection.

Was it because the testimony of a woman was not acceptable? Was it because the word of two people was not sufficient? Was it because the news was second-hand? Or was it because sometimes we would rather sit in our sorrow than rise to new life?

Jesus is risen, and so are we. We can no longer hide behind our self-made walls of fear, despair or the sense of inadequacy. If we believe that he is risen, there is only one path before us. We must become evangelists. We must share with the world our conviction that death is conquered, that we are freed from the fear of oblivion; and that grace of God, eternally present to us, is now the truth in our hearts and the message on our lips.

"He is risen, He is risen! Tell it out with joyful voice;
He has burst his three-days' prison; let the whole wide earth rejoice.
Death is conquered, we are free, Christ has won the victory."

First Century Evangelism

Peter, standing with the eleven, raised his voice and addressed the multitude, "Let the entire house of Israel know with certainty that God has made him both Lord and Messiah, this Jesus whom you crucified." Now when they heard this, they were cut to the heart and said to Peter and to the other apostles, "Brothers, what should we do?" Peter said to them, "Repent, and be baptized every one of you in the name of Jesus Christ so that your sins may be forgiven; and you will receive the gift of the Holy Spirit. For the promise is for you, for your children, and for all who are far away, everyone whom the Lord our God calls to him." And he testified with many other arguments and exhorted them, saying, "Save yourselves from this corrupt generation." So those who welcomed his message were baptized, and that day about three thousand persons were added. (Acts 2:14a, 36-41)

I was a bit of a klutz as child, prone to asthma, twisted ankles and stumbling over my own feet. So when it came time for choosing up teams at recess, I knew I would be among the last to be picked. There was one exception. If the game involved some degree of fearless self-destruction – like "Red Rover" – mine was the first name called. I couldn't hit or throw, and I wasn't very fast, but I could throw myself at the nearest target and not cry when I got hurt.

That's kind of how I imagine the Church's first efforts at evangelism. With neither the time nor the inclination to soften the message, Peter just stood up and told everyone what he wanted them to hear. No matter that it made some folks furious, and got him arrested more than once; Peter knew what was at stake and he knew where his skills lay. Argument, exhortation, and impassioned preaching were his gifts. And it worked.

But not so much today. This is about more than how many people are converted and baptized. It is also about how to include those folks who stand on the margins and whose names are not being called by the established religious teams. This is good news for everyone. "For the promise is for you, for your children, and for all who are far away, and everyone whom the Lord our God calls to him." We need more preachers like Peter because I think that we miss the point of the Good News when we are too busy focusing on how to build a strong and sustainable (read "financially viable") Church. We need a message that is delivered to all people. We need messengers who are willing to throw themselves into the fray. In fact, we need some good old-fashioned 1st century evangelism.

Fulfilling our Vows

*How shall I repay the LORD * for all the good things he has done for me?*
*I will lift up the cup of salvation * and call upon the Name of the LORD.*
*I will fulfill my vows to the LORD * in the presence of all his people.*
(Psalm 116:10-12)

I first started reading the Psalms on a daily basis about thirty years ago. Each time this one came up (Morning Prayer on the 24th day of the month), I would cringe. *"I will fulfill my vows to the Lord in the presence of all his people."* Did that mean, publicly? Does the expression of gratitude in a life of faith need to take place in the presence of all the people?

Now, to be fair to my own story, this was also the time during which I was discerning a call to ministry and preparing to go away to seminary. The process toward ordination is a very public one involving a great deal of self-disclosure, and for an introvert like me, it was very challenging. I longed for quiet prayer and silence. Still, God had done, and was doing wonderfully good things in my life; and I was genuinely thankful. I was just not certain that I had it in me to be so publicly demonstrative. I had every intention of living a life that would express my gratitude, at least in part because I believe that unexpressed gratitude is a waste. But wouldn't it be enough to be quietly grateful?

That, of course, is one of the challenges of being part of a liturgical community in the 21st century. We tend to privatize our faith, and rely on the shared words and actions of prayer book liturgy and music to communicate our gratitude. And that anonymity is fine, most of the time. But what do we do when we are genuinely moved to express our faith, our joy, and our gratitude? And how do we make spiritual space for those among us who are naturally enthusiastic and joyful?

We Anglicans have, on occasion, been referred to as "God's Frozen Chosen." We don't do well when our "personal boundary" space is challenged. And we have little patience with others whose spirituality is freely expressed. But for Heaven's Sake! If Easter is not a time to be enthusiastic and demonstrative, I don't know what is! So, let's all lighten up a bit. Sing louder. Enjoy the Alleluias. Even toss in an "Amen!" if you feel like it. The roof won't fall in, and you might be surprised at how good you will feel.

Genuine Mutual Love

Now that you have purified your souls by your obedience to the truth so that you have genuine mutual love, love one another deeply from the heart. You have been born anew, not of perishable but of imperishable seed, through the living and enduring word of God. (1 Peter 1:22-23)

I wonder what the writer of this Epistle means by "genuine mutual love." In fact, I wonder whether it is even possible to tell if the love we experience from the other person is either genuine or mutual. What I do know is that we are expected to our best to love one another, and that the "love" in question is not an emotional state of being. I have always understood such love to be an act of will by which we desire what is best for the "beloved" without placing any conditions or expectations on loving. But who am I to determine what is best for another?

I guess it has something to do with that line about "obedience to the truth."

If God is present with us in the Incarnation, and if we order our lives to be in accord with that fact, then it will certainly make a difference in how we treat each other. We will love the "other" as they deserve to be loved...not because they are good, but because they are in the image of God.

The place where I come down on this is "the golden rule" and the Great Commandment. Love your neighbor as yourself. If we love our neighbor as we ought to love ourselves, then we are, at a minimum, providing one another with those things necessary for a safe, healthy and meaningful life. We are respecting one another's dignity. We are constructively confronting issues of injustice and violence. And we are sharing and embodying the Good News in their lives.

And who knows? If we do this long enough, we may not only build the habit of being loving, we may actually start to feel really good in the process.

Table Fellowship

As they came near the village to which they were going, he walked ahead as if he were going on. But they urged him strongly, saying, "Stay with us, because it is almost evening and the day is now nearly over." So he went in to stay with them. When he was at the table with them, he took bread, blessed and broke it, and gave it to them. Then their eyes were opened, and they recognized him; and he vanished from their sight. (Luke 24:28-31)

There is something profoundly meaningful about a shared meal. The gift of hospitality offered to the guest is not only biblical, it is one of the deepest expressions of what it means to be a human. We all must eat to survive; but it is by eating in community that we thrive.

Even more important in this reading is the way in which the hosts were blessed by the presence of the guest. When someone honors us by accepting our invitation to break bread – to share a meal, they are also honoring and expressing thanks for our common humanity.

Most likely the couple with whom Jesus breaks bread in Emmaus was also present with him at the Last Supper. They recognize him through the action of breaking bread and they immediately return to Jerusalem to share the news with the others. Clearly they had broken bread with him before.

So, do we recognize Jesus when we come to the table at Holy Communion? Probably. But do we also recognize Jesus in the breaking of the bread at our tables at home? Through his actions at the Last Supper, Jesus has forever changed our relationship with bread and wine. In fact, he has changed our relationship with food, period.

He has reminded us that being fed is both a physical and spiritual action and that the two are neither easily nor wisely separated.

When you prepare a meal, be mindful of what you are doing, and prepare the meal with love and care. And when you share a meal, look for the presence of Christ at the table, and especially in the faces of those around you.

God's Knock-Out Punch

"Love's redeeming work is done, fought the fight, the battle won.
Death in vain forbids him rise; Christ has opened paradise. Alleluia!"
(Charles Wesley)

There is an adage among preachers that it really doesn't matter so much what you say in a sermon so long as the final hymn affirms it. That is because very few folks remember the exact words of a sermon but we all go home singing the final hymn. So, thank you to Charles Wesley. He has captured the message of Easter in two lines. Not only that, but they rhyme and are set to a couple of the most beautiful and stirring tunes in the hymnal.

These two short lines hold so much joy! Love's redeeming work IS done. It is finished. The war is over, and God won. As my late Church History professor, Dr. Donald Armentrout was wont to say, "Resurrection is God's knockout punch!" Fight over.

Enough said.

Eyes of Our Faith

"O God, whose blessed Son made himself known to his disciples in the breaking of bread: Open the eyes of our faith, that we may behold him in all his redeeming work; who lives and reigns with you, in the unity of the Holy Spirit, one God, now and for ever. Amen." (Collect for the 3rd Sunday of Easter)

Tomorrow we will begin the service by asking God to open the eyes of our faith. Can you imagine what might happen if we all really meant it? What might God accomplish through us if we were all willing and suddenly able to see the work of redemption in the world around us?

To be redeemed is literally to be bought back from servitude...to be freed. And God in Christ is continually at work around us doing just that. When we are in bondage to sin, or despair, or grief, Christ stands before us and says, "You are redeemed". When we are starved for the bread of life and the cup of salvation, he pours his Spirit into our hearts and our bodies through the Eucharist. When we are lonely, he comes to us in the presence of our sisters and brothers and in breaking bread with us, reminds us that in him we are never really alone.

His love frees us. And when, by the grace of God we see freedom, we see that our Lord is its source, its beginning and its end. May we all pray that the eyes of our faith are opened to the glorious redemption that surrounds and enfolds us.

Teaching, Fellowship, Breaking of Bread and Prayers

Those who had been baptized devoted themselves to the apostles' teaching and fellowship, to the breaking of bread and the prayers. Awe came upon everyone, because many wonders and signs were being done by the apostles. All who believed were together and had all things in common; they would sell their possessions and goods and distribute the proceeds to all, as any had need. Day by day, as they spent much time together in the temple, they broke bread at home and ate their food with glad and generous hearts, praising God and having the goodwill of all the people. And day by day the Lord added to their number those who were being saved.
(Acts 2:42-47)

Does this passage sound familiar? It is the description of a Christian's worship life -- *"Those who had been baptized devoted themselves to the apostles' teaching and fellowship, to the breaking of bread and the prayers."* It is also the text of the first promise of our Baptismal Covenant. The practice of our faith requires education, fellowship, communion, and prayer, and those four things together equip the baptized to become living examples of the continuing presence of Christ in the world.

Everything else flows from that foundation. In the Apostles' teaching, we learn to give, to share, to exercise hospitality, to and to offer healing and reconciliation. In fellowship we learn to love and forgive, to encourage and to constructively challenge. In breaking bread we honor the priority of hospitality and remember the obligation to feed the hungry; and in prayer we open our hearts to God in Thanksgiving, Intercession, Petition, Repentance, and Praise.

Best of all, such a life results in a spirit of gladness and generosity; and gladness and generosity are very effective methods of evangelism! *"Day by day, as they spent much time together in the temple, they broke bread at home and ate their food with **glad and generous hearts**, praising God and having the goodwill of all the people. And day by day the Lord added to their number those who were being saved."* When people experience Christians as loving, open-hearted, and joyously faithful, they are far more inclined to receive the Good News in their own lives.

Don't you want to be living with a glad and generous heart? The answer is right here!

The Power of Shepherding

The LORD is my shepherd; I shall not be in want.
He makes me lie down in green pastures and leads me beside still waters.
He revives my soul and guides me along right pathways for his Name's sake.
Though I walk through the valley of the shadow of death,
I shall fear no evil; for you are with me; your rod and your staff, they comfort me.
(Psalm 23)

We all need a shepherd now and then. In those times when we feel lost or adrift, when we are faced with very challenging choices, or when the stress of life threatens to overwhelm us, we may find ourselves longing for some firm, well-intentioned shepherding.

Unfortunately for most of us, as soon as the moment of need passes, we tend to revert to our normal patterns of wandering off or climbing through the fence.

What this psalm reminds us about is our continual need for the guidance and protection of God. Left to our own devices, we may succumb to the fears and tensions of our lives. We may lose the willingness to trust that God is present with us and will provide for us. We may, in fact, altogether abandon the relationship with our Good Shepherd. That is when disaster ensues.

The sheep that wanders away from the flock and ends up falling off a cliff does not intend to destroy itself. It merely forgets the fact that it needs the guidance and protection of the shepherd. The person who only trusts the Good Shepherd in times of trouble is far more likely to find herself standing at the edge of the cliff than if she had remained within the protection of the fold.

Our Good Shepherd is the Risen Christ, and he will never abandon us.

Feasting in the Midst of Danger

You spread a table before me in the presence of those who trouble me;
you have anointed my head with oil, and my cup is running over.
Surely your goodness and mercy shall follow me all the days of my life,
and I will dwell in the house of the LORD for ever. (Psalm 23)

I suppose that when we become truly aware of the blessed presence of God, we will have no trouble moving serenely through whatever life throws at us. But I am clearly not there, yet! I have a difficult time imagining how I could sit down and enjoy a feast if I were surrounded by enemies. Still, my admitting it also reveals that I am on a journey of learning to trust God.

But, the Psalmist, a man well-acquainted with dangerous enemies, rises above his circumstances as he presents us with a gloriously positive affirmation of what God will do for us. His confidence in the goodness and mercy of God has rung out through the centuries, and become a creedal statement for countless people of faith: *"My experience may be terrible right now, but I am not alone. I dwell in the house of the Lord!"*

There is a reason this Psalm is known to so many people, is recited at so many sickbeds and funerals, and is the most often quoted piece of Scripture in cinema. It gives voice to the deepest cry of the human spirit. We need, sometimes desperately, to know that God is with us, and that nothing, not even death, will defeat us if we walk with God and dwell in God's presence.

There is also a note of defiance in the 23rd Psalm. *"Sheltered by the goodness and mercy of God, I can go anywhere that God calls me."*

It is the work of our lives to learn to trust the truth of those words.

The Inevitability of Suffering

It is a credit to you if, being aware of God, you endure pain while suffering unjustly. If you endure when you are beaten for doing wrong, what credit is that? But if you endure when you do right and suffer for it, you have God's approval. For to this you have been called, because Christ also suffered for you, leaving you an example, so that you should follow in his steps. "He committed no sin, and no deceit was found in his mouth." When he was abused, he did not return abuse; when he suffered, he did not threaten; but he entrusted himself to the one who judges justly. He himself bore our sins in his body on the cross, so that, free from sins, we might live for righteousness; by his wounds you have been healed. For you were going astray like sheep, but now you have returned to the shepherd and guardian of your souls. (1 Peter 2:19-25)

It is safe to assume that people with normal self-preservation instincts neither enjoy pain nor actively pursue it; and Christian teaching declares that it is sinful to seek martyrdom. So we can be confident that this passage does not glorify suffering. What it does do is remind us that being a Christian is not always easy, and that in the course of following Jesus, we may encounter resistance, hostility, or in extreme cases, violence. When we do, we are admonished to remember why it is that we suffer, and do our best to see that our behavior is at all times in keeping with what we profess to believe.

It is actually quite a responsibility – one in which we are required to be certain that if we suffer for the sake of our faith, we do so with humility and patience. We are also called to be equally committed to being the best representatives possible of the redeeming love of Christ. In other words, don't be obnoxious about your faith. Don't provoke others with self-righteous, judgmental, or manipulative behavior. If we do, we may indeed suffer, but it won't be because we were following Christ. We cannot convincingly proclaim love from a hateful heart.

Jesus gives us the example we need. Tell the truth compassionately. Love others as you would like to be loved. Leave judgment to God. And if, while doing that, we suffer, trust in the abiding presence of God.

What Kind of Shepherd?

Jesus said, "Very truly, I tell you, anyone who does not enter the sheepfold by the gate but climbs in by another way is a thief and a bandit. The one who enters by the gate is the shepherd of the sheep. The gatekeeper opens the gate for him, and the sheep hear his voice. He calls his own sheep by name and leads them out. When he has brought out all his own, he goes ahead of them, and the sheep follow him because they know his voice. They will not follow a stranger, but they will run from him because they do not know the voice of strangers." Jesus used this figure of speech with them, but they did not understand what he was saying to them. So again Jesus said to them, "Very truly, I tell you, I am the gate for the sheep. All who came before me are thieves and bandits; but the sheep did not listen to them. I am the gate. Whoever enters by me will be saved, and will come in and go out and find pasture. The thief comes only to steal and kill and destroy. I came that they may have life, and have it abundantly." (John 10:1-10)

Not all shepherds are good shepherds. Some are actually thieves and bandits whose aim is not salvation, and whose motive is not love. With disturbing regularity, we read or hear of such shepherds who sole intent appears to be to fleece the flock. So how do we know if someone who purports to be speaking for Jesus if really doing so? How do we know what preaching and teaching is trustworthy and true?

The Church provides us with a very clear way of knowing. What fruit does this teaching produce? Specifically, does it produce the fruit of discipleship? Does it build up the community? Are the hungry fed, the naked clothed, and the despairing offered hope? Is the Good News proclaimed?

Jesus says that his sheep know his voice. That means that we have the ability to recognize his voice and to discern his message.

Jesus also tells us that he comes to bring abundant life. It is a good thing to remember that abundant life does not mean prosperity. Abundant life is not about wealth or power or influence. Abundant life means knowing the fullness of God's love and presence in any and all circumstances. Wealth, power and influence are exterior. Abundant life is interior. But just because it is interior does not mean that it is hidden. Those who experience abundant life have something about them that makes it visible to those around them.

So, if we are uncertain about the authenticity of any shepherd, all we need to do is pray, watch and listen. We will know who to follow.

Called by Name

O God, whose Son Jesus is the good shepherd of your people: Grant that when we hear his voice we may know him who calls us each by name, and follow where he leads; who, with you and the Holy Spirit, lives and reigns, one God, for ever and ever. Amen. (Collect for the Fourth Sunday of Easter)

If you ever spend any time around sheep, it is easy to understand why some folks resist the idea of being referred to as part of a flock. Sheep are neither the smartest, nor the most cooperative of livestock. In fact, some sheep seem down-right intent on self-destruction.

But the individual sheep and the flock as well stand a far better chance of surviving if the shepherd has managed to spend enough time with them to learn their names and to teach them to hear and respond to his voice. And yes, a good border collie helps as well!

So, it seems to me that there are two points to this passage. One is that we are all capable of recognizing his voice. The other is that it is often easier to hear the good shepherd if we stay in community. In community there will probably be someone around who can give us a nudge and say, "Didn't you hear him call you?"

It is also true that at least until we learn wilderness survival skills, following is safer and easier than trail-blazing. That is not to say that everyone should be docile and compliant, only that it is better to learn the basics and determine the destination before striking out on our own.

Preaching Outside the Envelope

Filled with the Holy Spirit, Stephen gazed into heaven and saw the glory of God and Jesus standing at the right hand of God. "Look," he said, "I see the heavens opened and the Son of Man standing at the right hand of God!" But they covered their ears, and with a loud shout all rushed together against him. Then they dragged him out of the city and began to stone him; and the witnesses laid their coats at the feet of a young man named Saul. (Acts 7:55-58)

This story seems at first a bit perplexing. The people of Jerusalem were very accustomed to street preachers and prophets. Whether from the temple steps or the street corners, they were used to hearing apocalyptic warnings and exhortations to repentance. And unlike today's pastors, first century preachers had no qualms about offending their audiences. Proclamation was a "no-holds-barred" sort of affair. So, what on earth has Stephen done that is egregious enough for the crowd to stone him?

He did the same thing that would result some decades later in the expulsion of Jewish followers of Jesus from the synagogues – Stephen identified Jesus as sitting at the right hand of God. He had, repeatedly, in his sermon attacked the established faith and practices of Judaism and accused them of murder and apostasy. They were already furious with him, but it was not until he described seeing Jesus in heaven with God the Father that they attacked him. In Judaism, God is spirit, not flesh, and to equate the ascended Jesus with God was unforgivable. To an observant Jew, this was not only unimaginable, it was blasphemy; and the penalty for blasphemy was death by stoning. Stephen met his end because he said and did the most provocative thing possible.

It is one thing to think of Jesus as Messiah, even if he failed at the task of liberation and died a shameful death. It is something else altogether to describe him as God and Savior.

What sort of faith do we possess? Who is this Jesus? Are we willing to proclaim him as God? Are we willing to challenge a mindset that seeks to demote him to merely prophet and teacher? Perhaps we are not foolhardy enough to consciously seek to offend others as Stephen did. But are we at least intuitive enough to realize along with Saul and the crowd, that God Incarnate in the person of Jesus is a very radical and very dangerous idea?

Irony of Trust

In you, O LORD, have I taken refuge; let me never be put to shame;
deliver me in your righteousness.
Incline your ear to me; make haste to deliver me.
Be my strong rock, a castle to keep me safe,
for you are my crag and my stronghold;
for the sake of your Name, lead me and guide me.
Take me out of the net that they have secretly set for me,
for you are my tower of strength.
Into your hands I commend my spirit,
for you have redeemed me, O LORD, O God of truth.
My times are in your hand; rescue me from the hand of my enemies,
and from those who persecute me.
Make your face to shine upon your servant, and in your loving-kindness save me."
(Psalm 31:1-5, 15-16)

"Trust in God in time of trial." Fortunately for most of us, we don't regularly have to exercise that degree of faith, because doing so sounds a whole lot easier than it is! We had far rather trust ourselves, our habits, and our assumptions. And, if we are of a certain temperament or personality type, we will rush headlong into the nearest source of comfort or the quickest solution to our problems, rather than abiding with God for the time required to discern what to do next.

Which is very ironic, because trust is required of us all the time. We trust that the food we purchase is clean and wholesome. We trust that the traffic lights are working properly every time we cross an intersection. To a greater or lesser degree, we even trust the knowledge and skill of our physicians, teachers and politicians.

Why then, is it so challenging for us to trust God as a rock, a castle, a refuge or a deliverer? Perhaps it is because tenuous as it may be, we at least have a relationship with those other entities. But do we really have a relationship with God – the sort that keeps us in regular contact and ongoing conversation? In other words, would we recognize God if we passed on the street? Trust requires relationship, and relationship requires an investment of self. God is always ready to receive us. The question is, are we ready to be received?

Living Stones

Like newborn infants, long for the pure, spiritual milk, so that by it you may grow into salvation-- if indeed you have tasted that the Lord is good. Come to him, a living stone, though rejected by mortals yet chosen and precious in God's sight, and like living stones, let yourselves be built into a spiritual house, to be a holy priesthood, to offer spiritual sacrifices acceptable to God through Jesus Christ. (1 Peter 2:2-5)

This passage reminds me of gymnasts and acrobats who, balancing and supporting one another's weight, construct elaborate towering human pyramids. It is only possible for them to do this because they understand and make use of the principles of architecture. They know that the foundation must be sturdy and solid, and that it must also be large enough to support the weight which will be placed upon it. They also understand that there is a limit to how tall the pyramid may be before it will collapse. True, these folks are very fit, and their skill and agility make it look far simpler than it actually is, but have you noticed that at the end of each performance, the pyramid comes down – either by those on the top gracefully tumbling row by row to the ground, or in a demonstration of the laws of physics, removing a central support and allowing the tower to fall?

So, this is more than a spiritual exercise. The writer of 1 Peter has employed a very athletic metaphor in referring to the faithful as living stones, building upon the cornerstone of Christ. And this means that the faithful must also be "fit" for the job. We must be strong, we must be prepared, and we must develop a sense of commitment and balance if we are to take our appointed place in the construction of God's house. This strength, of course, is not based simply on physical size or ability, this strength is dependent upon our stamina, our endurance, and our faith in the purpose of the work to which we are called. It also demands our trust that God will not only put us in the appropriate place in the construction of the house, but that God will shape and form us to fit into that spot.

We living stones will need all the strength, agility, and cooperation that our faith can provide. But what a privilege to be called to stand upon the foundation of Jesus Christ our cornerstone in the building of the reign of God!

The Way, the Truth and the Life

Jesus said to him, "I am the way, and the truth, and the life. No one comes to the Father except through me. If you know me, you will know my Father also. From now on you do know him and have seen him." (John 14:6-7)

In these two short verses, Jesus effectively demystifies God. If we know Jesus, we know God. If we see Jesus, we see God. We neither know nor worship some utterly transcendent force or being. When God became Incarnate in Jesus, we were invited to look upon the face of God. Jesus is the "way, the truth, and the life" because he is the avenue through which we directly experience God the Father, and his humanity is the vehicle through which we see God. Of course, because Jesus himself is also God the Son, we see God directly in Jesus. And because we have not been left comfortless, God the Holy Spirit is known to us through the Church, and the Body of Christ becomes our most immediate means of seeing and knowing God.

If we believe this, everything changes. God not only loves us enough to become one of us, God also entrusts us with the responsibility of showing God to others. With God's self-disclosure in Jesus Christ, access to the divine is placed before us. Once we have seen it, we are called to share it with others – through our own lives and actions. Limited though we may be, we are reflections of God's loving presence in the world; and if we are willing to become living stones in building the reign of God, others will be able to see God in and through us. That vision will be imperfect but it will be sufficient!

We do the Body of Christ in the Church a great disservice when we dwell on its imperfections. Of course we are imperfect, but that does not relieve us of the calling to proclaim Christ and seek to embody the love of God. Nearly everyone who comes to God these days does so through the ministry of fellow human beings. Some may be blessed to have a direct revelation of God; but most of us glimpse the holy through the ministrations of others.

Let us always remember that in our baptismal covenant we promise to "seek and serve Christ in all persons." We would not be called to do so if he were not present in them.

True Prayer Agrees with God

Philip said to him, "Lord, show us the Father, and we will be satisfied." Jesus said to him, "Have I been with you all this time, Philip, and you still do not know me? Whoever has seen me has seen the Father. How can you say, `Show us the Father'? Do you not believe that I am in the Father and the Father is in me? The words that I say to you I do not speak on my own; but the Father who dwells in me does his works. Believe me that I am in the Father and the Father is in me; but if you do not, then believe me because of the works themselves. Very truly, I tell you, the one who believes in me will also do the works that I do and, in fact, will do greater works than these, because I am going to the Father. I will do whatever you ask in my name, so that the Father may be glorified in the Son. If in my name you ask me for anything, I will do it." (John 14:7-14)

One of the greatest challenges of preaching is helping folks see just what this passage does NOT say. It does not promise us that the faithful will be granted anything for which they ask. Nor does it mean that invoking the name of Jesus compels Him to do our bidding.

What it does mean is this. When our prayers are in accord with God's will, they are to God's glory, and they are answered. So, our task is to get on board with God's will. Our prayer is to be "thy will be done." Our prayers do not instruct God. Nor do our prayers change God's mind. God will do what God will do.

True, praying only for God's will is much more challenging than pleading with God or sending in a memo concerning what we believe God ought to be doing. But ordering our lives and our prayers around seeking God's will and then submitting ourselves to that will, not only guarantees that our prayers will be answered, it also strengthens our souls as we develops trust, discernment and obedience.

Try it. Bring to mind something for which you pray. Now pray only these words. "Your will be done, O God." Now stop and take stock of what you are thinking, feeling, and expecting. This is the beginning of true prayer.

God's Map

Almighty God, whom truly to know is everlasting life: Grant us so perfectly to know your Son Jesus Christ to be the way, the truth, and the life, that we may steadfastly follow his steps in the way that leads to eternal life; through Jesus Christ your Son our Lord, who lives and reigns with you, in the unity of the Holy Spirit, one God, for ever and ever. Amen. (Collect for the Fifth Sunday of Easter)

Have you ever been somewhere that was so alien to you that you were totally dependent upon someone else to guide you? Perhaps a place where you did not understand the language or customs? Or perhaps a place where you did not feel safe or confident that you could find your way home?

We don't like feeling helpless or dependent. We're certainly not fond of radical trust. Most of us want to believe that we have the freedom to go where we would like and the competence to find our way around in even the most unusual terrain. And because we so often manage to arrange things to work out that way, we tend to project our confidence out into eternity assuming that we can also find our way to the reign of God.

But this prayer calls that state of mind into question. Jesus shows us the way to God and having blazed a clear and direct path for us, he expects that we will follow it. We don't need to find another route – this one leads to eternal life. So, unless we are looking for another destination, why not follow his steps? He is for us the way, the truth and the life. We need only follow.

How Many Gods are There?

Paul stood in front of the Areopagus and said, "Athenians, I see how extremely religious you are in every way. For as I went through the city and looked carefully at the objects of your worship, I found among them an altar with the inscription, `To an unknown god.' What therefore you worship as unknown, this I proclaim to you. ..For `In him we live and move and have our being'; as even some of your own poets have said, `For we too are his offspring.' (Acts 17:22-23, 28)

One Sunday a year I play a game with the church school children called "Stump the Rector." They get to ask me any question they'd like and if I can't answer it, they get their name and the question printed in the parish newsletter. Every year I can pretty much predict that one of the questions will be a variation of "with so many religions in the world, how many Gods are there and who's right?"

As this passage demonstrates, it's an ancient and universal question. The people of Athens asked it themselves; and in order to hedge their bets against inadvertently neglecting any deity, erected an altar to "an unknown God."

And one day just last week, I had a conversation with an adult who asked me "If there is only one God, how can we all be worshipping the same one when we believe different things?" I responded, "What we believe about God does not define God."

There is only one God, who self-discloses to creation as he chooses. We know him through our Scriptures, our relationship with Jesus Christ and our experience of his presence in our lives. Others may know him differently. Others may know him as "her". For it is very true that in him we live and move and have our being, and that all people are indeed the offspring of God. The important thing is that we are all seeking God with all our hearts and that we are loving our neighbors as ourselves.

This awareness is what allowed St. Paul to speak to the people of Athens and to affirm their reverence and faith. It is also what allowed him to preach the Gospel and reveal Jesus Christ to them. He made a connection that led them to believe. That is a good model for evangelism, and for life.

What Does God Require of Us?

*Bless our God, you peoples; *make the voice of his praise to be heard;*
*Who holds our souls in life, *and will not allow our feet to slip.*
*For you, O God, have proved us; *you have tried us just as silver is tried.*
*You brought us into the snare; *you laid heavy burdens upon our backs.*
*You let enemies ride over our heads; we went through fire and water; **
but you brought us out into a place of refreshment.
*I will enter your house with burnt-offerings and will pay you my vows, **
which I promised with my lips and spoke with my mouth when I was in trouble.
I will offer you sacrifices of fat beasts with the smoke of rams;
**I will give you oxen and goats.*
*Come and listen, all you who fear God, *and I will tell you what he has done for me.*
*I called out to him with my mouth, *and his praise was on my tongue.*
*If I had found evil in my heart, *the Lord would not have heard me;*
*But in truth God has heard me; *he has attended to the voice of my prayer.*
*Blessed be God, who has not rejected my prayer, *nor withheld his love from me.*
(Psalm 66:7-18)

Because the Psalms are prayers, they give us a glimpse into the interior life of those wrote them and those who prayed them. Our ancestors in the faith were much like us – they experienced the highs and the lows, the trials and the blessings that come to each of us. But the most striking feature of the Psalms is the manner in which they can shift gears midstream, moving from fear to joy, from regret to jubilation. Spiritually speaking, such transitions are only possible when our faith relationship is constant and continuous. We cannot move from thesis (Life is wonderful!) to antithesis (Why is this happening to me?) to synthesis (God is with me no matter what happens.) if we are not in relationship with God throughout the process.

That is what makes this Psalm such a good example of what a life of prayer and worship looks like when it is undertaken with the awareness of abiding in God through all the times of our lives. Such awareness allows us to "Praise God at all times, and in all things." Are we living through a time of trial? Praise God, not for the trial, but for God's presence in the midst of it. Are we experiencing a period of joy and happiness? Praise God, not just for the joy and happiness, but for God's presence in the midst of it. Are we sailing on peaceful seas? Praise God, and do not neglect to pray just because things are going well. For the truth is this: the loving presence of God is steadfast and trustworthy.

Honey or Vinegar

Now who will harm you if you are eager to do what is good? But even if you do suffer for doing what is right, you are blessed. Do not fear what they fear, and do not be intimidated, but in your hearts sanctify Christ as Lord. Always be ready to make your defense to anyone who demands from you an accounting for the hope that is in you; yet do it with gentleness and reverence. Keep your conscience clear, so that, when you are maligned, those who abuse you for your good conduct in Christ may be put to shame. (I Peter 3:13-16)

As I read these verses, I remembered a particularly perverse interpretation of this passage I often heard as a child. It had to do with rubbing salt in wounds and attracting flies with honey rather than vinegar. The point seemed to be that being good carried with it the reward of feeling superior to those who were not.

Now it is perfectly possible (perhaps even likely) that I misunderstood what I was hearing. But I do know that the emphasis was not so much on sanctifying Christ in my heart as it was on coming out ahead in the race to holiness.

And even if the emphasis had been on gentleness and reverence, I still very much doubt that those who malign others for their conduct in Christ are ever really shamed in this life.

So it seems to me that this passage is not about getting the best of a tormentor. It's not even about suffering unjustly. This passage is about knowing what we trust and hope for, and being willing to embody the Good News for an antagonist who demonstrates no real interest in learning about it. And the only way to successfully do that is with gentleness and reverence – not just toward the subject matter, but toward the individual with whom you are speaking.

To respond with gentleness and reverence to those who may malign is to "seek and serve Christ in all people." Indeed, the reward for that is a clear conscience. And with a clear conscience we need not be tempted to see someone put to shame!

What Saves Us?

And baptism, which this prefigured, now saves you-- not as a removal of dirt from the body, but as an appeal to God for a good conscience, through the resurrection of Jesus Christ, who has gone into heaven and is at the right hand of God, with angels, authorities, and powers made subject to him. (1 Peter 3:21-22)

My early years were spent in a denomination which practiced Adult Baptism for the forgiveness of sin. Once was sufficient for salvation, but fully aware that we would all sin again after baptism, it was not only possible, but more or less likely that most of us would need to be baptized again at some point later in life when the weight of our failures had burdened us to the point of our needing to be reminded of God's cleansing love. Re-Baptism in that context was actually what we Episcopalians do at every baptism when we re-new our Baptismal Covenant, or more specifically when we choose to re-affirm those vows in the presence of a Bishop.

Baptism itself does not save us. Our Baptisms are our response to the fact that God has already saved us. So, it is not that baptism conveys some sort of grace that requires God to accept us no matter what. Baptism is a sign that we know we are already accepted and that by choosing to be baptized we are permanently initiated into the Body of Christ and his family. In fact, the obligation to honor the event lies not upon God, but upon us. We are promising to live in a certain manner, to honor and respect Christ in all persons and to actively engage in the work of justice and peace. We are obliged to honor those promises and to do so with the grace and the help which God provides.

Being creatures who are embodied spirit, it is quite natural that we associate the cleansing of our hearts with the cleansing of our bodies. While it is certainly possible for a good, clear conscience to inhabit a grungy body, most of us feel a greater sense of congruity when our outward appears reflects and inward experience. Or as the Psalmist writes:

"Purge me from my sin, and I shall be pure;
wash me and I shall be clean indeed."

Proof of Love

Jesus said to his disciples, "If you love me, you will keep my commandments. And I will ask the Father, and he will give you another Advocate, to be with you forever. This is the Spirit of truth, whom the world cannot receive, because it neither sees him nor knows him. You know him, because he abides with you, and he will be in you. "I will not leave you orphaned; I am coming to you. In a little while the world will no longer see me, but you will see me; because I live, you also will live. On that day you will know that I am in my Father, and you in me, and I in you. They who have my commandments and keep them are those who love me; and those who love me will be loved by my Father, and I will love them and reveal myself to them." (John 14:15-21)

This passage describes a moment with which all of us can resonate. "Don't just say you love me, show me!" Or "Don't apologize, change!" Whether we are speaking of children, lovers, or politicians, we know that words without actions are meaningless.

So, when Jesus speaks to his disciples, he tries to impress upon them the absolute necessity of their putting their faith into action in their lives...and to do so by obeying his commandments. What commandment? "Love each other."

It is not that we must love one another simply to be obedient to Jesus' command. The truth is that we cannot love God unless we love one another, and that even though the Spirit of Truth, the Advocate, hovers constantly among us, we cannot recognize or benefit from that Spirit unless we are dwelling in love.

It is only when we are in Love that we are capable of truly knowing God and of making God known to others. Love requires action. Action builds love.

Keeping Things in Balance

O God, you have prepared for those who love you such good things as surpass our understanding: Pour into our hearts such love towards you, that we, loving you in all things and above all things, may obtain your promises, which exceed all that we can desire; through Jesus Christ our Lord, who lives and reigns with you and the Holy Spirit, one God, for ever and ever. Amen. (Collect for the Sixth Sunday of Easter)

The key to solid theology is keeping things in balance. It is when we veer off into the outer edges of an idea that we are most likely to get lost or forget what it was that we were trying to say in the first place.

This has often happened when folks talk about the Nature of God. Is God totally "other" or "out there" (what theology refers to as transcendent); or is God completely accessible to us or even within us (immanent)? It is especially important to keep those two in balance when we are speaking of knowing and loving God. This collect does just that.

We do, in fact, know of God through creation. Some degree of the self-disclosure of the Divine occurs in all things. But that does not make them God, and to love God in only that way and to that degree is a temptation toward idolatry.

But to limit our love of God to only "above all things" is a temptation toward indifference to the created order and to God's ongoing revelation.

It is only when we seek to love God in all things and above all things, which by the way is when we begin to understand Jesus' promise "Lo, I am with you always", that we begin to receive the gifts that surpass understanding and exceed all that we can desire.

Inquiring and Discerning Hearts

When the apostles had come together, they asked Jesus, "Lord, is this the time when you will restore the kingdom to Israel?" He replied, "It is not for you to know the times or periods that the Father has set by his own authority. But you will receive power when the Holy Spirit has come upon you; and you will be my witnesses in Jerusalem, in all Judea and Samaria, and to the ends of the earth." (Acts 1:6-8)

Who? What? When? Where? How? I learned in Junior High that asking and answering those questions was the key to competent writing, whether it was a book report, a news article or later in life – a sermon.

These questions are also the building blocks of most conversations and entertainment – because after all "inquiring minds want to know!"

We even include this idea in our baptismal service. The prayers over the newly baptized include these words "give him/her an inquiring and discerning heart."

Imagine, then the frustration of the disciples when Jesus sends them out to be witnesses to all the world but tells them that they are only to speak of what they already know. What they know is sufficient for their witness and for the evangelization of the world. They do not need to know the times or the periods of the restoration of the earthly kingdom. That is up to God and is in God's hands. Their job is to tell others what they have experienced of Jesus and of the reign of God that is already present and growing in the world.

They will not be able to predict the future, but they will receive the power of the Holy Spirit. They will not receive the facts that they may desire, but they will most assuredly receive the power to be trustworthy and effective witnesses to the liberating power of the gospel.

So, the question for us is simple – what do we know and are sharing it with others?

Storm Trooper Evangelism?

*Let God arise, and let his enemies be scattered; **
let those who hate him flee before him.
*Let them vanish like smoke when the wind drives it away; **
as the wax melts at the fire, so let the wicked perish at the presence of God.
But let the righteous be glad and rejoice before God;
let them also be merry and joyful.
(Psalm 68:1-3)

Most of the time, the lectionary chooses the least violent options for use on Sunday mornings. It's only if you read the Psalms in a monastic cycle that you encounter the curses and anathemas on a regular basis. But for some reason, this portion of Psalm 68 has been picked for the last Sunday of Easter season.

I have personally never thought that storm trooper evangelism is effective. And it's more than a little unsettling that the righteous should be rejoicing and making merry while the wicked are melting like wax. I can't imagine anyone who is taking Jesus seriously when he says that we are to love our neighbors as ourselves finding edification in merrymaking among the corpses. Something is seriously amiss, here.

So, what are we to do with these verses? Maybe we should stop focusing on who might be an enemy of God. Maybe we should consider the possibility that WE are the wicked. Maybe we should ask ourselves whether or not our lives and actions are congruent with what we profess to believe. And if they aren't maybe we should repent.

Thomas Jefferson thought that the only way to make the Scriptures useful was to edit them to remove the parts that he found unacceptable. His attempts resulted in a very truncated and basically insipid collection of useful aphorisms. I think that a better approach to these troubling texts would involve serious self-examination, and acknowledging that violence does not spring from the heart and mind of God. Let's stop projecting it onto God and start taking responsibility for the violence and hatred that threatens to infect each human heart. Christ suffered, died, was resurrected and ascended to show us the way home. Let's get on the road.

Popularity or Fidelity

Beloved, do not be surprised at the fiery ordeal that is taking place among you to test you, as though something strange were happening to you. But rejoice insofar as you are sharing Christ's sufferings, so that you may also be glad and shout for joy when his glory is revealed. If you are reviled for the name of Christ, you are blessed, because the spirit of glory, which is the Spirit of God, is resting on you. (1 Peter 4:12-14)

How do we know when we are being faithful to the Word of God? When we are not universally popular. That realization took decades to sink in, but it's true. If we are really being faithful, we will not be able to please everyone all the time. If that were the case, the world would be completely redeemed and there would be no need for the inconvenient truth of the Gospel.

The Gospel compels us to be uncomfortable, and among the treacherous comforts of life these days, complacent affluence is perhaps the most dangerous.

So, unless we are willing to make ourselves, and others, uncomfortable (or a least a bit uneasy) about the disparities of contemporary life we are not suffering with Christ or sharing in his work. How can we shout for joy when others are in despair? How can we be full and comfortable when others languish in hunger and preventable illness?

The people who Peter addresses in this passage are being persecuted for their beliefs and for their insistence on sharing those beliefs. By doing so, they are identifying with the suffering of Christ. There is nothing inherently good in suffering. The good, when it comes, derives from having endured the suffering for the sake of participating in the work of Christ.

The fact that we are so seldom aware of the suffering of Christ, let alone sharing that suffering, is largely due to the fact that we are not calling into question the inequities and sinfulness of our world and our culture. If we were to actively do so, we would learn very quickly just how unpopular a Christian can be.

Today, will you risk discomfort for the sake of the Gospel?

Meeting Jesus at Worship

Almighty God, whose blessed Son our Savior Jesus Christ ascended far above all heavens that he might fill all things: Mercifully give us faith to perceive that, according to his promise, he abides with his Church on earth, even to the end of the ages; through Jesus Christ our Lord, who lives and reigns with you and the Holy Spirit, one God, in glory everlasting. Amen. (Collect for Ascension Day)

When asked why they join a worship community, most folks will say something about the sense of family, the welcome they received, or the content of the worship itself. But every now and then someone says, "Because I feel the presence of Christ in this place."

That is how we all should feel. Everyone attending any service in a Christian Church ought to meet Jesus there; and if that doesn't happen, we have to wonder why. Is it because the individual was too distracted or in too much pain to notice? Or was the community too wrapped up in its own experience to be available to make Christ's presence known to others? Or perhaps the liturgy has become an end in itself and does not allow for the spontaneity of worship?

The wonderful thing about Jesus' ascension is (as the collect above states) that by leaving the specificity of 1st century Israel behind, Jesus is now everywhere at all times. He has filled all things. All we need do is avoid things which might obscure his presence. He is with us, always, even to the end of the ages. Such a gift is to be cherished and shared, and that truth should be abundantly clear to any who enter a church anywhere. In fact, that truth should be evident to anyone who encounters a Christian at any time or in any place. May it be true of us.

To Know God

Jesus looked up to heaven and said, "Father, the hour has come; glorify your Son so that the Son may glorify you, since you have given him authority over all people, to give eternal life to all whom you have given him. And this is eternal life, that they may know you, the only true God, and Jesus Christ whom you have sent. (John 17:1-11)

I love stories about time travel, but I have to admit that I generally end up with a headache when I try to understand how it might possibly work. I'm not alone, I know, because most of the authors who write about time travel end up having to use some sort of literary device like "and then a miracle happens" in order to avoid having to explain the unexplainable.

I suppose that is why I was so happy to learn in seminary that eternal life does not mean one moment after another after another without end. In fact, eternal life is not about temporal reality at all. Eternal life is about fullness of life and abundance of life. It is a metaphor used to attempt to describe what it is like to be completely taken up into God. To be totally united to the divine. To experience the infinite in an instant.

When our hearts and minds grasp who Jesus is and what it is to know him, we know all that there is to know of life. That experience produces an awareness of God that is not dependent on who we are or how we are faring at the moment. It is truly a moment of ecstasy – a moment out of time and out of our physical surroundings.

It is also the experience of heaven that we are promised. When we are in God, there is no need for anything else. To know God is to be in heaven.

WHERE IS JESUS?

O God, the King of glory, you have exalted your only Son Jesus Christ with great triumph to your kingdom in heaven: Do not leave us comfortless, but send us your Holy Spirit to strengthen us, and exalt us to that place where our Savior Christ has gone before; who lives and reigns with you and the Holy Spirit, one God, in glory everlasting. Amen. (Collect for Easter Seven)

As an undergraduate English major I really appreciated Samuel Taylor Coleridge's phrase "the willing suspension of disbelief". The only way to enjoy much of the poetry of the English Romantics was to grant some degree of credibility to what was often outrageously incredible. I got pretty good at doing that and in the process became a life-long fan of fantasy and science-fiction.

But I have to admit that I am not quite so tolerant when it comes to this collect. *"Do not leave us comfortless, but send the Holy Spirit to strengthen us and exalt us…"* I don't need to "forget" that Pentecost is coming or that the Holy Spirit, the Guide, the Advocate, the Paraclete is already with us. I rejoice that it is already true ad that it will happen yet again this year.

So it always seems odd to me that the opening Prayer of the Seventh Sunday of Easter suggests that unless we ask for the coming of the Spirit, God may rescind the comfort. I know that is not what the author of this collect intended, but it is what I think when I read it.

How different our lives and our faith might be if we could learn to receive the annual recapitulation of the liturgical year with gratitude and open arms. What we pray shapes what we believe. What if this prayer read, instead, "we thank you that you have never left us comfortless having given us the strengthening and renewing power of the Holy Spirit"? ….just asking.

PENTECOST

Tell Me about Pentecost

When the day of Pentecost had come, the disciples were all together in one place. And suddenly from heaven there came a sound like the rush of a violent wind, and it filled the entire house where they were sitting. Divided tongues, as of fire, appeared among them, and a tongue rested on each of them. All of them were filled with the Holy Spirit and began to speak in other languages, as the Spirit gave them ability...`In the last days it will be, God declares, that I will pour out my Spirit upon all flesh, and your sons and your daughters shall prophesy, and your young men shall see visions, and your old men shall dream dreams. Even upon my slaves, both men and women, in those days I will pour out my Spirit; and they shall prophesy. (Acts 2:1-4, 17-18)

Imagine how insurmountable the task of evangelism must have seemed to Jesus' disciples. They had already witnessed what had happened to him – and they knew that if anyone could communicate the Good News, he could. A miracle was needed if they were to be able to fulfill their mission of going into all nations preaching and baptizing in the name of God.

And a miracle was provided. With the descent of the Holy Spirit upon them they were empowered to proclaim the Gospel in ways that others would understand. Their tongues were loosened. But the miracle seems to have worked on the listeners as well. Each of them was enabled to hear and to understand the message that they received.

I really think that the greater miracle occurred in the ears of the listener's. I often have a dream that I am in possession of an extremely important letter but that I cannot read it. I see the paper, I recognize the letters of the words, I even know some of the words, but I simply cannot make sense of it.

For many people, hearing the Good News of God in Christ is a bit like that. The most gifted preacher on earth may be speaking to them. But until the Holy Spirit opens their ears to understand, they cannot comprehend what is being proclaimed.

But God provides all that is needed. The disciples were given the gifts of preaching, prophecy and exhortation, and the people were given the gifts of discerning and understanding the word. It takes hearers as well as speakers to proclaim the word.

Breath of God

O LORD, how manifold are your works!
in wisdom you have made them all; the earth is full of your creatures.
You send forth your Spirit, and they are created;
and so you renew the face of the earth. (Psalm 104:25, 31)

In the creation stories of the Book of Genesis, it is the Spirit/Breath/Ruah of God that moves over the face of the waters heralding the beginning of God's work in bringing life and order out of chaos. It is that same Spirit which creates and renews us amidst the chaos of our own lives.

When we are feeling isolated, confused or bereft, the Spirit of God hovers near us offering peace and solace. When we are stuck in the ruts of our lives, the Spirit challenges us to new ways of thinking and acting. When we are joyous and purposeful, the Spirit shields and protects us and allows our joy to be observed by others.

Because God's work of creation is not yet finished. In the wisdom of God, new things are coming to life and to light. God is not restricted. God is not contained. And because of that, creation is not stagnant. It is through the active, ongoing process of creation and renewal that the Holy Spirit calls us out of ourselves and onward into greater life. By hearing and responding to that call, we become witnesses to just how manifold God's works are.

Today, give thanks for the wisdom through which God creates, and take the time to see the flowering of the Spirit in your own life. Remember that you are created, you are renewed, and that you are living proof of the ongoing work of the Spirit.

Making Up the Body

To each is given the manifestation of the Spirit for the common good. To one is given through the Spirit the utterance of wisdom, and to another the utterance of knowledge according to the same Spirit, to another faith by the same Spirit, to another gifts of healing by the one Spirit, to another the working of miracles, to another prophecy, to another the discernment of spirits, to another various kinds of tongues, to another the interpretation of tongues. All these are activated by one and the same Spirit, who allots to each one individually just as the Spirit chooses. (I Corinthians 12:7-11)

We have all heard the phrase, "count your blessings" – most often when we are feeling as though life is just not treating us fairly. But this passage challenges us to take that a bit further, to make it a thoroughly positive statement and to actively celebrate our blessings and our gifts.

What a blessing it is to be in a community where the Holy Spirit has distributed gifts and talents among so many for the good of all. We have those gifted with wisdom, knowledge, faith, healing, works, prophecy, discernment, communication and interpretation in our midst. Together, we have everything that we need; and no one of us is either able or expected to do it all. That is cause for celebration!

We need only look around to see the abundance of grace in our communities, but how often do we take the time to appreciate and celebrate our own gifts? How often do we say, "thank you, God, for giving me the gift of ___? And even more importantly, how often do we allow others to know that we have that gift? Gifts of the Spirit are not private, nor are they to be hidden away. They have been distributed for the good of all and are meant to be exercised in that context. And we all have them. No one is left out – it is just a matter of identifying and exercising the gifts with which we have entrusted.

So, accept your giftedness and share it with the community for the benefit of the Body of Christ and for the world to which we are called to witness.

One Body – One Spirit

For just as the body is one and has many members, and all the members of the body, though many, are one body, so it is with Christ. For in the one Spirit we were all baptized into one body-- Jews or Greeks, slaves or free -- and we were all made to drink of one Spirit. (I Corinthians 12: 12-13)

Most of us have seen the definition of family change significantly in our lifetime. In my opinion those changes have been for the better. I can remember teaching an undergraduate class a few years ago and counseling a student whose parents had disowned her for marrying someone from another branch of the same denomination. In my own family we have in the last two decades gone from strict homogeneity to a rainbow family of race, creed and gender orientation. To be sure, our culture has become more accommodating of such diversity, but it is by no means a "modern" concept. The Body of Christ is intended to be multi-cultural, embracing people of all races, nations, and states of life. We are all members of the same body and that body is the family of God.

It wasn't an easy concept in the first century and it certainly isn't easy today. Most of us are willing to share worship with folks who differ from us, and some of us can even expand our circle of acceptance to allow us to share communion with the "other" -- though not from a common cup! Where the challenge becomes most obvious, however, is in areas of economics. Few congregations (let alone few individuals) would be willing to significantly reduce their own standard of living in order to improve that of another. The problem is endemic and has affected everything from voluntary giving for missions to the way in which clergy pension plans are administered. (Pensions are based on years of tenure of course, but the primary determiner is annual compensation.) Our choices may make perfect sense from the perspective of sound business practices, but are they in keeping with the spirit of this passage from Corinthians?

Today, let's all ask ourselves "Do I honestly believe that we are all part of one body in Christ? What difference does that make in my life?"

Receive the Holy Spirit

When it was evening on that day, the first day of the week, and the doors of the house where the disciples had met were locked for fear of the Jews, Jesus came and stood among them and said, "Peace be with you." After he said this, he showed them his hands and his side. Then the disciples rejoiced when they saw the Lord. Jesus said to them again, "Peace be with you. As the Father has sent me, so I send you." When he had said this, he breathed on them and said to them, "Receive the Holy Spirit. If you forgive the sins of any, they are forgiven them; if you retain the sins of any, they are retained." (John 20:19-23)

In the Body of Christ, every encounter, every conversation and every task is predicated on peace. Jesus greets us with a word of peace. We are to greet one another with the same attitude. We are meant to meet and to part in peace.

Now, peace does not mean the absence of conflict. Some degree of tension or conflict is inevitable, even in the Body of Christ. But being in peace does mean that we are aware of and doing our best to abide in the presence of Christ no matter what the circumstances. The disciples are hiding in terror for fear of the authorities, but the first words of Jesus to them are "Peace be with you."

And these are not empty words. Jesus immediately follows his admonition for peace with a mission. "Go, tell others. Bring the peace of God to them."

How were they to do that? Indeed how are we to do that? By the graceful presence of the Holy Spirit. That Spirit gives us grace to proclaim the good news and to offer others the peace and forgiveness that God alone can give. It is a peace which frees and liberates. That is why Jesus tells them that they have to power to offer peace, reconciliation, and forgiveness to others. If we do not offer peace, it may be that no one else will, and the individual is stuck carrying the burdens of the day with whatever dis-ease they may bring.

Often the gift of peace is given in spontaneous and completely unexpected ways. I was in a market recently after work when the clerk who was packing my groceries said, "You're a preacher, right?" We chatted briefly and as I left, she said "Peace be with you." She beamed when I replied, "And also with you." And the Holy Spirit was with us.

Promises Kept

Almighty God, on this day you opened the way of eternal life to every race and nation by the promised gift of your Holy Spirit: Shed abroad this gift throughout the world by the preaching of the Gospel, that it may reach to the ends of the earth; through Jesus Christ our Lord, who lives and reigns with you, in the unity of the Holy Spirit, one God, for ever and ever. Amen. (Collect for the Feast of Pentecost)

The history of God is the story of promises kept. Covenants are made and renewed. The steadfast presence of God abides with us, even when we ignore it. And the arrival of the Holy Spirit, promised by Jesus comes with empowering and renewing grace to those who will receive it. It is this grace which prepared the disciples to bear witness to the Truth and which gives them the language with which to do it. And it is this same Spirit which calls us to help fulfill God's promise that the message should reach to the ends of the earth.

It is very important to realize that the way of eternal life was not closed to other races and nations prior to the coming of the Holy Spirit at Pentecost! The way to God and to eternal life is and always has been open to any who wish to enter in. The reason that this collect is able to proclaim the opening of the road to eternal life is that on this day the disciples – all of us – are given the means and the ability with which to proclaim it. <u>It is our willingness to speak that truth that allows others to hear and receive it.</u> On this day we are reminded of our calling, and are reassured that we are worthy to fulfill it. God gives to us the language and the zeal to make it known.

Remember that you are a disciple. You are called to follow Jesus and to proclaim him. And near or far, there is a corner of the world and an end of the earth that is waiting to hear from you.

Creation and Sabbath

Thus the heavens and the earth were finished, and all their multitude. And on the seventh day God finished the work that he had done, and he rested on the seventh day from all the work that he had done. So God blessed the seventh day and hallowed it, because on it God rested from all the work that he had done in creation. These are the generations of the heavens and the earth when they were created. (Genesis 2:1-4a)

"Give it a rest!" Have you ever wondered why that phrase is only used in exasperation? There was a time when rest was a precious thing – a time when the frenetic pace of life and the ceaseless demands of work were at least partially balanced by a period of quiet. Even God rested at the end of a project! But, something has happened to us as a people which has reduced the concept of rest, of "Sabbath" to simply the reduction of irritation. We no longer seek refreshment – the cessation of aggravation or the reduction of stress seems to be all that we hope for.

We know such behavior is counter-productive. We are even aware that it is dangerous. And yet we feel trapped and compelled to stay on the perpetual motion treadmill.

But we are not trapped. It is within our power to wrest back the sanity-supporting benefits of Sabbath-time. All of us are completely capable of recognizing the difference between habit and necessity – between compulsiveness and emergency. And God knows that we need to discern that difference!

Today, take a look at your own life. Are you receiving the gift of Sabbath? Are you honoring the image of God within you by embracing a sense of balance between work and rest? If not, pray about it. And then do something about it. Take the time to be "off." It will not only lower your blood pressure, it will raise your spirit.

Good, Better, Best?

God saw everything that he had made, and indeed, it was very good. And there was evening and there was morning, the sixth day. (Genesis 1:31)

"That's very good" is what Genesis tells us that God said on the sixth day of creation.

Of course, we sometimes forget that just because it was the sixth day does not mean that God was referring solely to the creation of humankind with the phrase "very good." After all, land animals as well as people were created on the sixth day.

The creation of people is not the culminating act of creation – we are good, like everything else – but God's increasing satisfaction with all of creation **is** cumulative. In fact, the text very clearly says that God saw "everything" that he had made and that it was very good.

That ought to tell us something about the interconnectedness, and the interdependence of all creation. We are all part of the whole system, and in making us made us stewards of creation, God has given us the responsibility of remembering our place in the created order while doing our best to nurture and protect all that God has made. Everything in the system has a part to play, and a function to fulfill – even when we experience it as massively inconvenient.

Besides, no matter how much we might wish it otherwise, we are creatures – not the creator. I try to remember that each year when the gnats and the mosquitoes start to swarm. I have no idea what God had in mind in creating them, but I know that if we were to get rid of them altogether (as though that were possible!) we would be risking chaos in the ecosystem. And I suspect that there are other species who feel the same about us.

So, today, give thanks for creation and for your place in it. Look around at the natural world and remember that it is pleasing to God and that you are part of it.

There's Glory for You!

*Glory to you, Lord God of our fathers; **
you are worthy of praise; glory to you.
*Glory to you for the radiance of your holy Name; **
we will praise you and highly exalt you for ever. (Canticle 13)

I think that the Church has mislaid the word "Glory" somewhere along the path of the last two thousand years. We have retained all sorts of adjectives and theology for the power of God, but when it comes to the *glory* of God, we get a bit Humpty-Dumpty-ish:

"There's glory for you!' `I don't know what you mean by "glory",' Alice said. Humpty Dumpty smiled contemptuously. `Of course you don't -- till I tell you. I meant "there's a nice knock-down argument for you!"' `But "glory" doesn't mean "a nice knock-down argument",' Alice objected. `When I use a word,' Humpty Dumpty said, in rather a scornful tone, `it means just what I choose it to mean -- neither more nor less.'" (Lewis Carroll, <u>Through the Looking Glass</u>)

To use another popular culture reference, we seem to have turned God into something akin to the tutu-wearing, head-standing deity presented a few years back in the wickedly irreverent film "Dogma."

Both approaches are fatally flawed of course. Glory is intended to evoke awe, to leave us speechless with wonder, and nearly blinded with radiance in the presence of holiness. While it is true that there is much in creation which may suggest the glorious, the Glory of God is utterly unique. A far more apt metaphor comes to us from Wordsworth's <u>Intimations of Immortality</u> *"but trailing clouds of glory do we come from God who is our home."*

When was the last time you had a glimpse of the glory of God? Today, remember that we worship the God of all creation and that in God's abiding presence (Shekinah) we encounter Glory.

God Is A Community

Finally, brothers and sisters, farewell. Put things in order, listen to my appeal, agree with one another, live in peace; and the God of love and peace will be with you. Greet one another with a holy kiss. All the saints greet you. The grace of the Lord Jesus Christ, the love of God, and the communion of the Holy Spirit be with all of you. (2 Corinthians 13:11-13)

These verses appointed for use on Trinity Sunday teach us that it is the very nature of God to be in community and in relationship within the Holy Trinity; and that by extension, we are to seek a similar unity and harmony within the Church. The three persons of the Trinity are One. That is why St. Paul is able to speak of the grace of Christ, the love of God and the communion of the Holy Spirit and still be speaking of the One God.

Eternal internal harmony and inter-relatedness exist within the Godhead. The persons of the trinity are inseparable. As St. Athanasius would write in the Quicungue Vult "...we worship one God in Trinity and Trinity in Unity, neither confounding the persons nor dividing the substance." (BCP, p.864)

So how is that instructive to the Church? This is not to say that there will never be any disagreement in the Body of Christ. Instead it reminds us that disagreements are not to be allowed to result in estrangement. Our calling is the proclamation of the Good News that God is with us and that the presence of God brings reconciliation. To the extent that the Church lives in true peace (peace not being the absence of conflict, but an awareness of the presence of God in the midst of all situations), she will be empowered to proclaim the Gospel with strength and love.

We don't have to understand the intricacies of the Doctrine of the Trinity in order to understand what God requires of us. But we do need to seek the unity of purpose that can only come from the creative, redemptive and sustaining love of the God.

Go Make Disciples

"Go therefore and make disciples of all nations, baptizing them in the name of the Father and of the Son and of the Holy Spirit, and teaching them to obey everything that I have commanded you. And remember, I am with you always, to the end of the age." (Matthew 28:19-20)

"Go make disciples." Twice a day, every day for three years, I sat in chapel at seminary where those words were emblazoned across the front of the room. They are part of the "Great Commission" and are Matthew's summation of the Gospel.

We are to make disciples – people who follow Jesus and whose lives are shaped by his teaching. We are to baptize them into his body and to instruct them in what he has commanded...that we love God with all our hearts and our neighbors as ourselves. And we are to do it all with the abiding presence of God to guide and sustain us.

Matthew states it very clearly. What we do and what we produce in the name of Jesus matters and has eternal consequences. Matthew cares that we live up to that commission and that train others to do so as well. His harshest criticism is reserved for those who ignore the needs of others (25:31-46), or squander the gifts that they have been given (25:14-30).

Matthew is concerned that we forge integrity between our words and our actions and that our own lives be examples which have the power to draw others to Christ.

Gift of the Trinity

Almighty and everlasting God, you have given to us your servants grace, by the confession of a true faith, to acknowledge the glory of the eternal Trinity, and in the power of your divine Majesty to worship the Unity: Keep us steadfast in this faith and worship, and bring us at last to see you in your one and eternal glory, O Father; who with the Son and the Holy Spirit live and reign, one God, for ever and ever. Amen. (Collect of the Day, Trinity Sunday)

Granted, this prayer is challenging to read aloud. It is also challenging to explain. But it comes down to this.

Our faith, once embraced, gives us the ability, even now, to see and know God. That vision is limited by our finitude but the vision is there none the less. And what it reveals to us is Glory. More than we can grasp at this time, but all that we need for now. And through a life of worship and of seeking God, we come to know God more deeply and more confidently, until at last we see the fullness of God in eternity.

So, when you receive a glimpse of Glory, know that it is the gift of the Trinity. When you feel the presence of genuine love and peace, know that it is a sign of the presence of the Trinity. And when you are tired and weary understand that you are being carried by the love of the Trinity.

All in One and One in All.

ORDINARY TIME

Power of Trust

But Sarah saw the son of Hagar the Egyptian, whom she had borne to Abraham, playing with her son Isaac. So she said to Abraham, "Cast out this slave woman with her son; for the son of this slave woman shall not inherit along with my son Isaac." The matter was very distressing to Abraham on account of his son. But God said to Abraham, "Do not be distressed because of the boy and because of your slave woman; whatever Sarah says to you, do as she tells you, for it is through Isaac that offspring shall be named for you. As for the son of the slave woman, I will make a nation of him also, because he is your offspring." So Abraham rose early in the morning, and took bread and a skin of water, and gave it to Hagar, putting it on her shoulder, along with the child, and sent her away. (Genesis 21:9-14a)

This passage could serve as an object lesson for the pitfalls of plural marriage. True, Abraham is not married to Hagar, but he is the father of her child and he loves the boy. In fact, until the birth of Isaac, Hagar's son is Abraham's heir. Now he is faced with a jealous wife demanding that any threat to Isaac's future be cast aside. With what seems a strange lack of intestinal fortitude, this patriarch of patriarchs appears paralyzed and unwilling to challenge Sarah. He actually takes her ultimatum seriously enough to consider it; and it is only with God's assurances that Ismael will also be the father of a nation that Abraham is able to act at all. And so a beloved child and his enslaved mother are cast aside.

But we know that this is neither the first nor the last time that Abraham has trouble making decisions. And in sympathy, we must remember that God has already asked a great deal of him, and that the stakes grow higher with each passing year. "Leave your home in Ur, and go to Canaan." "I know that you don't have an heir, but be patient and I will give you a son." "Go ahead, send your eldest son and his mother away." And eventually, "Now that you have a son, kill and offer him as a sacrifice to me." Abraham has every right to be uncertain.

Before we rush to accuse either God of callousness or Abraham of a lack of faith, we need to ask ourselves – just how strong would we be in similar circumstances? In fact, just how strong and certain are we in the normal, everyday challenges that come to us? And we need to remember that above all, Abraham is a man of prayer. Each of the challenges he receives come to him through conversations with God. He prays, God instructs, then he decides whether or how to obey. Abraham is in a continually growing relationship with God and from that relationship he learns the power of trust, even when he does not know how things will turn out.

Enough to Go Around

When the water in the skin was gone, she cast the child under one of the bushes. Then she went and sat down opposite him a good way off, about the distance of a bowshot; for she said, "Do not let me look on the death of the child." And as she sat opposite him, she lifted up her voice and wept. And God heard the voice of the boy; and the angel of God called to Hagar from heaven, and said to her, "What troubles you, Hagar? Do not be afraid; for God has heard the voice of the boy where he is. Come, lift up the boy and hold him fast with your hand, for I will make a great nation of him." Then God opened her eyes and she saw a well of water. She went, and filled the skin with water, and gave the boy a drink. God was with the boy, and he grew up; he lived in the wilderness, and became an expert with the bow. He lived in the wilderness of Paran; and his mother got a wife for him from the land of Egypt. (Genesis 21:15-21)

Have you ever noticed the number of people for whom a mentality of scarcity is the default position? Children provide an excellent example of this phenomenon. They don't start out that way of course. Most children begin with a sense of unbounded optimism. They assume that whatever they want or need is available and is theirs for the taking. It is only when we adults and parents begin to instruct them in behaviors like sharing and delayed gratification that they begin to be fearful. And often, our best efforts at teaching them to share, to be generous, and to work for a reward simply reinforce their fears that at some level they are being cheated.

Hagar and Ishmael are wandering in the desert without water because Sarah, (who of all people ought to understand waiting for something) is afraid that her son will be shortchanged in his inheritance. Even Hagar is trapped in this worldview. So far as she knows, she and her child are both going to die. It is God alone who can break through her grief to compel her to stand up and see the water that is just in front of them.

In God's economy there is always enough to do what is needful and there is always enough to go around. It is only when we succumb to the fear of scarcity that we make scarcity a reality. What might happen in your life if you decided that you would no longer be directed by fear? What if you could open your heart and hands enough to share your abundance with others? What might happen if you were to open your eyes to see the gifts that are right before your eyes?

When Do You Pray?

Give ear, O LORD, to my prayer, and attend to the voice of my supplications.
In the time of my trouble I will call upon you, for you will answer me.
(Psalm 86:5-6)

It is said that there are no atheists in foxholes. True enough. When we are scared enough, or have truly reached the end of our own abilities, we will almost always turn to someone of something greater than we are. The only problem with that approach is that we waste a great deal of time trusting in something less than God while things are going well. That is not to say that God does not hear us when we are in need. Nor does God withhold love from us when we have been less than faithful. It just seems wrong and very short-sighted to wait until trouble begins to initiate a conversation with God.

Prayer is not a back-up plan. Prayer should be an everyday reality. The purpose and intention of prayer is to bring ourselves before God. Each day we are able to bring God our concerns, our thanksgivings, our petitions, our praise, and whatever else is going on in in our lives.

And God always hears us. God listens. It is important for us to listen as well, not just for God's answer but to the content of our prayers. What are we asking for? Do we mean what we are saying? Why have we waited until we have exhausted every other option before turning to God?

None of that changes the outcome of prayer from God's perspective, but it can certainly change our experience of praying. If we honestly and humbly come before God each day, and we do our best to trust in the abiding presence of God in our lives, then the specific answers to our prayers become less important than the prayer relationship itself. We won't wait until the time of trouble to turn to God, and we will learn to trust in God's love in all things, even when we don't get the answer we want

.

Dead to Sin

Should we continue in sin in order that grace may abound? By no means! How can we who died to sin go on living in it? Do you not know that all of us who have been baptized into Christ Jesus were baptized into his death? Therefore we have been buried with him by baptism into death, so that, just as Christ was raised from the dead by the glory of the Father, so we too might walk in newness of life. (Romans 6:1b-4)

The point of salvation is not escaping punishment. The point of salvation is a new life – a life in which we are no longer captive to sin. We still sin, of course, but when we do we are aware of it, and we are aware that we have chosen sin rather than the better option.

That is probably what St. Paul was trying to communicate in this rather sarcastic introduction to the 6th chapter of Romans. It is as though he is saying "If the grace of God abounds in response to the human need for forgiveness, then let's all sin as much as we can so that grace and forgiveness will flow down upon us! NOT."

Understanding the depth and breadth of the love of God in the Incarnation of Jesus Christ ought to make a difference in our lives. It ought to remind us that our lives, have been changed. Indeed the whole world has been changed. We have been baptized into the death of Christ, not an ordinary death in which life ceases, but a death which triumphs over death and which resurrects us to new beginnings, new life, and freedom.

Such a gift and such an awareness demands a new response. Cherish the grace and the forgiveness but do not hoard it. Offer it freely to all who are still in chains, and help them to see salvation themselves.

All Shall Be Revealed

Jesus said, "Are not two sparrows sold for a penny? Yet not one of them will fall to the ground apart from your Father. And even the hairs of your head are all counted. So do not be afraid; you are of more value than many sparrows. (Matthew 10:29-31.)

There seems to be something about the human psyche that often makes it difficult for us to believe that others really care. And if we do not believe that others care, it will be nearly impossible to trust them. And if we do not trust them, then how can we learn to trust God?

Trusting involves vulnerability. It also involves honesty. Most of all, it requires that we learn to move outside our deeply held conviction that we are unworthy. We even put it into our prayers, "Lord, I am not worthy."

What is God's answer? "I already know that. Now, get over it."

Jesus explains it this way... If God cares about the sparrows, and knows how many hairs are on your head, what makes you think that God doesn't cherish each one of those hairs? Besides, it is really not about worthiness, it's about love.

The good news is that we can't make ourselves worthy because God does not judge worth the same way we do. We are innately worthy because God made us. That's enough.

When confronted with the truth that God loves us, there can be only one response – "Act like it."

There Is No Doer but God

O Lord, make us have perpetual love and reverence for your holy Name, for you never fail to help and govern those whom you have set upon the sure foundation of your loving kindness; through Jesus Christ our Lord, who lives and reigns with you and the Holy Spirit, one God, for ever and ever. Amen. (Collect for Proper 7, BCP)

The wonderful thing about the prayers in the Episcopal Book of Common Prayer is the way that they give God the credit for everything. If we really believe that God is God, then we have to accept that God is ultimately responsible for everything. That's why our prayers contain so many petitions, of course, and why every collect has some form of praise or doxology, but my favorite portions of these prayers are the places where we subtly (or not so subtly) remind God of what God has always done, and what we sincerely hope that God will continue to do. But we have to admit that it sometimes sounds awkward, and seems to indicate that we're not really sure how reliable God is.

It's really not that we don't trust God to continue being God, loving and caring and creating and providing for creation. It is rather a manner of praying that acknowledges a deep and abiding truth. God is God, and we are not. But because we are not God, we find it challenging to believe that God really does have the time and the inclination to look out for all of us.

That is where radical trust comes in. God doesn't need our reminders. If God doesn't care about each of us, then God is not God. So, our job is very easy and very difficult -- we have to trust that God does care, and remember when we pray that we are reminding ourselves of what God does.

The Lord Will Provide

When they came to the place that God had shown him, Abraham built an altar there and laid the wood in order. He bound his son Isaac, and laid him on the altar, on top of the wood. Then Abraham reached out his hand and took the knife to kill his son. But the angel of the LORD called to him from heaven, and said, "Abraham, Abraham!" And he said, "Here I am." He said, "Do not lay your hand on the boy or do anything to him; for now I know that you fear God, since you have not withheld your son, your only son, from me." And Abraham looked up and saw a ram, caught in a thicket by its horns. Abraham went and took the ram and offered it up as a burnt offering instead of his son. So Abraham called that place "The LORD will provide"; as it is said to this day, "On the mount of the LORD it shall be provided."

There are many stories in the Hebrew Scriptures, which if taken literally, are extremely disturbing. The idea that God would require a parent to sacrifice a child is, and even then was, outrageous. God neither permits nor condones human sacrifice; the idea that God would require it is absurd. In fact, a major portion of the development of the covenant relationship of the Children of Israel with Yahweh God, is in response to the practice of child immolation in the religious practices of the ancient Middle East.

So, what is the writer of Genesis trying to tell us in this narrative? I believe the message is this: all meaningful human relationships are to emerge from and to be modeled upon a radical trust in God. God does not test our faith with horrific demands. God cements our relationships with God and others with the demonstrations od providence that God provides. Only by imagining something as extreme as the near sacrifice of Isaac is the narrator able to show us the absolute importance of trust in God.

The story is not to be taken literally. Nor is it to be viewed as a test of faith. It is a reminder that no matter how dire the situation, how hopeless the outcome may seem, or how trapped we may feel, God is present and God provides what is needed.

That makes this text far more powerful than if it were a literal account.

How Long, O Lord?

"How long, O LORD? Will you forget me for ever?
How long will you hide your face from me?" (Psalm 13:1)

There are few things in life more painful than feeling as though we have been forgotten or abandoned. The absence of caring, responsive people in our lives is spiritually debilitating; and we all know how such loneliness can contribute to a sense of despair.

How much worse it feels if we begin to think that God has turned away from us! We know, of course, that God does not turn away from us. We are continually in the presence of the One who makes, loves and keeps us; even when we are in too much pain or fear to remember it.

But, to be honest, as incarnate beings, we need other people to remind us of the presence of God. We need other people to embody that presence, to mediate the love of God in our lives, and to hold onto us when we are slipping away.

That's what Incarnation means, and it is what Incarnation requires of us as we work to be the Body of Christ in the world. We have to be the love, the hope, and the reminder that our fellow creatures need.

Today, be aware of those who may think that God has forgotten them. Pray for them, and then, act on their behalf. Give them tangible proof that God is with us and that you are a living reminder of that blessing.

Slaves to Righteousness

"Do not let sin exercise dominion in your mortal bodies, to make you obey their passions. No longer present your members to sin as instruments of wickedness, but present yourselves to God as those who have been brought from death to life, and present your members to God as instruments of righteousness. For sin will have no dominion over you, since you are not under law but under grace. What then? Should we sin because we are not under law but under grace? By no means! Do you not know that if you present yourselves to anyone as obedient slaves, you are slaves of the one whom you obey, either of sin, which leads to death, or of obedience, which leads to righteousness?" (Romans 6:12-16)

I often wish that St. Paul didn't put quite so much emphasis on the frailty of the flesh, but I have to admit that he really nails the point in the last verse of this quotation. The thoughts of our hearts may not always be visible, but it's really difficult to hide the truth when we give physical expression to our passions. So, to my short list of pithy sayings about how to tell where one's priorities really lie such as "The proof is in the pudding"..."follow the money"..."seeing is believing"... I have added, "Slaves to the one you obey." And to quote Jesus, we can say whatever we like about how we structure our lives, "but no one can serve two masters!"

Our bodies are a glorious expression of divine art, and they deserve to be treated with care and respect. But how often do we push ourselves beyond the limits of common sense? How often do we try to convince ourselves that to be truly righteous is to be more spiritual than physical? Why do we want to believe what we do with our material being and our material wealth is of secondary importance to what we do with our hearts and souls?

In truth, what we do with our bodies reveals what we really believe in our hearts. We are simultaneously enfleshed spirit and spirit-filled flesh. There is no way around it. The work we have to do is found in living in a harmonious whole – one in which, if we are enslaved to anything at all, we are enslaved to righteousness.

The Reward of Discipleship

Jesus said, "Whoever welcomes you welcomes me, and whoever welcomes me welcomes the one who sent me. Whoever welcomes a prophet in the name of a prophet will receive a prophet's reward; and whoever welcomes a righteous person in the name of a righteous person will receive the reward of the righteous; and whoever gives even a cup of cold water to one of these little ones in the name of a disciple-- truly I tell you, none of these will lose their reward." (Matthew 10:40-42)

In these two compact and fascinating verses, Jesus moves from the cosmic to the mundane. He reveals of the core of the truth of his teaching. And he leaves us no room to wriggle off the hook. How we treat one another has eternal consequences.

We are pretty sure that if what our faith teaches us about the nature of God and of Jesus is true, (that they are one) then we'd better be very careful about how we respond to the Holy. And we understand that prophets and righteous folk call forth from us a prophetic and righteous response. And we even recognize that Evangelists and Disciples may come to us in disguise. But do we really believe that responding to the most basic needs of others is a form of righteousness? Do we seek and serve Christ in all persons? Do we see Jesus in the faces and lives of those who lack even the comfort of a cup of cold water?

Most often, we do not. The clamor of the world and the sheer weight of unrelieved suffering in the lives of so many people has the power to beat our best intentions into submission. And yet, when we care for the least among us, we are doing the work of a disciple, in the name of a disciple, and are preserving our reward precisely because we do not know that we are doing so.

One human soul, one human hand reaching out to another is the work of discipleship, and the effects of that act of faithfulness travel all the way to the throne of God.

Christ the Cornerstone

Almighty God, you have built your Church upon the foundation of the apostles and prophets, Jesus Christ himself being the chief cornerstone: Grant us so to be joined together in unity of spirit by their teaching, that we may be made a holy temple acceptable to you; through Jesus Christ our Lord, who lives and reigns with you and the Holy Spirit, one God, for ever and ever. Amen. (Collect for Proper 8)

This is a very interesting metaphor for the architecture of faith. The Church – the Body of Christ – like our own bodies, is the temple of the Lord. The Church is the place where God visits us and where God dwells among us. Not the only place, of course, but the primary place in which we have learned to recognize the presence of God, Father, Son, and Holy Spirit.

Jesus, God Incarnate, is the chief cornerstone of the Church/Temple (the Body of Christ). And the structure of the Church/Temple is proclaimed and maintained by the teaching of the apostles and prophets.

An awful lot is dependent, then, upon just what we believe the teaching of the apostles and prophets to be. In other words, our temples will look like what we proclaim, and the degree of their acceptability to God will be determined by that proclamation as well.

Just what is that proclamation? And how do we know if we are faithfully preserving it? Does our proclamation produce unity of spirit? Does it emerge from the cornerstone Himself? Are we building upon a foundation that will survive the millennia?

There is a simple way to know. If what we proclaim is "Love God with all your heart and your neighbor as yourself" we are being true to the message of Jesus. And if we live that proclamation in our daily lives and in our common worship, our temple is acceptable. If we are not, then perhaps we need to re-build.

The Church's One Foundation

"Yet she on earth hath union with God, the Three in One,
and mystic sweet communion with those whose rest is won.
O happy ones and holy! Lord give us grace that we
like them the meek and lowly, on high may dwell with thee."
(Samuel John Stone, 1839-1900)

Despite all our foibles and all our failings, the Church is both the Body and the Bride of Christ. The Church is the beloved of Christ. The Church, past, present and future is eternally joined to our God and Savior. That is wonderful news! And it is true. It's true because God says so.

This hymn is a wonderful affirmation of our trust in the unbreakable bond between all those who base their faith upon the foundation of Jesus Christ. Ours is a marvelously diverse body, prone to all the challenges of human life, but led, guided and strengthened by the saving love of God in Christ. Even now, in this form in our earthly lives, we are in union with God. Even now, before we have all the answers or even the inclination to seek them, we are in communion with those who have gone before us. And even now, before we have truly learned to sing God's praises, we are showered with the grace that will teach us how.

No wonder this is one of the best-loved hymns of our faith. No matter what is going on in our lives, we are already in union with God and one another.

And will be forever. Amen.

Signs from God

"I came today to the spring, and said, `O LORD, the God of my master Abraham, if now you will only make successful the way I am going! I am standing here by the spring of water; let the young woman who comes out to draw, to whom I shall say, "Please give me a little water from your jar to drink," and who will say to me, "Drink, and I will draw for your camels also" -- let her be the woman whom the LORD has appointed for my master's son.' (Genesis 24:42-44)

I have always been of the opinion that asking a sign from God is a risky business. After all, once I have asked, how to do I know that what happens next is really a sign from God? What if I need another sign to ratify the accuracy of the first sign? And it doesn't end there. How do we know what to ask and how do we avoid exhausting God's patience with our uncertainty?

Abraham's faithful but unnamed chief servant does not share my fears. He is being sent to the land of his master's relatives to find a suitable wife for Isaac. The only instruction he has received is that she be willing to leave Haran to come to Isaac so that he will not be required to abandon his birthright by leaving Canaan. How will he make the right choice? With those instructions the servant could easily have chosen the first of Abraham's female relations who was willing to set up housekeeping in a new place. But he does not do that. Instead he asks a sign of God and makes it one that will demonstrate the character of the young woman. She needs to have a generous spirit and a sense of hospitality. She will go beyond the normal expectation that women draw and carry water. When asked for a drink, she will provide it. But she will not stop there. She will also offer to draw water for his camels. She will be a good helpmate to Isaac.

The servant's request for a sign is not an idle one. Like Abraham before him, the servant must trust that God will provide that which is needful. But he must also **ask** for what is needful. He has to know what is needed, have the courage to ask for it, and trust to accept the answer when it comes.

Perhaps it isn't that God does not give us signs. Maybe we don't know how to ask. The process requires wisdom, discernment and trust. Do we know what it is that we need? Do we know how to ask for it? And most importantly, are we willing to trust the answer when it comes?

Lord and Master

"Hear, O daughter; consider and listen closely;
forget your people and your father's house.
The king will have pleasure in your beauty;
he is your master; therefore do him honor. (Psalm 45: 11-12)

Very few women in this nation today would permit such a song at their weddings, because thank God, very few of us are still considered property to be transferred from one male relative to another. And fewer still are bartered into marriages intended to cement dynasties or consolidate businesses. So I have to ask myself why this particular coronation/marriage psalm appears in the Revised Common Lectionary at all. By the time I work my way through the apparently intended metaphors, my perception is way too clouded by offended sensibilities to pay much attention to deeper meanings.

But as an act of discipline, I wonder. Does the concept of master have any positive place in our culture today? Perhaps in the military, but certainly not in the secular world. We are a people of contracts, agreements, and relationships. We may speak productively of attaining mastery over a subject of study or a recalcitrant animal, but not over other people.

So, what about faith and theology? Have we lost any sense of God exercising mastery over us? Is there, in fact, much of anything to which we give that sort of authority these days? How about Jesus Christ, Lord and Master? OK, we'll do that liturgically – but only so long as it doesn't actually interfere with our own desires. Only so long as we can leave it behind when we leave the house of worship.

But faith is not a contract. Faith is at best a covenant, and in a covenant, one party accepts the terms of a more powerful party. The more powerful party sets the conditions and terms. That is certainly the case in our own Baptismal Covenant. We make the promises, we agree to bend our will to God's requirements and we promise to honor God by keeping the promises.

Maybe that is why the Church is called the "Bride of Christ."

Challenge of Choosing

I do not understand my own actions. For I do not do what I want, but I do the very thing I hate. So I find it to be a law that when I want to do what is good, evil lies close at hand. (Romans 7:15, 21)

There is a wonderful line in an old Marty Feldman film. Portraying a monk who is being tempted to break his vow of chastity, he prays in exasperation: "Lord, if you wanted us to avoid sins of the flesh, why did you make us out of meat???"

That question can be edited for any number of situations involving human choice. Most of us, by the time we reach adulthood, know the difference between what is right and wrong, necessary or merely expedient. We also know how tempting it is to make the easy decision, especially when we are relatively certain that we won't be found out.

St. Paul knows that too, and no doubt he committed his fair share of sins. But there is an edge to St. Paul that seems to prevent his rationalizing his behavior when he knows it is wrong. As in so many other instances, he seems to lack the internal filters that allow us to wear moral blinders when convenient. He is right there in the middle of the struggle.

Notice, too, that he does not blame anyone or anything else for his choice. He admits that evil is close at hand, but he also sees it for what it is, temptation rather than inevitability. St. Paul's admission of failure comes from a place of genuine integrity. Not because he ends up doing what is right, but because his choices, even when they are wrong, are part of an examined life.

He doesn't try to hide from reality any more than he tries to hide from himself.

Rest from Our Burdens

"Come to me, all you that are weary and are carrying heavy burdens, and I will give you rest. Take my yoke upon you, and learn from me; for I am gentle and humble in heart, and you will find rest for your souls. For my yoke is easy, and my burden is light." (Matthew 11:28-30)

We all know what it is like to have had a harsh, dictatorial or unfeeling teacher. On the other hand, I hope that most of us also know what it is to be taught by someone who is gentle and encouraging even while demanding our very best efforts. Which of the two types of teachers we end up with makes all the difference in the world.

Jesus does far more teaching than preaching or healing, and in the gospel accounts his teaching emerges from the deep wells of compassion and hope within him. In his humanity he knows the weight of the burdens that we carry and the tendency of the yoke to chafe. But in his divinity he knows the untapped potential within us and the spark of the divine that makes us human. He know that we were created with the ability not just to live but to thrive – if the load is properly distributed.

The gentle and humble teacher in Jesus uses the image of a well-fitted yoke. His yoke is easy because it is shared. We neither carry nor experience it as solitary individuals. We do so in community with him and with one another. We share the load, and thereby ease the burdens of all. Imagine a bucket-brigade in which instead of passing buckets hand to hand, each person ran for a bucket, filled it, carried it back to the fire, threw it at a burning building, then ran back and passed the empty bucket to the next member of a relay team. Pointless, right? It is also pointless to assume that we are doomed to carry all the burdens of life without help, support or rest, and that broken bones and bleeding backs just come with the territory.

If your yoke chafes, take it to Jesus and trade it in for one of his.

Price of Liberty

Lord God Almighty, in whose Name the founders of this country won liberty for themselves and for us, and lit the torch of freedom for nations then unborn: Grant that we and all the people of this land may have grace to maintain our liberties in righteousness and peace; through Jesus Christ our Lord, who lives and reigns with you and the Holy Spirit, one God, for ever and ever. Amen. (Collect for Independence Day)

Depending upon when and where you grew up, you may have been taught that the price of freedom is eternal vigilance. That's true. Few things slip away so easily as those we take for granted, and few things can be stolen from us with such catastrophic consequences. Vigilance is necessary.

But fear of loss can very easily become a self-fulfilling prophecy, and a posture of defensiveness can render us incapable of bending when bending is preferable to breaking. Perhaps that is why the authors of this collect choose to remind us that our liberties are best preserved from a place of righteousness and a commitment to peace. To be righteous is to be in "right relationship" with God and one another. That requires trust and interdependence, cooperation and compromise. And to live in peace does not mean achieving a society in which there is no conflict. It means a nation in which conflict is addressed and settled with as little violence or loss of dignity as possible.

As we give thanks on this day for the blessings and freedoms we enjoy, may God help us to remember that these benefits were purchased at great cost and that their peaceful preservation and just distribution is our greatest civic duty as we gratefully remember those who have made this day possible.

One Commandment

O God, you have taught us to keep all your commandments by loving you and our neighbor: Grant us the grace of your Holy Spirit, that we may be devoted to you with our whole heart, and united to one another with pure affection; through Jesus Christ our Lord, who lives and reigns with you and the Holy Spirit, one God, for ever and ever. Amen. (Collect for Proper 9)

A few years ago there was a very popular self-help book titled, Everything I Needed to Know in Life I Learned in Kindergarten. It was a book about common sense for life, sharing, taking responsibility for your own actions, and learning to be a good person. What this prayer points out is that Jesus "*wrote the same book*" over 2000 years ago.

Jesus' version wasn't terribly original either. It was handed down to him in two of the traditions of his Jewish faith and heritage. "Love God with all your heart and mind and strength and soul." And "Love your neighbor as yourself."

This combined form, the "great commandment" is not just the summary of the law, it is also the means by which the law is obeyed and fulfilled. There is no question of law or ethics which cannot be examined and illuminated through the lens of this commandment. Is it loving toward God and others? Does it demonstrate care for others? Does it honor and respect the rights of others? If it doesn't then with the grace of the Holy Spirit it needs to be re-worked so that it does.

It doesn't get much simpler than that. As wise Rabbi Hillel is reported to have said, "Everything else is commentary."

A Family Divided

Isaac prayed to the LORD for his wife, because she was barren; and the LORD granted his prayer, and his wife Rebekah conceived. The children struggled together within her; and she said, "If it is to be this way, why do I live?" So she went to inquire of the LORD. And the LORD said to her,
"Two nations are in your womb, and two peoples born of you shall be divided;
the one shall be stronger than the other, the elder shall serve the younger."
When her time to give birth was at hand, there were twins in her womb. The first came out red, all his body like a hairy mantle; so they named him Esau. Afterward his brother came out, with his hand gripping Esau's heel; so he was named Jacob. Isaac was sixty years old when she bore them. (Genesis 25:20-26)

Sibling rivalry is nothing new, although it generally does not begin in the womb. But in the case of Esau and Jacob, that rivalry is so intense as to cause Rebekah to wonder if death might not be better than pregnancy. Her two sons, representative of two ways of life, and of two nations, seem destined to be in conflict with one another from the moment of conception. Their lives enact this conflict, and their ancestors today have done little to end the discord.

But such conflict is not limited to nations, religions or groups of people. It has been said that the absence of conflict is not peace, but death. Conflict is the nature of life, and each of us knows what it is to seek wholeness, even within ourselves, while experiencing the ambivalence that comes from something as basic as the competing desires of our own hearts. Human life is complicated and peace of mind and balance are not easily attained.

How then, do we pursue peace in our own lives? Perhaps we should start by not obsessing about it. The more energy we put into fixing things just the way we want them to be, the less likely we are to be open to the learning which can only come to us through living with and working through the problem.

Rebekah did not have much choice about the wrestling match going on in her womb, and we don't have much choice about the competing desires of our own hearts. But peace comes through understanding the conflict and being willing to live in the tension until we can sort it all out.

The Lost Birthright

When the boys grew up, Esau was a skillful hunter, a man of the field, while Jacob was a quiet man, living in tents. Isaac loved Esau, because he was fond of game; but Rebekah loved Jacob. Once when Jacob was cooking a stew, Esau came in from the field, and he was famished. Esau said to Jacob, "Let me eat some of that red stuff, for I am famished!" (Therefore he was called Edom.) Jacob said, "First sell me your birthright." Esau said, "I am about to die; of what use is a birthright to me?" Jacob said, "Swear to me first." So he swore to him, and sold his birthright to Jacob. Then Jacob gave Esau bread and lentil stew, and he ate and drank, and rose and went his way. Thus Esau despised his birthright. (Genesis 25:27-34)

Isn't it amazing how easily we can convince ourselves that what we want is what is best for us? Esau is not really starving, he's just really, really hungry. And if he had only walked a few steps further into camp he would no doubt have found another cooking fire and someone who would give him something to eat. Esau has no concept of delayed gratification – he wants to eat, and he wants to eat now! Even worse, his lack of common sense gives his conniving younger brother the perfect opportunity to swindle him out of his birthright. It's a grand drama, and it demonstrates the dangers of not thinking things through.

But such things are not limited to Bible Stories or to family quarrels. How often do we lose sight of the big picture and things that really matter for the sake of a momentary reward? We resonate with this story because we know how easy it is to sell ourselves short and to end up losing our own spiritual birthright. Yes it is difficult to keep the promises we make. Yes, it is challenging to be faithful in our prayers, our work and our relationships. And yes it is far too easy to convince ourselves that those things don't really matter all that much.

And so we risk losing them. Not because we have a devious younger sibling waiting in the wings. Not because the tempter stalks our every move. We risk them because we cannot distinguish between genuine hunger and the involuntary response of our bodies to scent of something tasty. Mainly, we jeopardize our birthrights because we really don't believe they are worth preserving.

Today is a good day to take stock of your priorities, and to examine your wants and your needs. Which is them is worth waiting and working for? Which of them will leave you satisfied for only a little while before you once again feel famished?

Lighting the Path

*Your word is a lantern to my feet **
and a light upon my path.
*I have sworn and am determined **
to keep your righteous judgments. (Psalm 119:105-6)

Will and I share a home with a much-beloved small black Schnoodle. His name is Rudy, but half the time I call him "underdog" because he is swift and quiet and remarkably adept at being underfoot, especially at night. In our house, it is neither safe nor wise to walk through a darkened room unless you know exactly where Rudy is. So we understand what it is to need a lantern to our feet and a light upon our path.

Of course the Psalmist is talking about learning how to navigate through a different sort of darkness, the type we encounter when we don't know what to do. But unlike some of us, who wish we could just open the Bible at random and have the answer pop up on whatever page we turn to (come on, admit it!) the writer of this Psalm is trying to be a serious student of the word of God. After all, this is the 105th verse of one Psalm. And he is right. The only way to have the Scriptures truly light our paths is to know them well enough to get the big picture. That can't be accomplished through a casual relationship.

It is only when we immerse ourselves in the word of God, studying it regularly (if not daily) and allowing it to percolate through our conscious minds and down into our hearts that we are able to most benefit from its light. Such study requires time and commitment, but it is its own reward. It is the work of a loving relationship to take Scripture seriously, and doing so is a genuine blessing.

And it really does lighten the darkness.

Setting the Mind

For those who live according to the flesh set their minds on the things of the flesh, but those who live according to the Spirit set their minds on the things of the Spirit. To set the mind on the flesh is death, but to set the mind on the Spirit is life and peace. For this reason the mind that is set on the flesh is hostile to God; it does not submit to God's law-- indeed it cannot, and those who are in the flesh cannot please God. (Romans 8:5-8)

Centuries ago when a woman was determined to find a husband, she was said to have "set her cap" for him. I'm guessing that meant that she was adjusting her hat and her ribbons to show off her best features, and maybe even tilting the brim to provide a bit of shelter for a stolen kiss or two. In any case, the phrase made it clear that she was committed to the task. We also talk about someone having their heart set on achieving something.

What St. Paul is talking about is similar, but not the same. What he suggests is that our attention cannot be divided, and that if it is directed toward anything other than God, it is pointing in the wrong direction.

I'm not convinced that things are quite that clear. Granted there are some folks who might be called materialist, and others who could be described as spiritual, but that creates a false dichotomy.

The flesh is not evil. It is the vehicle through which we conduct our physical lives. And the spirit requires the presence of the flesh in order to be human. But to be completely absorbed in either the spirit or the flesh is to be less than human.

Maybe a balanced life is the answer.

Hearers of the Word

"Hear then the parable of the sower. When anyone hears the word of the kingdom and does not understand it, the evil one comes and snatches away what is sown in the heart; this is what was sown on the path. As for what was sown on rocky ground, this is the one who hears the word and immediately receives it with joy; yet such a person has no root, but endures only for a while, and when trouble or persecution arises on account of the word, that person immediately falls away. As for what was sown among thorns, this is the one who hears the word, but the cares of the world and the lure of wealth choke the word, and it yields nothing. But as for what was sown on good soil, this is the one who hears the word and understands it, who indeed bears fruit and yields, in one case a hundredfold, in another sixty, and in another thirty." (Matthew 13:18-23)

Ever notice how the same child who will stomp around in the mud for hours on one day, will on another day start to fuss when they get the least bit messy? We're all like that. Sometimes we are bold, sometimes we are timid; sometimes we hear and receive the word of God, sometimes we hear and receive but do not remember. That's doesn't mean that God loves us any less, it just means that we are human.

Because the point of this parable is not that some people get it and some don't. The point is that until things are firmly established in our hearts and incorporated into our lives, we remain susceptible to drifting or wandering away. In the end, the best way of knowing and judging something is by the fruit that it yields. A sound, healthy faith will produce a stronger, healthier witness – and just as it takes time for a grape vine to mature to the point of producing a reliably consistent fruit, our faith must mature as well. If we invest the time, prayer, energy and study that is needed, we will grow in the practice of faith and in the strength of our commitment to the Word of God.

God has made us all with the potential to be good soil. Developing and maintaining that potential is one of the works of faith.

Think and Do

O Lord, mercifully receive the prayers of your people who call upon you, and grant that they may know and understand what things they ought to do, and also may have grace and power faithfully to accomplish them; through Jesus Christ our Lord, who lives and reigns with you and the Holy Spirit, one God, now and forever. Amen. (Collect for Proper 10)

Those of us who were in grade-school in the 1950's and 60's will remember learning to read with "Dick and Jane" primers. Even then they were "pre-nostalgic" and not at all representative of American culture or family life. But Dick and Jane and Baby were cute, had a lively puppy (Spot) and unlike the rest of us were not taking part in the duck-and-cover school drills of the cold war. A series of workbooks accompanied them and the one I most remember some 60 years later is "Dick and Jane Think and Do." In fact, I think of it every summer when this pray comes around in the lectionary.

When it comes to a life of faith, we have to think and do. Just as God has created us as both physical and spiritual, God has also given us the responsibility to understand what we proclaim and to embody what we proclaim. We can't just think about God, we have to act on what we know and believe. And we can't just act out a faith that is unexamined. We are neither gurus nor robots. We are living entities engaged in the process of knowing God and one another as fully as possible even as we work to act upon what we have discerned.

It's a good system. And just as we did not learn to read and write without the help of teachers, textbooks and parents, we do not become the people God desires us to be without the grace and power that God provides, and the community that sustains us along the way.

By Any Other Name

"Surely the LORD is in this place-- and I did not know it!" And he was afraid, and said, "How awesome is this place! This is none other than the house of God, and this is the gate of heaven." So Jacob rose early in the morning, and he took the stone that he had put under his head and set it up for a pillar and poured oil on the top of it. He called that place Bethel. Genesis (28:16b-19a)

There really is something in a name – so long as the name is truly descriptive and is in a language that we understand. Bethel means "house of God". Imagine what it was like for everyone who passed that place to know that Jacob had met God there, consecrated the spot, and marked it with a name that served as a continual reminder. That sort of naming is bound to make a difference in the behavior and expectation of visitors.

But what if we don't know what a name means?

The challenge we face today is that so many of the meanings of names are simply unknown to us. The folks who named them (and often those who named us) were intentional about naming. Most of us know that the Quakers who named Philadelphia were hoping for a city of brotherly love, but would we know it if we did not live here? And does "Malvern" summon up images of a bare mountain? If we spoke Welsh it would.

The names we give to things and places will very often determine how we treat them. Perhaps the church would do a better job of teaching and evangelism if there were a clearer, stronger connection between what we call ourselves and what we do. Maybe the same thing would be true in our own lives. Being a Christian means being a follower of Christ. Does it show?

Where Can I Go?

Where can I go then from your Spirit? Where can I flee from your presence?
If I climb up to heaven, you are there;
if I make the grave my bed, you are there also.
If I take the wings of the morning and dwell in the uttermost parts of the sea,
Even there your hand will lead me, and your right hand hold me fast. (Ps 138:6-9)

As young children we need the almost constant reassurance that our parents or caregivers are right at hand. As adolescents we do our best to escape their notice and their authority. As young adults we convince ourselves that we are free to come and go as we please. Until finally in our later years, we realize that not only is God continually present, but that we really don't want it to be any other way.

Not everyone feels that way, of course. One who does not believe in God might never think about it all. But for those who do profess a faith in God, it is incredibly important to remember that we cannot escape the presence of God. It has even been said that hell is being in the presence of God and not liking it.

The Psalmist certainly knows this, and Jacob learned it when he fell asleep at Bethel and spent the night wrestling with the Angel of God who refused to let him go.

That is not to say that God stalks us. God simply refuses to abandon us. God does not give up on trying to reach us. God loves us and calls us even when we are doing our best to hide and ignore.

We might as well stop running and start listening.

The Coming Glory

"I consider that the sufferings of this present time are not worth comparing with the glory about to be revealed to us." Romans 8:12-23

This is one of those verses that is obviously intended to provide comfort. But I am not at all sure that it succeeds for most of us. Most of us are mentally parked in whatever place allows us to do the most worrying possible. Think of how much time we spend obsessing about the past, dwelling on our present troubles, and worrying about the suffering we may someday experience. Besides, who really believes that things are going to be better? Apparently St. Paul believed that and expects that we will believe it too if we can manage to take it seriously.

This is not a denial of reality. Of course, suffering is real. And this is not invitation to pretend otherwise. It is a reminder that suffering is not all there is. But when we are in the midst of suffering, it is very difficult either to remember a time when we were not suffering, or to look forward to when the present difficulties will be only a memory. Pain has a way of settling in and redecorating our lives.

Nor is this one of those really off-putting or patronizing "c'mon now, is it really all that bad?" moments. Both the suffering and the glory are absolutely true. The glory to be experienced is all the more glorious because we have come through the suffering and have the memory (and the scars) as a benchmark against which to compare the joy.

That is not to say that suffering is the price to be paid for glory. It is simply St. Paul's attempt to help us put it all in perspective – and to remind us that in God's economy, the least glimmer of glory in the presence of God eclipses the total of all the worst that can ever happen.

Wait For It

For in hope we were saved. Now hope that is seen is not hope. For who hopes for what is seen? But if we hope for what we do not see, we wait for it with patience. Romans 8:24-25

I have often wondered, what exactly is it that we are hoping for when we try to follow Jesus? Is it rescue from suffering, doubt, or uncertainty? Is it comfort and blessing in this life or the promise that everything will be better in heaven if we are faithful believers here on earth? Or is it just enough grace to get through the next twenty-four hours? I think that all of those are true for all of us at one time or another.

But what we are all really looking for is hope. Because when we have hope, we are able to see beyond the confines of our own momentary experience. We are blessed with just enough light to remind us of the promise of dawn. That light is not the dawn, but it serves as a promise that dawn will come, and calls us to patiently abide until then.

And that is where things get really tough.

We all know how extremely difficult it can be to be patient. We know what we want. We know what we need. And we do not wish to wait for it. When we say, "Just tell me what I have to do to bring this about and I will do it" we do not wish to hear, "Just be patient. Everything will work out."

Hope requires reinforcement. Hope requires renewal. And hope requires Incarnation. None of us are able, by force of individual will alone, to remain indefinitely in a posture of waiting. We need others to walk alongside us as living examples that we do not travel alone, and that each of us carries within ourselves the light of God's love.

Yes we are called to patience and hope. But thanks be to God, we are also surrounded by others who are on the same journey home.

Letting the Weeds Grow

Jesus put before the crowd another parable: "The kingdom of heaven may be compared to someone who sowed good seed in his field; but while everybody was asleep, an enemy came and sowed weeds among the wheat, and then went away. So when the plants came up and bore grain, then the weeds appeared as well. And the slaves of the householder came and said to him, `Master, did you not sow good seed in your field? Where, then, did these weeds come from?' He answered, `An enemy has done this.' The slaves said to him, `Then do you want us to go and gather them?' But he replied, `No; for in gathering the weeds you would uproot the wheat along with them. Let both of them grow together until the harvest; and at harvest time I will tell the reapers, Collect the weeds first and bind them in bundles to be burned, but gather the wheat into my barn.'" Matthew 13: 36-43

Any gardener knows that weeding is a full-time job. It is also true that by the time you finish weeding one row, there will be new weeds in the spot where you began. Weeds are like that. So it seems rather odd that the householder would tell the servants to let the weeds grow until the harvest. In fact, the weeds are likely to choke the wheat long before harvest time arrives.

Clearly, Jesus is talking about something other than gardening here.

Jesus is talking about the patience of God. In God's thinking, all the plants start out with the same potential. They even look alike. Every day that the "weeds" and the "wheat" are left together is another day in which the weeds just might start to grow into something else. There is no need to rush to judgment while the growing season is still upon us. Who knows what may yet happen? Yes, the time for harvest, for judgment, will surely come. And at that point it will be very easy to tell the wheat from the weeds.

This passage is a not-too-subtle reminder to us that God the master gardener watches and waits to see how we will turn out.

A Thumb on the Scale

Almighty God, the fountain of all wisdom, you know our necessities before we ask and our ignorance in asking: Have compassion on our weakness, and mercifully give us those things which for our unworthiness we dare not, and for our blindness we cannot ask; through the worthiness of your Son Jesus Christ our Lord, who lives and reigns with you and the Holy Spirit, one God, now and for ever. Amen. (Collect for Proper 11)

If we were to judge humanity by this collect, we would have to admit that we are a dismal lot indeed! Ignorant, unworthy, weak and spiritually blind. And on the whole, there is not much that we can say to dispute that description. We're a mess. But while it is good to be truthful about our failings as a species, despair will not benefit us either.

But that is only half the prayer. The other half shows us that God intends to do for us all that is necessary, whether we deserve it or not. God appreciates honesty but does not require groveling, especially if that groveling is the end of the conversation. We need to retain enough hope to get up, dust ourselves off and keep trying.

That is why the mercy of God is such a boundless blessing. God does not look the other way and pretend that there are not any problems. God acts on our behalf and intends that we learn and grow from the experience. We can clearly see how large the debt is, but that is not the point. We don't leave prayer and worship with an ever growing stack of past-due notices. In fact, when we admit our need for help, it is as though God quietly lays a thumb on the scales to balance out our deficits.

As You Sow...

Laban said to Jacob, "Because you are my kinsman, should you therefore serve me for nothing? Tell me, what shall your wages be?" Now Laban had two daughters; the name of the elder was Leah, and the name of the younger was Rachel. Leah's eyes were lovely, and Rachel was graceful and beautiful. Jacob loved Rachel; so he said, "I will serve you seven years for your younger daughter Rachel." Laban said, "It is better that I give her to you than that I should give her to any other man; stay with me." So Jacob served seven years for Rachel, and they seemed to him but a few days because of the love he had for her. (Genesis 29:15-28)

Jacob is about to discover just how easily we can be duped when we really want something and do not take the time to count the cost. Just as he tricked his ravenously hungry brother out of his birthright, Jacob will find himself with a wife he wasn't looking for and a 14 year stint of indentured servitude before he marries Rachel. And when he finally leaves Laban, the trickery continues.

Many things in life are worth working for, and more than a few are worth a major investment of time and energy. But I wonder, how many of the things that consume our time, energy and spirits are actually in that latter category. And how many of them have we thought through before we begin the process of acquiring them?

Commitment is a spiritual choice. Those things to which we commit ourselves may not be spiritual in nature, but the investment of our selves is a spiritual matter deserving of prayer and deliberation.

If you find yourself feeling exhausted and more than a little frayed at the edges, ask yourself "where am I expending my spiritual energy?" and "am I doing so because of a conscious choice?" Many of the things in life which demand our attention are necessary, but if they weigh on our spirits, a good long look at our priorities may be in order. It is possible to do the things that we must do without giving them unnecessary power in our lives. And it is possible to tell the difference.

...So Shall You Reap

Then Jacob said to Laban, "Give me my wife that I may go in to her, for my time is completed." So Laban gathered together all the people of the place, and made a feast. But in the evening he took his daughter Leah and brought her to Jacob; and he went in to her. (Laban gave his maid Zilpah to his daughter Leah to be her maid.) When morning came, it was Leah! Genesis (Genesis 29:21-25)

Poor Jacob. "When morning came, it was Leah!" That verse is one of the three funniest lines in Scripture. (The other two, in my opinion, are Exodus 32:24 and Jonah 4:9.) I suppose it is possible that Jacob was so smitten by the prospect of having Rachel that he did not notice Laban's switch until the next morning, but really? One can just hear the laughter and giggles circulating around the tents in Laban's settlement. The trickster Jacob has met his match – at least for the moment. But maybe not – after all, he is going to need more than one wife, isn't he?

What is more interesting in this passage is the manner in which Jacob, even when he is not exercising good judgment, continues to prosper. Jacob knows an opportunity when he sees one. Over the years of his servitude to Laban, he will acquire wives, concubines, and livestock. He will have to work hard, but there is a shrewdness about Jacob which reveals that he is a master at making lemonade from Laban's gifts of lemons.

No one today would use Jacob as a model for the best husband, father or relative. But the passage gives us an object lesson concerning the often inscrutable nature of how God works in our lives. For all his warts (and they are numerous!) Jacob will wrestle with God and hold his own in the contest. Like so many others, he is a major character in our story because he refuses to give up. He prospers, but he also suffers like the rest of us. Jacob becomes a Patriarch, not because he is particularly good or pious but because he stays in the conversation and the relationship with God.

Are you still talking to God?

Who Would You Tell?

Give thanks to the LORD and call upon his Name; *
make known his deeds among the peoples. Psalm 105:1

Isn't it odd how we decide what information we will share with others? And more importantly what we won't share? We are fine with announcing that we finished the PhD. or that we are setting a new business. We love sharing the news that we are getting married or expecting a child or grandchild. But what about announcing the amount of an annual bonus or winning the lottery? Not so much. And the oddest thing of all is how reluctant we are to talk to others about our relationship with God.

"Make known his deeds among the people." Now, that's a real challenge. This is not something like "Thank God that's over." Or "Thank Goodness I found my keys before I was late to work." This is actually telling others how the active presence of God in your life has made a difference. This is exhorting others to remember all the times of blessing in their own lives. This is knowing and sharing the salvation story and sharing it with others who may not yet know it. This is evangelism.

All of us are called to be evangelists. There is no getting around that. If the Good News of God in Christ is really good news then we have no option about whether or not we will share it. That is not to say that everyone must become a preacher, but it is to say that everyone must bear witness. Using the gifts that God has given us, everyone must be willing and able to give an account of the faith that is within us.

Start simply, but start today. Tell someone something about how God has acted in your life. You don't have to write a book or make a speech, just tell them. You will be amazed at how often the opportunity presents itself in the simplest of everyday encounters. And if you can honestly say that you have no opportunity, perhaps God is telling you that you need another set of friends, neighbors or co-workers.

The Big Picture

We know that all things work together for good for those who love God, who are called according to his purpose. For those whom he foreknew he also predestined to be conformed to the image of his Son, in order that he might be the firstborn within a large family. And those whom he predestined he also called; and those whom he called he also justified; and those whom he justified he also glorified. Romans 8:28-30

This is one of those instances where it is really important to finish the sentence. How many times have you heard someone say "all things work together for good for those who love God" and then stop. Period. There are few things more troubling or misleading that making such blanket statements about God.

Of course God intends good for us. Of course God is working in and through us. But God is no more orchestrating every detail of our daily lives than sending us some magic formula that will turn all the painful and unpleasant things we experience in life into the DNA of eternity.

What St. Paul is getting at (when we let him finish his sentence) is that we are chosen by God to be part of the family of God and the Body of Christ and that nothing can take that away from us. God's purpose is to call us all home. No one is left out of that invitation. We can ignore that if we wish, but if we fail to respond it will be because we chose to do so. In the end, God desires that all be reconciled, healed and glorified.

"All things working together for good" does not guarantee a pain-free life for the faithful. But it does guarantee that all the good that God intends will be made manifest.

The New and the Old

"Therefore every scribe who has been trained for the kingdom of heaven is like the master of a household who brings out of his treasure what is new and what is old." (Matthew 13:52)

This comment occurs at the end of a string of metaphors which Jesus has used to describe the Kingdom of Heaven to his disciples...a mustard seed, a measure of yeast, buried treasure and a great catch of fish. In each case, a seemingly small investment yields a very great return. But the metaphors mean more than that. Jesus employs so many of them to remind his disciples that they must have the ability to speak to people using language that the people can understand.

The scribe trained for the kingdom of heaven knows how to tell the story and how to illustrate it appropriately. That scribe will also have a sense of balance and an intuitive approach. In a day and age in which so much of the world sees and is seen in black and white, this is good advice indeed. It is not that we need more shades of gray, but that we need color!

No one is likely to be won to Christ by a brilliant exposition of the doctrine of the Trinity. That is why St. Patrick is reputed to have used a shamrock to explain things to the Irish. It wasn't that they were incapable of understanding the theology, it was that there was no point of connection. But when Patrick brought out a new use for an old image (the Irish knew all about three natures in one substance) he was well on his way to converting a nation and a culture.

We all need to follow this example, and be prepared to use whatever image presents itself to us when we are sharing our faith with others. The simplest of metaphors is capable of communicating the greatest of truths.

Eyes on the Prize

O God, the protector of all who trust in you, without whom nothing is strong, nothing is holy: Increase and multiply upon us your mercy; that, with you as our ruler and guide, we may so pass through things temporal, that we lose not the things eternal; through Jesus Christ our Lord, who lives and reigns with you and the Holy Spirit, one God, for ever and ever. Amen. (Collect for Proper 12)

I have a retired clergy friend who used to say that as far as he was concerned the surest place to lose your soul was in church, and especially at the altar. He was not being facetious, but he was being ironic. As this collect reminds us, there are myriad things in life that have the power to distract us from those things that really matter; and if we are not vigilant, we may mistake the small and the mundane for the great and the eternal.

This is true, even within a worship community. For example: Which causes more anxiety in a church – meeting the budget or sharing the Good News?

But missing the point, and ultimately perhaps even the prize, is an even greater temptation in our daily lives. Does prayer show up on our daily agendas? Can we remember the last time we were able to make a clear and comfortable distinction between what we wanted to do and what we felt compelled to do? Will our obituaries be filled with achievements or with accounts of the lives we touched?

God has secured our salvation. God has made it so. We will not lose that. But what we are in danger of losing is our joy. We need not wait until eternity to experience abundance of life. After all, the meaning of our lives is this: we are members of the family of God. In the end, everything else will pass away.

Tenacity

Jacob was left alone; and a man wrestled with him until daybreak. When the man saw that he did not prevail against Jacob, he struck him on the hip socket; and Jacob's hip was put out of joint as he wrestled with him. Then he said, "Let me go, for the day is breaking." But Jacob said, "I will not let you go, unless you bless me." So he said to him, "What is your name?" And he said, "Jacob." Then the man said, "You shall no longer be called Jacob, but Israel, for you have striven with God and with humans, and have prevailed." Genesis 32:24-28)

The things with which we wrestle are often the things which define us. In Jacob's case, the wrestling match began before his birth as he and Esau struggled in Rebekah's womb. His life story is one of conflict – with his brother, wife, in-laws and with God. But Jacob was not rewarded for his contentiousness. Instead it was his tenacity and his endurance which won for him and his people the name Israel.

That distinction is an essential one. Conflict may be inevitable in life, but it is foolhardy to seek it out. Tenacity, however, is a virtue when it allows us to remain engaged in seeking the good that we desire. Even when it means that we are marked by the struggle. Jacob's hip was put out of joint, but he refused to abandon his search for the blessing.

Jacob the trickster finally learned how to fight for what he wanted.

He could not win the blessing by cheating Esau out of his birthright. He was unable to prevail over Laban in the first round of a battle of wits over a wife. And although he ultimately tricked Laban out of most of his livestock, it took Jacob years to do so. But none of those things were what he really wanted. The blessing Jacob really desired was not bestowed until Jacob had proven his determination.

God alone can provide the blessing we seek. And sometimes we have to work for it.

The Highest Court

Hear my plea of innocence, O LORD; give heed to my cry;
listen to my prayer, which does not come from lying lips.
Let my vindication come forth from your presence;
let your eyes be fixed on justice. (Psalm 17:1-2)

Just as Jacob is determined to wrestle with God until he wins the blessing, the Psalmist is set on achieving justice. He is willing to put everything – life, reputation, and future – on the line in his attempt to receive vindication. And he trusts that it will work. What inspires such confidence?

He has searched his heart and knows that he is right; and he believes that God knows the truth and will reward his integrity. He trusts that God is the Highest Court. In fact, his trust is so complete that he almost seems to be daring God to prove him wrong.

Do we have such confidence? Such trust? Few of us would dare to call ourselves righteous these days. We are far too wedded to the misconception that righteousness equals purity; and we are all very much aware of our failures. But righteousness is not defined by purity, it is defined by the state of our hearts and our intentions to be in a right relationship with God.

If purity were the standard of righteousness, the Psalmist would not have dared to ask for the justice he demands. He is aware of the brokenness in his life, but that does not deter him from believing in the power of the truth that is God. This is not self-justification. No matter what else may have happened in his life, he knows that in this case he is right. So, as any good attorney might, he insists that the only admissible evidence is the evidence immediately before the court – his own truthfulness in this instance.

Who knows what our world might be like if we were to be able to focus on the truth of the moment? Perhaps it would free us all from the burden of self-justification, and empower us to learn to live without it.

It Is Enough to See You

But at my vindication I shall see your face;
when I awake, I shall be satisfied, beholding your likeness. Psalm 17: 16

The same writer who early in this Psalm has insisted on the truthfulness of his plea, ends his prayer with this statement: *When I receive justice I will see the face of God. When I see God my plea for justice will be satisfied.* What a glorious assertion of faith. God and Truth are One.

It has been said that heaven is being in the presence of God. No more need to worry about whether or not our theology was correct, or whether we will be reunited with those we have loved and see no more. All those things, as important as they are, will fade by comparison to the splendor of being taken up into the divine. We will see the face of God. And the face of God will be revealed as Truth, even as the truth of our lives will be revealed by the same Truth.

That last part is the definition of judgment. Judgment is being shown the truth. When the truth is revealed, all is known. There is nothing left to do. It may make us nervous to think about that right now, because we have not yet learned to trust that the truth and the judgment of God are grounded in divine love.

But truth is also vindication. And when we are vindicated, we have justice and we shall be satisfied. It will be enough. For when we have everything there is nothing more to desire.

A River in Egypt

I am speaking the truth in Christ-- I am not lying; my conscience confirms it by the Holy (Romans 9:1)

I remember the first time I heard the phrase "Denial is not a river in Egypt." It was about 30 years ago and since then I have seen it on coffee cups, t-shirts, and book covers. But no matter how often I see it, the phrase still resonates. Just as some few people will believe pretty much whatever they hear, for the rest of us, denial is the default setting for life. Much of the conflict of contemporary society stems from our unwillingness to accept something until it is empirically and irrefutably proven. Since such proof is seldom provided, argument and disputation are the rule of the day – especially when we are attempting to avoid what we suspect is a painful or inconvenient truth.

But it appears that this is nothing new. St. Paul, himself, a lawyer and a Pharisee, must preface his remarks to his Jewish and Christian brothers and sisters in Rome with the assurance that he is telling the truth as he knows it to be. He even makes this statement an oath by invoking the name of Christ and of the Holy Spirit. He implores them to believe him and the truth of his message.

There is a reason for that of course. They, too, believe that they have received the truth of God through the Covenant, the Torah and the Law. Who is this person to tell them otherwise?

I cannot help but wonder if we might all be better off if we learned to be more open-minded. None of us will know the truth about God until we meet God face to face. In the meantime, we all need to remember a cartoon by Charles Schultz. Snoopy sits atop his doghouse typing his theological opus. Charlie Brown asks him what the title will be. Snoopy replies, "Has it ever occurred to you that you might be wrong?"

Just Do It

When he went ashore, he saw a great crowd; and he had compassion for them and cured their sick. When it was evening, the disciples came to him and said, "This is a deserted place, and the hour is now late; send the crowds away so that they may go into the villages and buy food for themselves." Jesus said to them, "They need not go away; you give them something to eat." They replied, "We have nothing here but five loaves and two fish." And he said, "Bring them here to me." Then he ordered the crowds to sit down on the grass. Taking the five loaves and the two fish, he looked up to heaven, and blessed and broke the loaves, and gave them to the disciples, and the disciples gave them to the crowds. And all ate and were filled; and they took up what was left over of the broken pieces, twelve baskets full. And those who ate were about five thousand men, besides women and children. Matthew 14:13-21

Over the years I have watched folks tie themselves in knots trying to explain what really happened on the hillside when Jesus fed the 5000 from one scant meal. The answers have ranged from “Well, they really had more food in the crowd but Jesus had to convince them to share” to “even the least little symbolic bit is enough when it is blessed and shared in the name of Jesus.” Fine. We are, after all, in the realm of religious metaphor here.

But if we spend a great deal of time and energy trying to arrive at the rational truth of the event, we are likely to miss Matthew’s real message. The truth of the passage lies in Jesus words “you give them something to eat.” Jesus is challenging the disciples to recognize that they are not powerless in the face of such need.

They are not ready to hear that, so they respond with denial – “there is not enough to go around.” But Jesus counters with “bring me what you do have.” He then proceeds to show them that there is enough. And not just enough for all who are present, but twelve baskets left over to use to feed the rest of the world.

Jesus still challenges us to recognize that we have what we need to feed others, figuratively and literally. It is just a matter of distribution. We have a spiritual truth to share. We also have the means to provide for the physical needs of our fellow human beings. I wonder, just how many times does Jesus have to remind us?

Bathed in Mercy

Let your continual mercy, O Lord, cleanse and defend your Church; and, because it cannot continue in safety without your help, protect and govern it always by your goodness; through Jesus Christ our Lord, who lives and reigns with you and the Holy Spirit, one God, for ever and ever. Amen. (Collect for Proper 13)

There is a wonderful song in J.R.R. Tolkien's The Hobbit, when at the end of a long and treacherous journey Bilbo and his friends are treated to the glorious ministrations of a leisurely soak in a hot tub.

Sing hey! For the bath at close of day
that washes the weary mud away!
A loon is he that will not sing:
O! Water Hot is a noble thing!

Tolkien, good Roman Catholic that he was, never missed an opportunity to write of the connection between spirit and flesh, body and soul. I am certain that he would appreciate the fact that this collect reminds me of his bath song.

We all need the healing effects of soap and water from time to time. They remind us that life is not all work, grime and sweat. There are times when we can relax and be restored to a kinder and gentler state of mind. And, as this collect reminds us, the church itself is on a long and arduous journey through time. She, too, needs the cleansing effect of God's mercy and defense.

And the truly wonderful thing is that the mercy of God does serve to cleanse, to defend, and to govern our lives – individually and in the Body of Christ; so that when we are caked with the weary mud of life and when our image is more than a little worse for wear, we can trust that God's mercy will bathe and cleanse us for the days and the work ahead.

Who Is the Favorite?

Now Israel loved Joseph more than any other of his children, because he was the son of his old age; and he had made him a long robe with sleeves. But when his brothers saw that their father loved him more than all his brothers, they hated him, and could not speak peaceably to him. (Genesis 37:3-4)

For Tommy Smothers, there was only one explanation for any problem. He would turn to his brother Dickie and say "Mom always loved you best." For those of us watching their '70's variety show, this petulant line was a humorous reminder that Tommy had never grown up. It is tempting to say the same of Joseph's brother's; but in this case, the observation is accurate. Jacob did love Joseph best, and Joseph knew it.

It is never a good idea (no matter how the parent feels) to let the children know that one child is loved more than another. Every child with siblings suspects that this is true, but most parents have the good sense to keep it hidden. They know what will happen to both the favorite and the runner-up; which makes me wonder why the authors of Genesis didn't keep that in mind when telling their own story.

Sarah preferred Isaac over Ismael. Rebekah preferred Jacob over Esau. Jacob preferred Esau. And Isaac clearly preferred Joseph over all the rest of his sons. No wonder the story of the people of Israel is founded on the assertion that God had chosen them over all the other nations. Even though they understand themselves to have been chosen as an example of covenant and obedience, and even though their history is one of trial and suffering, they retain the consolation of having been chosen by God – to which the rest of the world has pretty much always said, "Chosen, eh? Here's what we think of that!"

The truth of the matter is that God does not have favorites. We are all of us loved equally. So we can no more hide behind feelings of rejection than we can claim the privilege of preference.

Dickie Smothers would regularly tell Tommy to "grow up!" That's pretty good advice for all of us.

Ways of God

They said to one another, "Here comes this dreamer. Come now, let us kill him and throw him into one of the pits; then we shall say that a wild animal has devoured him, and we shall see what will become of his dreams." But when Reuben heard it, he delivered him out of their hands, saying, "Let us not take his life." Reuben said to them, "Shed no blood; throw him into this pit here in the wilderness, but lay no hand on him" -- that he might rescue him out of their hand and restore him to his father. So when Joseph came to his brothers, they stripped him of his robe, the long robe with sleeves that he wore; and they took him and threw him into a pit. The pit was empty; there was no water in it. (Genesis 37:19-24)

When Jacob's sons conspire to kill their brother, two of Joseph's brothers speak to spare his life. Reuben and Judah. In these verses we hear that Reuben intends to rescue Joseph and take him back to Isaac. A few verses later, Judah suggests that it makes more sense (and profit) to sell Joseph into slavery. Aside from an unwillingness to kill their own kin, we don't know anything more about their motives or their actions.

But we do know that without their intervention, Joseph would not have lived, and the saga of Jacob and his family would have ended in fratricide. There might well have been no going into slavery in Egypt, no Moses, no liberation, or Exodus. In fact, there might never have been anything like Judaism, Christianity or Islam.

All of which, of course, assumes that the book of Genesis is a literal history.

For those of us who do not read Genesis as literal history, the fact that Joseph's own brothers plot his death points to a truth about the providence of God. God works in all things and nothing is beyond the reach of God's redeeming embrace. Joseph's arrogance, Reuben's reluctance to shed blood, and Judah's apparent greed are all part of the foundational story of Israel, and in both cases, God takes human imperfections and turns them to ultimate good.

God continues to work with our imperfections. We do not know how things will end, but we do know that in the end, God's will is done.

Seeking God's Face

Search for the LORD and his strength; continually seek his face. (Psalm 105:4)

To see the face of God is to court death – at least according to a host of admonitions in the Hebrew Bible. And yet, the Psalmist tells Jacob' descendants to do just that. Jacob has wrestled with God and earned a new name, "Israel." And as a result of that wrestling match, all the children of Israel, and we by extension, are exhorted to seek the face of God. Not because we no longer fear the consequences of bumbling into the presence of utter holiness, but because it is now our purpose in life to know God. We are to know God, not as a faceless power, but as the source of our life, our strength and our hope. We are to spend our entire lives, continually seeking to have the same sort of experience that Jacob had – to know the blessing of wrestling with God and being named by our Maker.

Yes, restriction on entry into the Holy of Holies will remain in place. And yes, anyone who unworthily or unwittingly touches the ark will be destroyed. But those outcomes are the consequence of a human encounter with the raw power of holiness, not because God wishes to remain unknown.

God desires that we seek and serve. God desires that we seek and see his face. That is the reward of a life of devotion. If we desire God above all else, then we shall see God. In so far as the Psalmist is concerned that is our highest calling and the purpose for which we were created.

Where Is Christ?

But the righteousness that comes from faith says, "Do not say in your heart, 'Who will ascend into heaven?'" (that is, to bring Christ down) "or 'Who will descend into the abyss?'" (that is, to bring Christ up from the dead). But what does it say? "The word is near you, on your lips and in your heart" (that is, the word of faith that we proclaim); (Romans 10:6-8)

Jesus repeatedly told all who would listen that the kingdom/reign of God is at hand. He had no use for something that might happen one day. Jesus was all about how we behave and what we believe right now. And when someone failed to understand what he was saying, he was likely to respond…."all right. But remember that the Kingdom of Heaven is already present."

St. Paul, who understands Jesus Christ to embody the Kingdom, the Word and the Salvation of God, uses the same theme. The Word/Christ is already here. He has not disappeared into the realm of the unknown and unknowable. The Word of God in Christ is as near to you as your lips and your heart. You are, in fact, swimming in it.

If God and the Word of God were not already present in this world, it is unlikely that any of us would be moved to seek it out, even if we thought that we might find it by traveling to the uttermost ends of the earth.

No, the presence of God is as near to us as the breath in our bodies. We need look no further, we only need to recognize what already its.

I Dare You

Peter answered him, "Lord, if it is you, command me to come to you on the water." He said, "Come." So Peter got out of the boat, started walking on the water, and came toward Jesus. But when he noticed the strong wind, he became frightened, and beginning to sink, he cried out, "Lord, save me!" Jesus immediately reached out his hand and caught him, saying to him, "You of little faith, why did you doubt?" (Matthew 14:28-31)

Sometimes we just don't know how to quit when we are ahead. When the disciples see Jesus walking "on the water" they are terrified and think that he is a ghost. But when he announces himself and tells them not to be afraid, Peter seems to need additional proof.

That's never made much sense to me. If I thought a ghost was approaching me I don't think I would dare it to bring me closer! But the real dare seems to come from Jesus and is issued in a single word. "Come." It is as though Jesus says to Peter "OK, if you really think that's what you want, go ahead and give it a shot." Peter does, and sinks like stone – which is a pretty good pun on his name – at least in English.

Peter is never in any physical danger. Jesus is there to pull him out of the water as he begins to sink. The real mystery is why Peter is asking for proof in the first place. By this point in the narrative, Peter and the rest of the disciples have surely seen enough of Jesus to know that walking on water would not tax his talents in the least.

Apparently, Matthew wants us, the readers to be able to relate to Peter, who no matter how hard he tries, just cannot seem to be able to get his faith and his actions in sync. I suspect he also wants us to wonder, "Lord, how many times have you had to pull me back into the boat?"

Create a Right Spirit within Me

Grant to us, Lord, we pray, the spirit to think and do always those things that are right, that we, who cannot exist without you, may by you be enabled to live according to your will; through Jesus Christ our Lord, who lives and reigns with you and the Holy Spirit, one God, for ever and ever. Amen. (Collect for Proper 14)

I often amaze myself with my ability to hold two utterly contradictory opinions at the same time. My response to this collect is an example. I readily admit that I cannot exist without God and that I am likely to make a colossal mess of things when I endeavor to live my life in a virtuous and obedient manner. And yet, judging from my behavior, I also seem to think that I am the sole arbiter of my spiritual desires and that the ability to make choices and follow through on them takes place entirely within my head.

Which of course turns prayer into a fallback position. If I can't or don't do the right then on my own, then I will ask God for help...both in doing the right thing and in cleaning up the mess.

As this collect points out, what we all need is the "spirit" to think and do the right thing; and asking for that spirit should not be Plan B. God has created us with the ability and even the desire to think and do what is right. But our history as a species and as individuals demonstrates just how unlikely we are to do so. What seems to be missing is the sustained will to follow through. I do not think that God left that part out. But I am extremely grateful that if I ask for a right spirit, God will grant it.

Busted!

Joseph could no longer control himself before all those who stood by him, and he cried out, "Send everyone away from me." So no one stayed with him when Joseph made himself known to his brothers. And he wept so loudly that the Egyptians heard it, and the household of Pharaoh heard it. Joseph said to his brothers, "I am Joseph. Is my father still alive?" But his brothers could not answer him, so dismayed were they at his presence. Genesis 45:1-3

From their perspective, Joseph's reunion with his brothers has to rank among the more awkward moments of family history. For all they know he died a slave a decades earlier. And whether or not they had repented of their murderous intentions toward him, they certainly never expected to see him again, let alone to be completely dependent upon him.

Dismay seems a rather mild description for what they must have felt. Shame, fear, guilt and dread come to mind. And while they are trying to sort all this out and think of a plan that won't get them killed, Joseph begins to cry hysterically. Not only are they "busted", but Joseph seems to have gone completely mad in the years since they have seen him.

What they don't know of course is that he has changed. But rather than driving him insane, his sufferings have made him a kinder and far more compassionate person. He loves them, and the whole elaborate scheme to get them all together in his presence is intended to keep the family together and alive during a famine. He is not trying to punish them. (Well, he's not perfect, so there may is a small bit of perversity at work here). But the point is that he has forgiven them and wants to help them.

They just don't know it.

Truth is Judgment

Then Joseph said to his brothers, "Come closer to me." And they came closer. He said, "I am your brother, Joseph, whom you sold into Egypt. And now do not be distressed, or angry with yourselves, because you sold me here; for God sent me before you to preserve life. For the famine has been in the land these two years; and there are five more years in which there will be neither plowing nor harvest. God sent me before you to preserve for you a remnant on earth, and to keep alive for you many survivors. So it was not you who sent me here, but God; he has made me a father to Pharaoh, and lord of all his house and ruler over all the land of Egypt. Hurry and go up to my father and say to him, `Thus says your son Joseph, God has made me lord of all Egypt; come down to me, do not delay. You shall settle in the land of Goshen, and you shall be near me, you and your children and your children's children, as well as your flocks, your herds, and all that you have. I will provide for you there-- since there are five more years of famine to come-- so that you and your household, and all that you have, will not come to poverty.' Genesis 45:4-11

"I don't blame you," Joseph says. "God was working through you." If Joseph's brothers were dreading what sort of revenge he might take upon them, these verses should put their minds at rest. We must also wonder what effect these words have on their hearts.

But notice what Joseph does not say to them. He does not say "It's OK. Don't worry about it." Joseph very specifically recounts exactly what happened and their part in it. He tells the truth. Sometimes judgment is nothing more nor less than just telling the truth.

The biggest problem for us seems to be that we always equate judgment with punishment. That is not to say that judgment is comfortable, especially if we have been lying to ourselves. But the truth has to be told before forgiveness can be genuine. If Joseph had merely brushed aside their guilt, they might never have been able to trust that he was sincere or that their reunion might lead to a restored relationship.

God does the same thing for us. We cannot escape knowing and dealing with the truth. And sometimes that knowledge and action are in themselves very painful. But God is not in the business of heaping punishment on top of responsibility. God sees our sinfulness as an injury sustained in the battles of life. To be sure, it is an injury which can only be healed through the administration of truth and justice. But God's intent is to heal us, not destroy.

Life for Evermore

Oh, how good and pleasant it is, when brethren live together in unity!
It is like fine oil upon the head that runs down upon the beard,
Upon the beard of Aaron, and runs down upon the collar of his robe.
It is like the dew of Hermon that falls upon the hills of Zion.
For there the LORD has ordained the blessing: life for evermore. (Psalm 133)

I once knew someone who considered herself so wronged that she said that if God forgave her recently deceased enemy and took her into heaven, she did not know how she would be able to enjoy heaven herself. She was not an evil woman. She was a believer. She simply could not imagine eternity without her anger, and she would not accept the idea of genuine reconciliation. Union and communion were too great a price to pay.

This Psalm is a song of celebration for the blessings and benefits of true community. Rare as such a thing may be, true peace and unity are as precious as the oil of anointing and as refreshing as the morning dew on a dry land. They are also metaphors for the reign of God and for the experience of heaven.

We are not to understand this as meaning that all difference is smoothed into homogeneity. Nor does it mean that the bumpy edges of human life cease to remind us that we are individuals with various hopes and needs. But it does mean that our differences and our conflicts are placed into their proper perspective. When viewed through the lens of the reign of God, our quarrels are paltry things indeed.

But so long as we refuse to let go of our sense of injury, or entitlement, or even guilt and shame, we render ourselves unable to see and to experience the unity that is at the heart of God.

My resistant friend has since died herself, and I am certain that in the presence of Christ she and her enemy can now laugh at themselves as they enjoy the blessings of life for evermore.

Trustworthy and Permanent

For the gifts and the calling of God are irrevocable. Romans11:29

This line comes from a passage in the middle of St. Paul's explanation of the fact that the Torah and the Covenant remain in force and that they are God's means of salvation for Israel. Unfortunately Paul the Pharisee seems bent on making the explanation as long and didactic as possible. It is often clear that he is dealing with his own doubts and fears; and heaven knows his life as an evangelist has often cast him in the role of arguing his own defense. But when Paul does get to the point, he lands there solidly and refuses to budge. The gifts and the calling of God are irrevocable. End of discussion.

Having grown up in a tradition where we were continually exhorted to be watchful lest we lose the blessing and find ourselves condemned, I was overjoyed to find discover this verse. I had spent years wondering about the state of my soul and looking for unconfessed and inadvertent sins which might be pushing me toward the fires of hell.

It was a blessing beyond measure to realize that while I might try to walk away from God, I could never force God to walk away from me. That meant that Jesus promise "Lo, I am with you always" included me. It also freed me from the obsessive fear that my ability to sin was beyond God's willingness or ability to love and forgive.

The words of our baptismal service include "you are sealed by the Holy Spirit and marked as Christ's own forever." That doesn't mean that we give each of the Baptized a "get into heaven free" card. Nor does it bind God to look the other way no matter what we do. But it does remind us that from God's point of view, that promise, with its gift and its calling are irrevocable.

Sometimes Laughter Is the Only Medicine

Jesus called the crowd to him and said to them, "Listen and understand: it is not what goes into the mouth that defiles a person, but it is what comes out of the mouth that defiles." Then the disciples approached and said to him, "Do you know that the Pharisees took offense when they heard what you said?" Matthew 15: 10-12

One of the fundamental skills of being a pastor, or a teacher, or pretty much anyone else in a position of leadership is learning when to laugh and when not to. These verses are example of a time when a hearty guffaw would be completely appropriate but not very helpful.

Jesus has just made a patently true observation about the power of words and language to hurt and defile. It's a though a pastor has just preached what she knows to be a solid, theologically and scripturally sound, and totally uncontroversial sermon on a subject upon which all the parish can agree. Before she can get to the coffee hour however, a member of the vestry rushes up and says "I need to tell that the Symthington-Erstwhiles and their five adult children were very offended by what you said today."

Incredulous laughter is the only sane response.

But isn't it representative of human nature that we are quickest to take offense when the truth is most obvious? And that laughter in the face of offense only seems to escalate the conflict. Of course, the alternatives can be worse. Suppose rather than reading the Pharisees the riot-act as he proceeds to do, Jesus had said, "On my, I am so sorry to have offended you. Would you like a public apology?" Some Messiah that would be!

Maybe the next time we find ourselves taking offense at something someone says, we might stop and ask ourselves why we are upset. Sometimes the truth can be very illuminating.

Following in His Footsteps

Almighty God, you have given your only Son to be for us a sacrifice for sin, and also an example of godly life: Give us grace to receive thankfully the fruits of his redeeming work, and to follow daily in the blessed steps of his most holy life; through Jesus Christ your Son our Lord, who lives and reigns with you and the Holy Spirit, one God, now and for ever. Amen. (Collect for Proper 15)

During one of last winter's snow storms, my niece posted a picture of her six year old son trudging across the yard in his new snow-boots. His two year old brother was trying to walk behind him in his footsteps. The only way he could manage that, in snow above his knees, was to crawl. There he was, moving along on all-fours with his backside in the air as he tried to keep his tummy out of the snow.

That's how I imagine we look to God sometimes when we try to follow in Jesus' steps. Hilarious but determined. And I also imagine that God feels just as kindly disposed toward our efforts as my niece and I felt toward the efforts of her son.

We need to keep a spiritual sense of humor, and a healthy dose of humility. We are not going to do things perfectly. But the only way we are going to learn to do them at all is to give it our best effort. We are truly grateful that Jesus has led the way and left a clearly marked path for us. But even if we learn to walk upright and follow along, we will never be able (or expected) to keep up with him.

Our job is to do our best to stay on the path.

A Doctor in the House?

"Is there no balm in Gilead? Is there no physician there?" (Jeremiah 8)

Like everything else, an individual's awareness of her own health falls somewhere along a continuum. At one end are those who are in a constant state of worry about every little ache and pain. In the middle are those who don't think about it so much but who monitor their health closely enough to know when they are ill, and when they need to see a doctor. At the other end of the scale are those who do their very best to ignore the messages sent to them by their bodies, and only seek medical attention when they are desperately ill. That is usually the point at which someone is called upon to shout "Is there a doctor in the house?"

"Is there a doctor in the house?" How many times has that phrase been used to frantic effect in films and plays? And real life? Most of us intuitively know that when genuine medical catastrophe strikes, real aid is required, and only the services of a professional will do. We may know how to offer comfort or support, but we also recognize the limits of our abilities and call for help.

Jeremiah's critique of Israel's health, physical and spiritual, is the plaintive cry of one in such a situation. He has called for faithfulness, but no one has come forward. It is not that there are no healers in Israel. Nor is there a lack of spiritual medicine. Help is available. Help has been requested. But Jeremiah's pleas for a restoration of the spiritual health of the nation have been ignored. In this passage the prophet stands as one who has witnessed a great public tragedy to which there has been no response.

He is heartsick at the suffering he has witnessed, especially to the indifference to the needs of the poor. He weeps fountains of tears over the people's idolatry. They have turned from God to a selfish and indifferent way of life and are now abandoned to the consequences of their neglect.

Jeremiah's truth remains true today. There is an unbreakable link between the spiritual health of a community or a nation and the health of the people who inhabit it. God offers us healing. Balm is available. But if the balm of God's healing and empowering love is not applied to the wounds of our sin, fear, and isolation, it can do us no good.

Blame Game

"We have become a reproach to our neighbors,
An object of scorn and derision to those about us.
How long will you be angry, O Lord? Will your fury blaze like fire for ever?
Pour out your wrath on the heathen who have not known you
And upon the kingdoms that have not called upon your name." (Psalm 79:4-6)

The children of Israel are suffering. Their homes have been sacked. The temple has been profaned, and many have died. But, there is a reason that the children of Israel find themselves living this way. They have been unfaithful to God, engaging in idolatrous behavior and abandoning the ethical demands of their faith. God is indeed furious with them and has left them to the consequences of their sin. God is waiting for repentance and amendment of life.

So, what do they do? They try to shift the blame from their own shoulders to those of their oppressors. *"If you're going to be mad at someone, God, why not these heathen who are trashing the place?"*

We would never pray for the love and mercy of God in our own lives and then secretly believe that someone else's suffering was deserved, would we? Of course we would. Because we are all subject to the temptations of idolatry, and most especially to the idolatry of thinking ourselves better than others.

Idolatry means placing first priority on anyone or anything other than God. It means worshipping someone, or something other than God, and that definition encompasses an almost infinite array of temptations.

Do you want to know where the temptation to idolatry lies in your life? Ask yourself, "What defines me? What do I value above all else? What do I fear losing?" And pay attention to your physical response to those questions. If they make you angry, or tie your stomach in knots, then you are probably onto something. And if you feel defensive, and start trying to justify your answers, you are most certainly onto something.

But remember, loving something or someone is not sinful. It is only when we place those things at the center of our lives, in the place that God alone should inhabit, that we lose our way.

Images of Christ

"For there is one God; there is also one mediator between God and humankind, Christ Jesus, himself human, who gave himself a ransom for all." (I Timothy 2:5-6a)

When I was in seminary, we often lightened the load of philosophical and theological reading by looking for Eucharistic metaphors in popular culture. One set of classmates even did a project about Christ figures in film, and listed Luke Skywalker and Zorro at the top of their lists.

But my favorite example had not yet been written. I had to wait for J.K. Rowling and Harry Potter. I am especially fond of the scenes when Harry, who is engaged in battle with a malevolent force, finds himself physically, spiritually, and emotionally depleted by the experience. That is the point at which a teacher or mentor hands him a piece of chocolate and says, "Eat this. It will help."

When we are fighting the spiritual battles of temptation to idolatry, Jesus hands us a remedy. "Take and Eat. Take and Drink." Jesus himself, as he comes to us in Holy Communion is the remedy. He is also the example of one who defeats idolatry. He refused to hold onto anything – not even his life. He allowed nothing to take the place of his love for God. And when we are struggling with the challenges of our own spiritual life, he says to us "Eat this. It will help."

When you come to the table, remember that in the bread and wine of Eucharist you receive the real presence of Christ to feed your soul, nourish your spirit, and strengthen your ability to go forth into the world proclaiming the Good News.

In Baptism and Eucharist, we are united/joined to God in a mystery and a miracle for the good of all the world. There is one God, and thanks be to God, it is the love, power, and grace of God that unites us to one another and to all creation.

Who Does God Love?

"First of all then, I urge that supplications, prayers, intercessions, and thanksgivings be made for everyone, for kings and all who are in high positions, so that we may lead a quiet and peaceable life in all godliness and dignity. This is right and acceptable in the sight of God our Savior, who desires everyone to be saved and to come to the knowledge of the truth." (I Timothy 2:1-4)

On the face of it, we might slip right over these verses and not recognize what they have to say to us about idolatry.

How about his example from an old western. Think of the hero (say John Wayne) sidling up to a bad guy and saying "Listen, pardner, this town ain't big enough for the two of us." In spiritual terms, that sort of attitude is a real temptation to the idolatry of self.

Is your religious system too restrictive to allow for the idea that God wants everybody to be saved? Is salvation contingent on certain beliefs or opinions, or actions, rather than on the all-embracing love and wisdom of God. In other words, we cannot presume to know how God sees the heart or faith of another. And when we seize upon the "my way or the highway" version of theology, we are seeking to limit God. In the vocabulary of faith, that sort of attitude is a real temptation to the idolatry of religion.

Yes, even religion can be idolatrous. If our understanding of God assumes that human sin, failing or even evil is greater that the ability of God to forgive and redeem, we are placing our religious understanding on a level above God and seeking to bind the divine.

Religious idolatry is very dangerous. It blinds us to the ongoing nature of God's self-disclosure. It rejects the possibility of divine revelation. And it makes us think that we are capable of rendering judgments that belong to God alone.

So, ask yourself, is my heaven large enough to hold everyone that God chooses to have there? If not, then beware. For, it may not be large enough to accommodate you either.

Cheating

So, summoning his master's debtors one by one, he asked the first, "How much do you owe my master?" He answered, "A hundred jugs of olive oil." He said to him, "Take your bill, sit down quickly and make it fifty." Then he asked another, "And how much do you owe?" He replied, "A hundred containers of wheat." He said to him, "Take your bill and make it eighty."

I love a really well-written mystery or detective story. The challenge of figuring out who did what to whom, and when they did it, while trying to unravel complicated plots has always intrigued me. But the one thing that constantly baffles me is the way that the villain always thinks she'll get away with it. Good grief! Doesn't she realize that she is leaving forensic evidence all over the place? Can't she understand that there is no such thing as the perfect crime? With all the cameras, electron microscopes, and DNA analysis available, only the less than intelligent, or the extremely arrogant would even try.

That's the thing about this parable. The dishonest manager is not only a crook, he is unbelievably arrogant. He really thinks he can pull it off, and that no one will be on to him. Well, he's got a problem with idolatry...the idolatry of self which is arrogance. In fact, he is so confident that he can pull a fast one on his master that keeps on cheating even after he's been caught.

But he's not alone. We're all subject to the temptation to think that God really doesn't have the time or inclination to pay attention to how we are ordering our lives. We're not that important, right? With so much real nastiness in the world, why should God notice or care about what we basically honest folk do? Those rules are there for the real sinners. They don't apply to us. Besides, there's always time to repent later, right? God loves us. God forgives us. It's all good.

And so we go blithely on, never considering the fact that with our small or daily breaches of ethics, we are gradually building the habit of dishonesty.

What we do matters. What we say has weight and consequence. And what we make of ourselves in this life is what we will carry with us into eternity.

High Anxiety

"Grant us, Lord, not to be anxious about earthly things, but to love things heavenly; and even now, while we are placed among things that are passing away, to hold fast to those that shall endure..." (Collect for Proper 20, Book of Common Prayer)

Each year hundreds of millions of Christians around the world hear this prayer read at the beginning of their Sunday worship – in every congregation in which the Revised Common Lectionary is used. People of enormously different backgrounds and cultures and ages all hear the same admonition. We might be entirely different from each other in every other way, but this much we have in common. *"Grant us not to be anxious about things that are passing away, but rather to hold on to things that endure."*

What is it that endures? In what can we truly, eternally trust? Not power, or reputation, or possessions, or wealth. All those things may make us momentarily happy or comfortable while we have them in our grasp. But they are not permanent. They can be taken from us in a heartbeat. How about health, comfort, or peace? Those, too, are inevitably subject to change. Nor can we place ultimate trust in religious or philosophical teachings. Even doctrine, dogma and truths carved in stone are malleable.

So when we share this prayer, what is it that we are called to hold onto? In the 13th chapter of First Corinthians, St. Paul lists the three things that we can count on. Faith, Hope, and Love.

Faith is the lived experience of our relationship with God.
Hope is the assurance of things as yet unknown.
Love is the presence of God, and the rock upon which our faith and hope stands.

The greatest of these is love. Not a warm feeling or a sentimental attachment -- neither a grand passion nor a tumultuous struggle -- but the unshakable awareness of the presence of God with us in all things and at all times.

Shadow of the Almighty

He who dwells in the shelter of the Most High abides under the shadow of the Almighty. He shall say to the Lord, "you are my refuge and my stronghold, my god in whom I put my trust. (Ps 91:1-2)

We independent thinking and acting 21st century folk would not normally consider it a good or helpful thing to be living in anyone's shadow. It is true that we are appreciative of shelter, but we far prefer to construct, maintain and own it ourselves. And when times are tough we want to know that our dwelling places are built to withstand the storms of life. At the very least, we try to have really good homeowners insurance.

It is little wonder then that so many of us have a difficult time entering into a spiritual relationship in which we have to understand ourselves as being under the protection and authority of God. We are raised and educated to take care of ourselves, and to cling fiercely to our autonomy.

But these lines from Psalm 91 challenge us to think differently. Rather than seek out God when we are in trouble or when it seems appropriate, our lives and the meaning of our lives are to be truly grounded in our trust in God. That relationship is to be source of our strength and comfort.

While the concept may be alien to us today, what the Psalmist is really talking about is utter reliance on the Almighty – not on an "as-needed" basis and certainly not in contractual terms. The one who continually dwells in the shelter of God, abides (stays) in the shadow of the Almighty. There is no safer place to be.

Imagine what your life could be like if you were able to embrace such an attitude of trust and intimacy. Imagine a way of being in which you remain yourself while continually seeking God's will for you and acknowledging the primacy of God in your life. It is in that place that we most truly find ourselves, as God has created us to be.

Deliverance

He shall deliver you from the snare of the hunter and from the deadly pestilence. (Ps 91:3)

Years ago a group of friends gave me a lovely translation of the Psalms by Nan Merrill, in which she recasts the Psalms as prayers of the human spirit. Today's verse reads:

"For you deliver me from the webs of fear, from all that separates and divides."

I had never thought of equating the snare of the hunter with the webs of fear, but it makes perfect sense. While there have been plenty of times in human history in which people have been the prey of slave traders, and many still find themselves caught up in the nets of human trafficking, we are for the most part blessed to be spared those evils.

We do, however, live in a culture in which we are often beset by fear, anxiety, and insecurity – in jobs, relationships, and finances. The gut-deep pressures of contemporary life take their toll as well, and in our fear, stress and exhaustion, we may find ourselves separated from our truest nature, and divided from one another.

But there is a remedy for this illness of alienation and fear. Those who trust in God and abide in the shadow of the Almighty do remain close enough to God to be continually reinforced by God's graceful presence. God is always present to us, but it is often true that we distance ourselves from the awareness of that grace. The cure for that unfortunate tendency requires building the habit of seeking God and remaining close to the source of our refuge.

Refuge

He shall cover you with his pinions, and you shall find refuge under his wings; his faithfulness shall be a shield and buckler. (Ps 91:4)

We are all familiar with the idea that being in a relationship requires faithfulness. Entering into any meaningful degree of closeness with another person carries with it the intention of giving the relationship priority in our lives, and of respecting the dignity of the other individual. We make a promise – we commit to being present – we agree to honor the claim that the other person has upon our loyalty.

But have you ever thought about what the concept of faithfulness means when it is being applied to God? God promises to be faithful to us, to remember us, and to be present to us. What is that like? In the words of the Psalmist, God covers us with his pinions and his faithfulness is shield and buckler. Shield? OK. God protects us. But what on earth are pinions and bucklers? And what do they have to do with the faithfulness of God?

Pinions are wing feathers of a bird, and a buckler is a small round shield which is held at arm's length to fend off an attacker. In these two images we see God acting on our behalf – sheltering us under protective wings while keeping danger away from us. God is actively faithful in keeping us spiritually safe through times of fear and challenge. God's faithfulness provides the environment in which we find shelter. And the faithfulness of God is a promise that we can trust. The word of God is absolutely reliable.

Do you believe that? Do you believe that God is your spiritual defense? Have you tried it? If you haven't, here is an experiment. Bring to mind something that you really fear or dread. Now imagine the faithfulness of God protecting your spirit and soul as you meet the challenge. Notice that there is no promise that the thing you fear will be destroyed or removed. Instead, God's faithfulness supports and sustains us while we go through the trial. God walks alongside us.

Our Deepest Needs

You shall not be afraid of any terror by night, nor of the arrow that flies by day; of the plague that stalks in the darkness, nor of the sickness that lays waste at mid-day. (Ps 91:5-6)

The manner in which we humans respond to the Psalms is gloriously counter-intuitive. Have you noticed that in the face of greatest danger, or deepest grief, we will remember and recite the words of a Psalm even when we know that what we are saying does not describe the physical reality that we are experiencing?

The best example I have seen of this comes from the Alistair Sim film version of "A Christmas Carol." Tiny Tim has died and been buried. His mourning family sits around the table, while the eldest son reads Psalm 91. "You shall not be afraid of any terror by night..." when clearly one would think that their lives have been shattered by the loss of this child.

I see this all the time in ministry. People trust and proclaim the promises of healing, strength, protection, and of the presence of God at times when that reality is least obvious to any observer. We claim the promise in the absence of proof. We proclaim health in the face of illness. We shout "alleluia" in the dark and fearsome hour of grief. And we do it precisely because we know the truth of eternity even when we cannot see or touch it.

Thank God for the Psalmist and his humanity. Thank God that this ancient Hebrew poet was so wonderfully honest about his hopes, dreams, fears and failures. For he speaks for all of us when he gives voice to our deepest needs.

Hope Summarized

Because he is bound to me in love, therefore will I deliver him; I will protect him because he knows my name. He shall call upon me, and I will answer him; I am with him in trouble, I will rescue him and bring him to honor. (Ps 91:14-15)

There it is – the summary of our hope. We are bound to God in love, and our faith is founded upon the belief that the love of God is stronger than anything, anywhere, anytime. God is with us. God will not leave us comfortless. God will answer us, rescue us, and bring us to honor.

How can that be true when we are constantly confronted with circumstances in which deliverance and rescue do not arrive? Yes. It is true. So long as we remember that the span of life and reality are eternal, and that God is continually, eternally working God's purpose out for us, with us, through us – regardless of any momentary experience.

We are bound to God in love. And all that God requires is that the relationship be personal. *"I will protect him because he knows my name."* Not because we keep all the rules, or makes spectacular sacrifices, but because we love God, and because we know God's name. God does not require perfection, as the Psalmist clearly knew. But God does require that we be willing to be perfected. God does not require success, only that we show up and take our part in the relationship. And that we ask for God's help when we need it.

In the end, it all comes down to relationship. Are you in a personal relationship with God? God wants you to be. All you have to do is call God by name, and the best way to do that is through prayer. So, pray, my friends. Open your heart and talk to God.

True Mercy

O God, you declare your almighty power chiefly in showing mercy and pity: Grant us the fullness of your grace, that we, running to obtain your promises, may become partakers of your heavenly treasure. (Collect for Proper 21)

Only the genuinely powerful can be merciful for mercy is the abridgment of power. God, who has all power, does not focus on judgment and condemnation. God gives us time to learn, opportunity to change, and the grace to recognize the need for growth.

God invites us to partake in the treasures of heaven, and to take our place at the Eucharistic table where we receive the medicine that heals our souls and strengthens us for the race we run.

But ours is not a race that merely exhausts us. Running for the promises of God is an exhilarating experience in which we can feel our bodies, our spirits and our minds functioning as a whole, working in unity, stretching forward toward the goal of knowing God, and of being fully known.

Toxic Texts

"Happy shall he be who takes your little ones, and dashes them against the rock." (Psalm 137:9)

In contemporary parlance, this last verse of Psalm 137 is "toxic." Even the framers of the lectionary seem to know this because when it turns up every three years, they offer an alternate option for those of us who would rather die ourselves than read it in worship. I am among that group. No matter when Psalm 137 appears in the assigned readings – on a Sunday or in the Daily Office at Evening Prayer on the 28th day of the month, I refuse to speak these words aloud.

Can we even begin to imagine the feelings going on inside the person who would say such a thing? What rage must he feel? What agony must be burning within her breast? Being able to applaud the slaughter of innocents is beyond the pale. The speaker has either embraced vengeance to the point of evil, or has been driven to a degree of insanity that we cannot imagine.

I cannot believe that I would ever react this way. I refuse to accept that I would ever condone the death of a child, an infant, a toddler. And yet, there it is, enshrined in Holy Scripture. The cry of a soul so bereft as to lash out in mindless vengeance – blessing the slaughter of children.

Why? The people are exiled, their identity has been killed. Their faith feels void and empty. They cannot remember how to sing, or to pray. In that feeling of utter lose, they lash out with curses. They are so out of touch with their own humanity that they are no longer capable of behaving humanely. Is that an excuse? No. It was not an excuse when the children of Israel found themselves in captivity in Babylon. Nor is it an excuse today when despair and ideology lead a young man to strap a bomb across his chest and go out to kill as many as possible in the name of his pain.

It is not an excuse. But it might be a blood-drenched invitation. An invitation to us to ask, why? Why, if it is not normal, not human, for a people to rejoice in the death of innocents, does it still happen? If we can find the courage to face the question head-on, perhaps we can finally learn how to erase this verse from Holy Scripture.

What's a Believer to Do?

"For this reason, I remind you to rekindle the gift of God that is within you through the laying on of my hands, for God did not give us a spirit of cowardice, but rather a spirit of power, and of love, and of self-discipline. Do not be ashamed then of the testimony about our Lord..." (2 Timothy 1:6-8a)

Has anyone ever asked you – point blank – if you are a believer, and if you are, what it is that you believe? I would imagine not. In the first place that would be considered rather intrusive, if not downright rude. Such a question would also carry with it the possibility that you might turn and ask the same question. And Heaven knows, most of us would really rather not talk about God – and certainly not about Jesus.

We tell ourselves that we do not want to give offense, or to appear pushy or judgmental. But I wonder...perhaps it is something else. Perhaps, to put the best spin on things, it is a failure of courage. We may fear that we are not worthy spokespersons for Jesus, or that we don't know enough to answer any follow-up questions. That fear is understandable.

But there may be a more troublesome explanation. What if we really don't know what we believe? Or we don't think that it matters enough to share? Or that God won't mind if we just go quietly on our way and let others find their own path?

And worst of all, what if we are ashamed to be people of faith? What if we are embarrassed to admit that we believe in God and that we follow Jesus? What if we don't want to be classified with those "other" people who make such a scene when describing their love or God?

But here's the thing. When we were baptized and/or confirmed, someone laid hands on us and we were commissioned as disciples and evangelists. We were not taken into the family of God for our own convenience or protection; we were brought into a living relationship of "power, and of love, and of self-discipline." With the mark of Christ upon our foreheads and the fires of the Holy Spirit within us, surely that gives us something to say.

I Am Persuaded

"I know not why God's wondrous grace to me He hath made known,
nor why, unworthy, Christ in love Redeemed me for His own.
But "I know whom I have believed, and am persuaded that He is able
to keep that which I've committed Unto Him against that day."
(Broadman Hymnal 1940 paraphrase of 2 Timothy 1: 12)

As a former Southern Baptist, I know that the best way in the world to learn Scripture is to sing it. By the time that I was ten years old I could sing more theology than I would learn in the next five decades. I probably didn't understand most of it, but I could belt it out with the best of them.

Long before I knew that 2 Timothy was a New Testament Epistle attributed to St. Paul, I knew that when I made my declaration of faith in Christ Jesus that it was held secure in his heart forever. And, although I often railed against the strictness of my fundamentalist childhood faith, I have always known what an incredible blessing it was to grow up secure in the knowledge that God loved me, and always would.

There is an element of intimacy in this Epistle that may sound startling to contemporary ears. Writing for all who will follow Jesus, St. Paul says that has cast in his lot with Christ, and come what may, he will not turn back. But Jesus is equally committed to the relationship, holding our love and devotion as the precious gifts that they are. Treasured and closely guarded, our trust is safely invested in him. He is not ashamed to accept us as his own, and we should not be ashamed to proclaim him as our Lord.

A Goodly Fellowship

"O God, by your grace you have called us to a goodly fellowship of faith. Bless our Bishops, and other clergy, and all our people. Grant that your word may be truly preached and heard, your Sacraments faithfully administered and faithfully received. By your spirit, fashion our lives according to the example of your Son, and grant that we may show the power of your love to all among whom we live; through Jesus Christ our Lord. Amen." (BCP, p. 817)

Most of us know St. Francis as the one who loved animals, who appreciated the glories of creation, and who cared for the sick, the untouchable, and the unlovable. But do we also remember that his vision for his religious order was so out-of-step with the times (12th century) that when he first asked for permission to found a mendicant (begging) order, the Pope refused permission?

Or that he was so firm in his convictions about the rule of poverty and simplicity in his new order that his monks turned against him and evicted him from his own monastery?

Why did he get into so much trouble? Because he seemed to go out of his way to identify with the poor, the wretched and the neglected. He identified so closely with the suffering of Christ that he is said to have suffered the wounds of Christ, the Stigmata, himself. If he did, it was not because he was exceptionally holy. It was simply because he refused to see the church and his order as anything other than an instrument of God's love and peace in the world – where it was most needed. He knew how it felt, and what it cost, to love the unloved.

Throughout the history of the Christian faith, it has fallen to certain people like Francis to remind us all that we are not called to be rich, or powerful, or even popular as a faith. We are called to follow Jesus and to proclaim the love of God to all.

Prayer of St. Francis

"Lord, make us instruments of your peace. Where there is hated, let us sow love; where there is injury pardon; where there is discord, union; where there is doubt, faith; where there is despair hope, where there is darkness, light; where there is sadness, joy. Grant that we may not so much seek to be consoled as to console; to be understood as to understand, to be loved as to love. For it is in giving that we receive; it is in pardoning that we are pardoned, and it is in dying that we are born to eternal life. Amen."

There is a phenomenon often witnessed by clergy praying at deathbeds. A person who is no longer capable of speech or conversation, who may in fact appear to be unconscious, will nonetheless join in praying the words of the Lord's Prayer, the 23rd Psalm, or the Hail Mary. Part of it is the lifelong experience of comfort that these words have delivered. Part of it is also the rote nature of the prayers which lift us out of conscious speaking and into the eternal realm of corporate prayer. But even more than that, these prayers have become part of the fabric of our lives and are articulations of who we are and what we believe.

I am confident that those who know St. Francis can add his prayer to the list of those they would recognize and pray on their own deathbeds. It is an extraordinary confession of the structure of the life of Christian Faith. Recognizing the tensions of human existence, this prayer offers a Christ-centered remedy to each of the polarities of human experience. And even more, this prayer is a commentary on the Gospel. Not so succinctly put as "Love God with all your heart, and your neighbor as yourself", it nonetheless gives us concrete examples of how to live the gospel and how to embody the love of God. This is a genuinely incarnational prayer.

True Prayer

"Almighty and everlasting God, you are always more ready to hear than we to pray, and to give more than we either desire or deserve." (Collect of the Day for Proper 22)

I have recently come up against the paradox of "scheduling prayer." I know that if I were not bound by vows to the practice of making time each day for morning and evening prayer, and for quiet contemplation, that I would find innumerable excuses for skipping it. On the other hand, the practice of having the time set apart has made it even more obvious to me that the time I spend in prayer is miniscule compared to the time that I spend on the treadmill of worry, and busy-ness.

This collect really speaks to me. Whether I am consciously on my knees in prayer, or leading worship, or hastily throwing intercessions toward heaven between appointments, God is always there, listening, and ready to hear. But that is not all, God already desires to give me much more than I can even imagine, let alone desire or deserve.

Prayer is a mystery. It is an action that joins the human soul to God and opens us to the possibility of being formed into that which God desires us to be. What we often forget is that no matter how much we may ask God to guide, direct, change or inspire us, we can never begin to approach an understanding of the blessings that God already intends for us.

True prayer is this. To put oneself in the presence of God and to ask for God alone. No bargaining, no promises, no desperate pleas. To pray is to say, simply, "Here I am God" and to be open to what God wishes to do.

Bloom Where You Are Planted

"Thus says the LORD of hosts, the God of Israel, to all the exiles whom I have sent into exile from Jerusalem to Babylon: Build houses and live in them; plant gardens and eat what they produce. Take wives and have sons and daughters; take wives for your sons, and give your daughters in marriage, that they may bear sons and daughters; multiply there, and do not decrease. But seek the welfare of the city where I have sent you into exile, and pray to the LORD on its behalf, for in its welfare you will find your welfare." (Jeremiah 29:4-7)

What a fascinating passage! God has sent the children of Israel into exile, allowing them to be torn away from all that they know and love. They are living in a strange land, bereft of the stability and foundation of home. They are grieving for what they have lost and dreaming of a day of restoration and return. So, what is God's word to them through the prophet Jeremiah?

"Bloom where you are planted."

That phrase always struck me as a bit trite and dismissive when it was so popular a few decades ago. What was it supposed to mean anyway? Make the best of things? I have to admit that it still strikes me as trite and dismissive, but only if we understand it to mean that ultimately we have control over what happens to us and how we respond. Clearly there are times when the former is not true, and the latter is not possible.

But what if it's about trusting God anyway? What if it means that even in times of exile and dislocation, we remain the people of God? The instruction to build homes and families is a form of assurance that life does continue, and that God is present with us. So, living and thriving are acts of faith. We do not wait until things get better, nor do we succumb to the temptation of despair when we cannot see just how things will turn out.

God has put us where we are. And God is with us where we are. That is wonderful news, because it reminds us that nothing that happens to us can separate us from God; and that in all times and places we can praise God for the blessings that we do have.

To Confess God's Goodness

"For you, O God, have proved us; you have tried us just as silver is tried.
You brought us into the snare; you laid heavy burdens upon our backs.
*You let enemies ride over our heads; we went through fire and water; **
but you brought us out into a place of refreshment." (Psalm 66:9-11)

Today's passage is the prayerful confession of the people we read about yesterday. But there is nothing trite or dismissive about their honesty or their willingness to accept responsibility for the conditions in which they find themselves. The Psalmist knows and accepts that human actions carry consequences. The Psalmist also knows that the first step in repentance and reconciliation is acknowledging responsibility.

But this is more than a confession of sin. This is also confession of the goodness of God. "You have proved us, you have tried us just as silver is tried." The result of the trials that the people endure – even when those trials are the result of their own sinful actions – is that the people learn and grow. They discover through their adversity that they are being refined into the precious metal that they have always been destined to be.

Without sugarcoating anything the people can admit that the consequences of their infidelity have been very hard to bear, but that the outcome is now a place of refreshment, rest, and self-knowledge. They know, now, that they were capable of a much greater, and deeper faith than they had exhibited. And so they are renewed in their spirit, and strengthened for the future.

The glory of confession is that it frees us to stop lying to ourselves, and it relieves us of the temptation to self-justification. I did it. I was wrong. I am sorry. I take responsibility for it. And now, I move on with trust in the love and guidance of God.

The tricky part is the moving on. Confession and absolution mean that we cannot hide behind guilt. Nor can we cower in fear. We can only pick ourselves up out of our self-imposed "time-out", and journey on.

For which we can all say, "Thanks be to God!"

Releasing the Word of God

"But the word of God is not chained. Therefore I endure everything for the sake of the elect, so that they may also obtain the salvation that is in Christ Jesus, with eternal glory. The saying is sure: 'If we have died with him, we will also live with him; if we endure, we will also reign with him; if we deny him, he will also deny us; if we are faithless, he remains faithful-- for he cannot deny himself.' Remind them of this, and warn them before God that they are to avoid wrangling over words, which does no good but only ruins those who are listening. Do your best to present yourself to God as one approved by him, a worker who has no need to be ashamed, rightly explaining the word of truth." (2 Timothy 2:9-15)

The "Word of God" is the Good News of God in Christ. The "Word of God" is also Jesus Christ, the Word Incarnate. So it does seem a bit obvious that we cannot chain, restrict or diminish the Good News.

And yet, we do sometimes try to bind the Spirit. And sometimes we do try to restrict the infinite blessings of the Gospel with our own narrow interpretations of what it means and to whom it is addressed. And very often, we do those things by wrangling over the words. Pre-destination? Transubstantiation? Parousia? We have a whole trunk load of words that have led to wrangling, bloodshed, and worse-yet, indifference to the message of the Good News.

Because the truly tragic thing about wrangling over words is that if we do it long enough, we drive away those who were thirsting for the word and were more than willing to receive the blessing. "Avoid wrangling over words, which does not good but only ruins those who are listening." They simply stop listening to us and wander away to more peaceful and edifying surroundings.

So, how do we "rightly" explain the word of truth? We tell the Good News. God is with us. God Incarnate is with us in Jesus Christ. Jesus Christ shows us the way to God.

How God accomplishes that task is God's concern, not ours. And when we find ourselves wrangling over one approach or another, we do so at the expense of those who are listening. Instead, let's invite them to the table, share the Word of God, and welcome them to the family.

A Great Equalizer

Then one of them, when he saw that he was healed, turned back, praising God with a loud voice. He prostrated himself at Jesus' feet and thanked him. And he was a Samaritan. Then Jesus asked, "Were not ten made clean? But the other nine, where are they? Was none of them found to return and give praise to God except this foreigner?" (Luke 17)

This this is one of those times when we must approach the Gospel as the counter-intuitive document that it is. What Jesus is talking about is the destructive effects of illness, history, and religious difference. These ten men, who in other circumstances and in the days before they were ill might have crossed the road to avoid contact with one another. They might have hurled curses across the path over the differences in their ways of worship. Jews worshipped in Jerusalem. Samaritans did not. Both groups considered the other's beliefs to be not only wrong but sinful.

But here they are, reduced to equals by an illness that made them unacceptable to either side. It seems that in illness, in extreme distress and need, that the walls and boundaries are eradicated. When all they have left is each other, then being together becomes acceptable.

Jesus is making a fundamental observation about what it means to be human, and about how divisive and pointless many of our rules and definitions have become. I think there is also something in this story about the hierarchy of human-ness. Does being a leper make someone sub-human? Or is having leprosy so devastating that it erases the human distinctions between cultures and methods of worship?

I do not think that Jesus wants us to believe that the Samaritan was a better or more faithful man. In fact, I am confident that if the story had been told the other way around and that nine Samaritans had been sent off to show themselves to their priests that the one who returned to give thanks would have been a Jew.

Each of them went and offered thanks where they could. Nine went to the temple and the one who could not go to the temple returned to Jesus. In all ten cases, they were healed. This gospel lesson isn't about foreigners, it is about recognizing the source of our healing and giving thanks.

Faith Heals Us

"Get up and go on your way; your faith has made you well." (Luke 17:19)

Faith is not about accepting a set of religious rules, methods or teachings. Faith is a relationship. The Samaritan leper has a relationship with Jesus. It is his gratitude toward Jesus that has compelled him to return and give thanks.

But we must be extremely clear about this. There are two things that this lesson does not say. First, it does not say that the other nine were not healed or that their healing was rescinded because they did not return to give thanks. Their healing was not conditional. All ten were healed. Second, it does not say that the Samaritan was healed because he believed. He was already healed when he returned to enter into a relationship of gratitude to Jesus. What the text does tell us is that his faith has made him *"well."* Not only has he been healed, he has been made well.

Wellness is so much more than physical health. Wellness is wholeness. It is a way of being in which there is a balanced relationship within all parts of our lives – emotional, physical and spiritual. That is not to say that we cannot be well unless we are physically healed. The physical is not the most important aspect of healing. It is healing of the spirit that is the most important. The best health in the world cannot compensate for a spirit in need of healing. It is the faith of the Samaritan – his grateful relationship with Jesus – that makes him whole.

When we see it that way, we are freed from the temptation of linking healing to faith. There is little that is more devastating to someone suffering an illness than being told that they cannot be physically healed because their faith is not strong enough. Such teaching is not only wrong, it is cruel and perverse.

Sometimes we receive physical healing. Sometimes we do not. In either case, our faith makes us well.

Three Little Words

God called to him out of the bush, "Moses, Moses!" And he said, "Here I am."

Three words, three syllables, one short sentence. And yet these words are among the most important words we humans can utter. Here I am.

We say those words in response to a lost or frightened child, to a suffering loved one, to a friend in need of help or companionship. Here I am. You are not alone. I am with you. These words are an assurance of presence, of availability and the promise that we are not only aware of the other but are paying attention to them.

They are also the best answer that we can give to the stirring of our hearts in the presence of God in prayer. "Here I am, Lord." But how often in the stress and rush of daily life to we spare the time to pray at all, let alone offer ourselves as ready and waiting to receive the word of God?

Moses might have turned aside to see the burning bush and then have gone on his way, excited to tell his family and friends of the strange sight he had seen. That would have made a good story. But had he not also paused long enough to hear God calling him, how different the story of the Exodus might have been. Had Moses missed that opportunity to listen, he would not have known to respond, and had he not been so awed by what he saw, he might have babbled on rather than simply replying "Here I Am."

The value of being in silent awe before God lies in our willingness to be known and to know the Holy. Try as we might, we cannot hear the voice of God amidst the clamor of our lives. It is only when we glimpse the burning bush and are willing to step aside to see it that we can give our full attention and the appropriate response.

Something in a Name

But Moses said to God, "If I come to the Israelites and say to them, 'The God of your ancestors has sent me to you,' and they ask me, 'What is his name?' what shall I say to them?" God said to Moses, "I AM Who I AM." (Exodus 3:13-14a)

Names have power; which is why in some cultures people have public as well as private names and are especially careful about to whom they divulge the private one. It is also true that the ability to name something grants power and assigns responsibility. In the Garden of Eden, God gives Adam the privilege of naming the animals of creation, but Adam also receives responsibility for their care and welfare.

That is why this passage is so striking. God's response to Moses is cryptic so that Moses will come to appreciate how this name is different. And notice that Moses does not get to name God. Furthermore, the Name of God is not a noun at all. It is a verb. God is being. God is action. God cannot be controlled. God is what God is. God will be what God will be. And the Name of God has the power to heal, to liberate, to save and to destroy.

When Moses says "Here I am" he communicates his attention, presence and availability. But the name of God --"I AM who I AM" -- communicates autonomy, power, and strength.

For those of us who may be in the habit of presuming upon God's friendship, the use of so formal and powerful a tone can be very challenging. We may prefer an approachable and accommodating deity; but we lose a great deal when we presume intimacy with the Divine on a regular basis. The God of Moses possesses unquestionable and unassailable authority. Such authority demands respect and reverence.

If you would like to understand this better, try this. In your prayer time today, honor the power and authority of God and with reverent awe, be still before the Lord who is the Source of all.

Seeking God

Search for the LORD and his strength; continually seek his face. (Psalm 105:4)

If, as we believe, God is present everywhere, why should it be necessary to search at all? Instead, it would seem that we might be in danger of bumping into God every time we turn around!

Of course, the truth is that while we are continually immersed in the blessed presence of the Almighty, most of us manage to remain oblivious to that fact. So the instruction to search for God and to seek God's face is for our benefit. It is a reminder that we must never take the presence of God for granted. We must learn to open our hearts as well as our eyes; and to be observant of the myriad ways God appears to us.

The presence and strength of God are made known to us in the face of a loved one, in the needs of others, in our own spirit (especially when our spirits are troubled) and in even the simplest and most ordinary events of the day. We know, for example, that morning will bring the light of dawn. But do we ever stop to thank the Creator of the universe for the new day with all its potential? Or are we so busy rushing headlong into what lies ahead that we do not see what is right before us?

And there is more. Seeking God's face is about the practice of prayer as well. It takes work and intentionality to search for the Lord; it is only by continually seeking the face of God, and opening ourselves to the encounter that we develop the spiritual muscle which transforms us from a "person who prays" to a "prayerful person." In time, the act of seeking God becomes automatic, and our awareness of God becomes part of our moment-to-moment lives.

For the more we see and know of God, the more we desire to be with God, and the more continually we will seek God's face.

Heads of Coals

"...if your enemies are hungry, feed them; if they are thirsty, give them something to drink; for by doing this you will heap burning coals on their heads." (Romans 12:20)

My mother and her mother both loved this verse – though I often wondered if perhaps there was more than a little perversity at work in their appreciation. Like all children I had been warned about the danger of hot coals, so it seemed odd to me that doing something nice would cause an injury, and that God (or at least St. Paul) would condone such action.

It wasn't until adolescence and the onset of attacks of acute embarrassment that I began to understand. My tendency to blush beet-red and to feel as though I were standing way too close to an open fire taught me what this verse really means.

Doing good things for our enemies, even when we don't feel like, may make them re-examine their own behavior, awaken their conscience, cause them to be ashamed, and change their behavior. That may not work for everyone, but doing the right thing and hoping for a good outcome is a whole lot better than responding in anger and defensiveness thereby increasing the conflict. At least that is how it is supposed to work.

But the question for us is different. Are we capable of feeling ashamed of our own actions? An awareness of our own shortcomings can feel a great deal like a heap of hot coals. We all know what that feels like. And perhaps that is God's way of reminding us that we all stand in need of repentance and forgiveness – and that we should cut others some slack, too!

That is what communion is all about. God is continually seeking to feed us with the bread of life and to offer us the cup of salvation. The difference is that the food and drink of Holy Communion, rather than shaming us into repentance, are signs of the forgiveness that is already ours if we will only receive it.

Confronting Temptation

Jesus turned and said to Peter, "Get behind me Satan! You are a stumbling block to me; for you are setting your mind not on divine things but on human things" (Matthew 16:23)

Within seven verses of this chapter, Jesus moves from naming Peter the rock upon which he will build his church to calling him Satan. What happened?

Satan, as Jesus is using the word here is the "tempter" or the one who shows us options, alternatives, and other paths to take – all with the intention of diverting our attention from what God is calling us to do. So, Peter, who has just demonstrated his love and faith in Jesus by proclaiming him as Messiah, very humanly blunders into acting the role of Satan when he tries to dissuade Jesus from traveling to Jerusalem and his death. Peter acts out of love, and fear for Jesus, but in his humanity, even Jesus must resist taking the easy way out.

I find this very comforting. Even Jesus, in his humanity, must deal with temptation. He must acknowledge and deal with those things which might on the surface seem to be good and helpful, but may not be the best choices.

How does he do this? He prays. He spends time in conversation with God, and in the practice of self-examination. He knows who he is, and he trusts in his relationship with God. Most importantly, Jesus derives strength from that knowledge.

As usual, his example is a good one.

Grafted on Our Hearts

Lord of all power and might, the author and giver of all good things: Graft in our hearts the love of your Name; increase in us true religion; nourish us with all goodness; and bring forth in us the fruit of good works; through Jesus Christ our Lord, who lives and reigns with you and the Holy Spirit, one God for ever and ever. Amen. (Collect for Proper 17)

Walking in the state park the other day, I passed a bench that was covered with carved initials, dates and entwined hearts. Some were decades old, others were newly etched into the wood. When we love someone, especially in the first rush of a new love, we are apt to cherish everything about them – even their name. We speak it, whisper it, shout it, and carve it into our hearts.

This collect asks God to do that for us. Graft in our hearts the love of your Name, O God. Make us so aware of you, we pray, that we love everything about you, including your name.

The Holy Name of God deserves that sort of attention, and that sort of respect. In some traditions the Name of God is too holy to be spoken aloud and a euphemism is used instead. In other traditions, the Name of God is invoked so frequently that we may wonder at the familiarity with which it is employed. Both approaches are attempts to demonstrate the holiness and the power of God. And both are indicative of the centrality of God in the human heart.

When we say this prayer, we might also wonder...Does God's Name occupy a place of such honor in my life?

Marching Orders

This is how you shall eat it: your loins girded, your sandals on your feet, and your staff in your hand; and you shall eat it hurriedly. It is the Passover of the Lord. (Exodus 12:11)

These days, most Passover meals are feasts at which Jewish families linger to share and cherish the memories of their lives and their faith, and the goodness and providence of God.

The first Passover was not such an event. The children of Israel ate hurriedly, packed up and dressed for departure. There was a sense of immediacy and a call to action. Be ready! Eat for the sustenance it will provide you, and be prepared to go forth at a moment's notice.

It is interesting that while the Episcopal Church does not retain the practice of a Passover Seder, it very much preserves the ethos of this verse in the prayer said each week at the end of the Holy Communion. There are multiple forms of this prayer, but each includes some variation on these two phrases: "you have fed us" and "now send us forth".

For Christians, Holy Communion is the Passover Meal. And while it is a joyful celebration of the saving love of God in Christ, it is also a reminder that we are to be a people on the move. We come to the table to be fed for the work ahead; and we come each week so that we may be continually prepared to meet the challenges and opportunities set before us.

When we do not come to the table each week, we risk being malnourished and becoming too weak to share the Good News.

You Are God's Pleasure

For the LORD takes pleasure in his people and adorns the poor with victory. (Psalm 149:4)

It is often difficult to remember that God takes pleasure in us. We are all too ready to remember and lament the times when we know that we have been a disappointment to God, or when we have felt ashamed or unlovable. But how often do we allow ourselves to rest in the unconditional love of God that continually surrounds us?

One of the most famous sermons of the 20th century German Theologian Paul Tillich was titled "You Are Accepted." In it Tillich confronts us with the sometimes uncomfortable truth that we cannot hide behind our own sense of unworthiness. God sees us as redeemed, as beloved, as accepted. That may of course sound like bad news to someone who fears having to live life as one who is loved and accepted. But feeling unworthy is no excuse. God loves us anyway.

God celebrates us. God delights in us. Just as we take delight in the face and voice and presence of those we love, God takes pleasure in us. All of us! What might our lives and our world be like if we took that to heart and behaved as though we believed it to be true? There is only one way to find out.

Stop looking for reasons why God may not like you (and while you are at it, stop looking for reasons why God may not like someone else). Instead, look at yourself and the world around you with appreciation, and with the sort of love that sees the truth and continues to love. We need not be perfect in order to be in the process of being perfected. We are made holy by the love and the word of God. God has all of eternity to do the work necessary to convince us that we are accepted. In the meantime, God already sees the finished project and delights in it.

Love Is All We Need

Owe no one anything, except to love one another; for the one who loves another has fulfilled the law. The commandments, "You shall not commit adultery; You shall not murder; You shall not steal; You shall not covet"; and any other commandment, are summed up in this word, "Love your neighbor as yourself." Love does no wrong to a neighbor; therefore, love is the fulfilling of the law. (Romans 13:8-10)

When we stop to think about it, love is the scariest thing on earth! Think of all the things that are easier than loving. Wars? Isolation? Fear? Anger? All these, even with their devastating consequences, are easier than loving. If that were not the case, why would we even need laws? Laws exist to command good and loving behavior – or at least to place a limit on the damage we might otherwise do. The sanctions of the law do not inspire love, but they do confront us with the consequences of disobedience. And knowing the consequences of breaking a law allows us to choose how far we will go and how much punishment we are willing to take. It's easy to figure out what it will cost us.

Love, on the other hand, is an all or nothing proposition. We may know of folks who find it difficult to say "I love you." Such people are often described as being incapable of commitment or trust. But perhaps they are simply more honest than the rest of us. They may not be willing to speak words that they are not willing to support by their actions.

If we understand love and if we attempt to live in love, then we are committing ourselves to the long haul of life in relationship to God. We relinquish the option of deciding who or what is worthy of love and we embrace the Biblical standard. Love your neighbor as yourself – which by the way also encompasses the command to love yourself as you deserve to be loved. Love does not discriminate in its demands.

Love fulfills the law because it moves choice from the individual to the universal. If I love, I must love everyone. If I cannot or will not do that, I still need the law to keep me from hurting another.

St. Paul might not have appreciated John Lennon's musical style, but I am certain that he would endorse his theme…"All you need is love."

Don't Try to Go It Alone

Jesus said, "If another member of the church sins against you; go and point out the fault when the two of you are alone. If the member listens to you, you have regained that one. But if you are not listened to, take one or two others along with you, so that every word may be confirmed by the evidence of two or three witnesses. If the member refuses to listen to them, tell it to the church; and if the offender refuses to listen even to the church, let such a one be to you as a Gentile and a tax collector. (Matthew 18:15-17)

This passage sounds fairly harsh, doesn't it? Point out the offense, give the offender several opportunities to repent, and if that doesn't work, cast her out of the community.

It would harsh if this were only about how to deal with injury and offense. But there is a much deeper meaning here. What Jesus is pointing out is the very serious nature of life in community. Living in community means that there will be many opportunities for personalities to bump up against each other. Nerves will fray and tempers will flare. Conflict will be inevitable, which is why we need a process for dealing with conflict. Such a process will provide stability, honesty and accountability. Without a means of addressing conflict the community will collapse.

The whole point of community is shared life around a shared purpose. And for Christians, the most visible sign of community (perhaps even more so than family) is the Church. The Church is the visible expression of the Body of Christ in the world and how its members behave is a reflection of what they believe about God. So we need to turn things around and see that this passage is not nearly so much about how to treat someone who has sinned against an individual, as it is an example of how far the community must be willing to go to seek reconciliation. We are to model our behavior for life in community on the example of Jesus who instructed his disciples to forgive a penitent brother a nearly unimaginable 7 x 70 times, but who also said "if they will not listen to you, shake the dust from your sandals and move on." We need to remember both.

All of us stand in need of repentance and forgiveness – those in community even more so.

Genuine Agreement

Truly I tell you, whatever you bind on earth will be bound in heaven, and whatever you loose on earth will be loosed in heaven. Again, truly I tell you, if two of you agree on earth about anything you ask, it will be done for you by my Father in heaven. For where two or three are gathered in my name, I am there among them." (Matthew 18:18-20)

Of all the places in Scripture where I am tempted to take things literally and completely out of context, this one ranks in the top five (along with "but not a hair of your head will perish"!) It would be great to know that God would hear and answer all my prayers if I just asked for everything in the name of Jesus.

Of course, Jesus is giving us the benefit of the doubt that we understand his meaning. When we ask for something that that is in accord with God's will and that God wants us to have, it will be granted. Not "stuff" of course, but an awareness of the presence and blessing of Christ in our lives, and the strength to do the tasks before us. Besides, this is a case where the majority clearly does not rule. It's not about the number of people who ask, but about the nature of the request. Religious history is strewn with the debris of inappropriate requests and the arrogance of power.

Also, the part about whatever you bind on earth will be bound in heaven is neither permission nor authority to control eternity. Jesus is just pointing out that our actions have consequences and that sometimes those consequences follow us for a very long time.

So, what is Jesus promising us? The exact same things he always promises. "I am with you." If we stop to think about it, that is more than enough.

With All Our Hearts

Grant us, O Lord, to trust in you with all our hearts; for, as you always resist the proud who confide in their own strength, so you never forsake those who make their boast of your mercy; through Jesus Christ our Lord, who lives and reigns with you and the Holy Spirit, one God, now and for ever. Amen. (Collect for Proper 18)

I have to admit that trusting God with my whole heart is a task I have never accomplished. There is a part of me that is always withholding some part of my heart – just in case God fails me and I have to step in and clean things up myself. It's sort of my contingency plan. Talk about proud!

But this collect points out the moral dangers of relying entirely on ourselves. Most of us grew up thinking that "God helps those who help themselves" comes from the Bible rather than from "Poor Richard's Almanac." And it is a sentiment that dovetails beautifully with the American dream of endless horizons and limitless possibilities for the rugged and stout of heart individual.

Humility does not come to us naturally; nor does trust. Anyone over the age of three has experienced enough disappointed wishes to be a bit skeptical. But that is precisely the point. Trusting completely in God is counter-intuitive; but trusting in God is what God requires of us.

So, although I have not yet succeeded in complete trust, I am now at least aware that I am holding back a part of my heart. And I am aware that I am doing so to my detriment. And perhaps that awareness is slowly and gradually helping me learn to offer God my humble and growing trust.

Fear of the Lord

Thus the LORD saved Israel that day from the Egyptians; and Israel saw the Egyptians dead on the seashore. Israel saw the great work that the LORD did against the Egyptians. So the people feared the LORD and believed in the LORD and in his servant Moses. (Exodus 14:31)

How can fear possibly be the foundation for a meaningful relationship? Even if, as we know, the meaning of the word "fear" has changed over the millennia and the scriptural use of the word is much closer to reverent awe and respect, why should we applaud the death of another, even if that person is our enemy?

The account of the Exodus from Egypt is rife with such "cringe" moments. Someone offends God – God acts to destroy the offender – the survivors rejoice and their faith is strengthened by the renewal of their fear.

Times have changed, I know; and the language and experience of one generation do not easily translate to that of another. But when we read these stories and feel the narrative crash over us like the returning waters of the red sea, it is challenging to see how a 3500 year old description of God as avenging liberator will appeal to a 21st century listener.

It is essential then, for each of us to know God through study, community, and the daily discipline of prayer. When we are thus prepared, we are able to see ourselves as part of a family whose understanding of the nature of God has been shaped by our history, and whose experience of one another is inextricably linked to our relationship to our Creator. And we will know that the violence of Scripture is rooted, not in the actions of God, but of the projections of humanity.

Lord of All Creation

What ailed you, O sea, that you fled?
O Jordan, that you turned back?
You mountains, that you skipped like rams?
you little hills like young sheep?
Tremble, O earth, at the presence of the Lord,
at the presence of the God of Jacob,
Who turned the hard rock into a pool of water
and flint-stone into a flowing spring. (Psalm 114:5-8)

These verses are a beautiful example of the manner in which the Psalmist views God's relationship to creation. The seas and mountains, rocks and waters, even the earth itself are aware of and capable of responding to the presence of God with appropriate reverence and delight. The metaphors are a lovely expression of the intimacy God shares with all things created.

And even more important, these verses remind us that in God's economy, we are all linked one to another. The providential hand of God cares for us and sustains us with the gifts of air, water and sea at the same time that we are charged with stewardship over these elemental blessings.

There is nothing outside the scope of God's love. There is nothing too large, or small, too lofty or too basic as to lie outside the sphere of God's attention or the reach of God's embrace. And if even these examples of inanimate objects carry the ability to praise and respect God, it certainly behooves us to remember that we, too, are to be vehicles of the wonder, love and praise due to our Creator.

The Path to God

Welcome those who are weak in faith, but not for the purpose of quarreling over opinions. Some believe in eating anything, while the weak eat only vegetables. Those who eat must not despise those who abstain, and those who abstain must not pass judgment on those who eat; for God has welcomed them. Who are you to pass judgment on servants of another? It is before their own lord that they stand or fall. And they will be upheld, for the Lord is able to make them stand. (Romans 14:1-4)

I have read that when we meet someone for the first time we make an almost instantaneous assessment of them. We judge them based on gender, age, race, physical attractiveness, and all the subtle cues of body language. This first impression decision is not only very often incomplete, it is frequently incorrect. So just what is it about being human that allows us think that we are qualified to make judgments about others?

I suspect that the cause is rooted in our own fears and insecurities. If the only way that I can feel certain that I am acceptable is to be aligned with the majority, then I will, at best, be condescending toward the minority. Worse, I may feel proud of my own comfortable status. Unfortunately, this tendency toward judgment is often most evident in faith communities. When the stakes are as high as our fears about our status in eternity, being "safe" is easily defined as being "right."

In this passage, St. Paul reminds us that there is much, much more to our faith than what we eat or wear or drink, even more than how we interpret a particular portion of doctrine. The only allowable standard is one which does not lie within the sphere of our ability to judge. As God welcomes us all, and as only God is worthy to judge, should we not be as loving, supportive and accommodating as possible?

After all, the only judgment with which we need to be concerned is God's opinion of our own lives and behaviors.

The Living and the Dead

We do not live to ourselves, and we do not die to ourselves. If we live, we live to the Lord, and if we die, we die to the Lord; so then, whether we live or whether we die, we are the Lord's. (Romans 14:7-8)

These lines appear in the opening anthem of the Burial Office and every time I read them at a funeral, I am struck by their utter simplicity. We are, all of us and all the time, in the hands of God. Our status, our future and our identity lies in that fact.

So, isn't it odd then how often we forget that our very being derives from the grace and power of God? Or that we spend so much time trying to make a name and a life for ourselves? We all do it, and I am certainly not disparaging our attempts to make a difference, to be cherished, or to live loving and meaningful lives; it just seems to me that if we were to remember these words each day, our lives would be happier and our hearts more peaceful.

As usual, it's a question of perspective. Do we begin and end each day with the conscious awareness of the sovereignty of God, or do we plow ahead with our own agendas until we are thwarted by life or crash into the wall of our own limitations?

God is not likely to see to it that I accomplish all that I set out to do; nor is God likely to approve each of my plans. The point is that if I start out with the acknowledgment that I am in God's hands no matter what, then my plans and choices might be more in line with the will of God.

Beyond Measure

Peter came and said to Jesus, "Lord, if another member of the church sins against me, how often should I forgive? As many as seven times?" Jesus said to him, "Not seven times, but, I tell you, seventy-seven times. (Matthew 18:21)

This is one of those passages when I can imagine the disciples shaking their heads in dismay at the extremism of Jesus. The more literal among them might ask, "Are you serious??? We might as well forgive everybody all the time." To which I can hear Jesus exclaiming, "Right! You are to forgive as many times as it takes."

That sounds like a morally and mentally expensive exercise. But the truth is that the real cost of such radical forgiveness lies in the loss of power over the offender. If we are to forgive as many times as it takes, then forgiveness ceases to be a bargaining chip in the game of life, and we abandon the option of making others pay for their mistakes. In essence we set them free.

But even more importantly, we also set ourselves free from the sin of holding a grudge, or assuming power over another person's life. Maintaining anger, holding a grudge, and taking charge of another's business are great consumers of psychic and spiritual energy. When that energy is freed up, we can focus it on the real work of the kingdom – proclaiming by word and example the Good News of God in Christ.

So, if you are carrying around the weight of refusing to forgive, set it down. It will only grow heavier with time. Besides, you will be utterly amazed at how much more time you will have for doing things that really matter.

Asking for Directions

O God, because without you we are not able to please you mercifully grant that your Holy Spirit may in all things direct and rule our hearts; through Jesus Christ our Lord, who lives and reigns with you and the Holy Spirit, one God, now and for ever. Amen. (Collect for Proper 19)

Gender stereotypes aside, some people simply refuse to ask for directions. They seem to think it a sign of weakness not to be able to figure out such things on their own. Others are all too willing to ask for directions but then simply ignore them because they figure their own way is better. Then there are those like me who ask and receive but get lost anyway. In each of these instances, something essential is missing. The first group is too proud to admit that they don't know, the second group is too arrogant to believe that someone else might know better, and the third group needs to learn how to listen to and follow directions.

The good news is that the folks in each group eventually find their way to where they were going. The bad news is that a great deal of time (not to mention peace of mind) is usually wasted in the process.

The same thing is true in terms of following God. In this collect, we acknowledge that none of us is able to do things perfectly. We all need help and direction. But God has provided that assistance through the work of the Holy Spirit. All we have to do is get over our pride and let the Spirit guide us.

Granted, that means that we have to let God rule in our hearts, and that may be even more challenging than asking for directions; but once we agree to let God be God, the burden tends to get lighter, and we find our way more easily.

A Venerable Tradition

The whole congregation of the Israelites complained against Moses and Aaron in the wilderness. The Israelites said to them, "If only we had died by the hand of the LORD in the land of Egypt, when we sat by the fleshpots and ate our fill of bread; for you have brought us out into this wilderness to kill this whole assembly with hunger." (Exodus 16:2-3)

Two truisms about human nature: Complaining about the actions of those in authority is a nearly universal human practice; and the shorter our memories the louder the complaint. Everyone needs something, has an opinion, or wants to register a grievance, and God help the leader who delays or disappoints. This is where Moses and Aaron find themselves when the journey into the wilderness turns into something other than a short stroll to a belly-buster of a picnic.

Is it possible that their memories are really that short? Have they already forgotten not only the misery of slavery but their miraculous deliverance from captivity? No, they haven't forgotten, but as with most of us, the best thing that has ever happened in their lives is part of a "Yes, but what have you done for me lately?" mindset. "Yes we are free now, but what good is that if we starve to death?"

Clearly, what is missing is trust. If the solution to their problem is not immediately obvious or the food is not yet on the table, how can they believe that God will provide? They know what God has already done, but they don't yet believe that the relationship is trustworthy. They can only behave as though it is true. That's a big part of learning to trust; and part of the growth of an individual or a nation is learning to wait in trust.

Imagine how much more enjoyable our lives would be if we were able to stop anticipating the worst and to end the practice of second-guessing everyone else's actions and motives. Once again, it depends on where we start. We can either start out doubting and expecting catastrophe or we can decide to trust until something demonstrates that our trust is misplaced. It might not have taken forty years to cross the Sinai desert if the people had trusted Moses and Aaron; and we might shorten our own years in the desert if we gave it a shot as well.

The Proof in the Pudding

The LORD spoke to Moses and said, "I have heard the complaining of the Israelites; say to them, `At twilight you shall eat meat, and in the morning you shall have your fill of bread; then you shall know that I am the LORD your God.'" (Exodus 16:11-12)

Complaining is a tricky business. You want to make sure that you get your point across but that you don't completely alienate the person or power to which you are complaining -- which is what makes God's words to Moses in this passage somewhat ominous. "I have heard their complaints. If meat and bread are what is required to convince them that I am their God, then they shall have meat and bread." (In the book of Exodus, the language is mild, but in Numbers 11:20 God tells Moses that the people shall have meat to eat until it comes out of their noses.)

Still, when I think of the times that hearing complaints has prompted me to alter my plans, and how I irritated I have been when that happened, I am utterly amazed at God's patience with the children of Israel -- as though they are complaining children who are too busy whining to be spoken to as adults.

The irony is that while the writer of Exodus states that God is testing the obedience of the people, they are also testing the patience of God with their demands – for food, water, shelter, protection, even for religious security (remember the golden calf). I shudder to think how often my own prayers and petitions resemble those of the children of Israel. "I need... I want... Please help me..."

If I stack them up side by side, I have to admit that my petitions far exceed my praises – just as my fears far outweigh my trust. God's loving presence with the people is physically demonstrated by providing for their basic human needs. Perhaps our love should be proven by our gratitude and trust.

God Remembers

For God remembered his holy word and Abraham his servant.
So he led forth his people with gladness, his chosen with shouts of joy.
Psalm 105:42-43)

For the children of Israel it probably seemed that God had forgotten them during the centuries they languished as slaves in Egypt. And it probably seemed that God did not remember them until Moses was sent to lead them from captivity.

But does God forget?

There is all the difference in the world between a human's ability to remember something and God's acts of remembrance. When we remember, we often do so because we have forgotten and are startled into awareness. From the divine perspective, however, memory is an ongoing process. God never "forgets" as we do. Instead, God continually holds us in remembrance. Because we function within the context of time, it may seem to us that God is focusing on something else at the moment, but for God that is not the case. God is always about the business of liberation, salvation and love, and God does not forget us.

It is very challenging to live "in time" while worshipping God who is "time-less, time-full, and outside of time." We have to trust that God always acts "in the fullness of time" and that God alone knows when that moment arrives. Then we, too, are led forth with shouts of joy.

Living Up to Our Potential

Only, live your life in a manner worthy of the gospel of Christ, (Philippians 1:27a)

I have heard a phrase at several funerals lately. "His/Hers was a life well-lived." In each case, the speaker meant that the deceased had been fully engaged in living, had loved and been loved, and had made a real difference in the lives of others. As it turns out, these were also folks who had loved God and had been devoted and faithful members of their worship communities. They had lived lives worthy of the people and ideas they cherished.

I think that is what St. Paul is talking about in this verse from Philippians. What does it mean to live a life worthy of the Gospel? The answer is surprisingly simple and enormously challenging. A life worthy of the Gospel is a life in which we love God with all our heart and our neighbors as ourselves. We will never be perfect, of course, but if we really love Jesus, our lives will show it and our actions will be demonstrations of our faith.

Living a life worthy of the Gospel requires a daily commitment to prayer and to action in the name of Christ. It requires a generosity of spirit, a sense of humility, an open and loving heart, the willingness to forgive and to seek forgiveness, and the ability to trust that the love of God embraces all people. And it takes a lifetime.

So it really is a help that it can be summed up in the simplicity of the Great Commandment: Love God with all your heart and your neighbor as yourself. And it is even more helpful that Jesus has shown us how and stands beside us as we seek to travel in his path.

A Very Narrow Lens

...they grumbled against the landowner, saying, `These last worked only one hour, and you have made them equal to us who have borne the burden of the day and the scorching heat.' But he replied to one of them, `Friend, I am doing you no wrong; did you not agree with me for the usual daily wage? Take what belongs to you and go; I choose to give to this last the same as I give to you. Am I not allowed to do what I choose with what belongs to me? Or are you envious because I am generous?' (Matthew 20:11b-15)

Grace that can be calculated or expected is no longer grace. And this passage is all about grace. That may be difficult for us to see because we are confused by questions of equality and justice and fair play. But this is not about labor practices. And it is certainly not about justice.

When Jesus begins this parable he says, "The kingdom of heaven is like a landowner." That should serve as an immediate clue that Jesus is about to set us up and pull the rug out from under us. Our rules and expectations don't apply here. In this parable the landowner has a personal relationship with each of the workers. Landowners don't generally go out to do their own hiring. They send an overseer or a foreman to do that. And landowners don't negotiate pay scales with individuals. Landowners do, however, have the right to do what they wish with their property.

The parable surprises us because the kingdom of heaven/reign of God supersedes human expectations. Grace is freely, even extravagantly, poured upon all whom God chooses. In fact, if we understand the concept of grace, there is absolutely no reason for any of us to question the abundance of its presence in the life of another. God loves because God chooses to love, not because the love has been earned.

Grace is a free gift and we would do well to concentrate on being grateful for the blessing of our own lives rather than worrying about whether we are being treated fairly.

A Non-Anxious Presence

Grant us, Lord, not to be anxious about earthly things, but to love things heavenly; and even now, while we are placed among things that are passing away, to hold fast to those that shall endure; through Jesus Christ our Lord, who lives and reigns with you and the Holy Spirit, one God, for ever and ever. Amen. (Collect for Proper 20)

It seems as though it is exactly at those moments when I am feeling most stressed out, frustrated, and ineffectual that I will encounter someone who is preternaturally calm, attentive and competent. Such as person is exhibiting what psychologists describe as a "non-anxious presence." I hate it when that happens – mainly because it reminds me of how anxious and easily distracted I am.

But, as this prayer points out, part of our Christian vocation is to learn to live our lives with one eye on heaven and one here on earth. Life is teeming with temptations to anxiety, and if we succumb to those temptations we may find ourselves perpetually trudging along on a treadmill of worry. That's why it's essential to be able to discern and cling to what is permanent and enduring rather than having our energy and spirits drained by things that will in time pass.

We can only do this through the grace of God, and that grace, which continually surrounds us, is most easily accessed by prayer. For those of us who are not by nature "non-anxious presences" a daily discipline of prayer and meditation is our best response. May God grant us the grace to let go of those things that we cannot fix or change, and to abide in the loving presence of God in the here and now.

Test and Quarrel

The Lord said to Moses, "Go on ahead of the people, and take some of the elders of Israel with you; take in your hand the staff with which you struck the Nile, and go. I will be standing there in front of you on the rock at Horeb. Strike the rock, and water will come out of it, so that the people may drink." Moses did so, in the sight of the elders of Israel. He called the place Massah and Meribah, because the Israelites quarreled and tested the Lord, saying, "Is the Lord among us or not?" (Exodus 17:5-7)

When my sons were small, I had much more patience for downright disobedience than for whining. After all, disobedience was at least an indication of initiative. But whining and wheedling drove me right up the proverbial wall.

I wonder if Moses felt the same way about the children of Israel, and if that is why he acted out his frustration by naming the water source Massah (test) and Meribah (quarrel). And I wonder if humanity's continual plea for proof of God's presence tries God's patience and mercy even more than our sins.

It seems that we are incapable of trusting God's word without instant responses to our perceived needs and constant demonstrations of favor. So test and quarrel remain apt descriptions of our spiritual nature. Not very complimentary, is it?

A different approach is embodied in this old Baptist Hymn.

When we walk with the Lord, in the light of his love,
what a glory he sheds on our way.
While we do his good will, he abides with us still,
and with all who will trust and obey.
Trust and Obey, for there's no other way
to be happy in Jesus but to trust and obey.

It isn't easy, but it will see us through many a journey through the wilderness.

Tell Me a Story

That which we have heard and known, and what our forefathers have told us,
we will not hide from their children.
We will recount to generations to come
the praiseworthy deeds and the power of the LORD,
and the wonderful works he has done. (Psalm 78:3-4)

It has been said that the family that prays together stays together. I think it is equally accurate to say that the family that shares stories is a stronger, healthier family. As parents we are admonished to read to our children so that they will learn to appreciate books. Shouldn't we also be encouraged to tell our children our family and cultural and religious stories so that they will know who they are and where they come from?

Stories are the life-breath of a people; and when the story is lost, much more than identity is sacrificed. Stories communicate values, history, dreams and challenges. They also teach us to look deeper than the surface. The same great-aunt who can no longer walk or who sits silently in the corner may have been an athlete, a singer, or an outspoken advocate for women's rights.
But no one will ever know if her story is not told.

That is why liturgy and worship must include narrative. Every Psalm, every song, every prayer tells a story of the people of God. And each of those stories contributes to the life-story of the listener, the singer and the prayer. That is also why Sunday School is so very important. We neither live nor die in a vacuum, and what one family or community may be lacking is preserved and presented to us through our faith stories.

God has made you a character in an unending story. It's up to you to play your part and to pass the story on.

The Test of Humility

If then there is any encouragement in Christ, any consolation from love, any sharing in the Spirit, any compassion and sympathy, make my joy complete: be of the same mind, having the same love, being in full accord and of one mind. Do nothing from selfish ambition or conceit, but in humility regard others as better than yourselves. Let each of you look not to your own interests, but to the interests of others. (Philippians 2:1-4)

Only very rarely is an individual naturally humble. It does happen that some folk are born with the ability to see and appreciate the importance of others, and the desire to quietly step aside so that others may move ahead. The rest of us are pretty much always defending our own turf, having our say, and demanding our share of attention and reward. Some would say that our innate drive for self-promotion is a biological necessity. St. Paul, who knew as much about pride and defensiveness as anyone, would disagree. For him the most important thing was the building up of the Body of Christ, and the example of loving consensus among its members.

St. Paul understood that the Church was under the constant scrutiny of those who could not believe that it was possible to live in harmony while embracing the teaching of Christ and the leading of the Holy Spirit. Having set so high and frequently unsustainable a standard for itself made the Church a natural target for accusations of hypocrisy. But that was not, and is not, an excuse for shaping the identity of the Church after that of the world.

Even if it does not come naturally we are, with the grace of God and the support of the Body, capable of choosing to behave with humility. We can learn to listen before speaking, to recognize and to temper our ambition, and to give the needs and desires of others as much standing as our own.

When we choose to behave with humility, we present a very different face to the world – imperfect, but not hypocritical.

Sharing the Mind of Christ

Let the same mind be in you that was in Christ Jesus, who, though he was in the form of God, did not regard equality with God as something to be exploited, but emptied himself, taking the form of a slave, being born in human likeness. And being found in human form, he humbled himself and became obedient to the point of death-- even death on a cross. (Philippians 2:5-8)

So, how do we, who are clearly imperfect, share the mind of Christ? For St. Paul the most important thing about the work of Christ in the world was something called "kenosis" or self-emptying. The two natures of Christ, human and divine, had to cooperate in relinquishing any power or privilege in Jesus' divinity, and any ambition and selfishness in his humanity. So Jesus declined to use his power as Son of God to do things his own way; and refused to succumb to any human inclination to take the easy way out. He lived, worked and died in obedient humility; and he did it all within the context of his humanity to show us that it was, with the grace of God, possible.

The Mind of Christ is focused on loving obedience to God, and obedience to God both requires and produces humility. Our orientation, then, is also to be toward seeking, discerning and acting upon the will of God – an orientation which can only be sustained with the model of Christ before us and the empowering presence of the Holy Spirit alongside us. But, as St. Paul clearly knew, such a life is far more easily lived within the context of community.

In community we are able to support one another in the work, to share the work of discernment, to lovingly correct one another when we go off track, and to spread the Good News to those who may not yet have heard it.

The Mind of Christ led Jesus to kenosis, to radical love, and ultimately to death. It is unlikely to lead us to physical death, but it will lead us to the death of pride and arrogance and into the new life of obedient humility.

Word or Deed?

"What do you think? A man had two sons; he went to the first and said, `Son, go and work in the vineyard today.' He answered, `I will not'; but later he changed his mind and went. The father went to the second and said the same; and he answered, `I go, sir'; but he did not go. Which of the two did the will of his father?" They said, "The first." (Matthew 21:28-31a)

Repentance trumps regret. It is quite possible that the second son felt really awful about promising to do something that he failed to do. It is also possible that there was a really good reason why he couldn't work that day or that he went to his father, apologized and explained his absence. But in none of those cases was he present where he said he would be when he promised to be there.

The first son, however, simply refuses to go. We don't know why he refused, and there may have been any number of legitimate reasons for his having done so. But we do know that in the end, he placed his father's will and his own filial responsibility above his own desires. He went to work.

Life is rarely as clear-cut as some of the parables that Jesus used to illustrate his teaching. But when it comes to discerning and obeying the will of God, such parables reveal an inescapable truth. Obedience is not a question of verbal assent. Obedience requires action.

Notice that Jesus does not say that one son was good and the other was bad. Nor does Jesus suggest that one was rewarded and the other punished. He simply presents the question of obedience as clearly (in fact starkly) as possible. One son did as he was instructed, the other did not.

Obedience may be based on fear, of course. But in this case, when both sons have a choice about what to do, it is evident that obedience is based on respect. One son chooses to respect his father and honors the father's command. The other son chooses to do as he wishes and acts in a way that neither honors nor respects his father's will.

Flights of Mercy

O God, you declare your almighty power chiefly in showing mercy and pity: Grant us the fullness of your grace, that we, running to obtain your promises, may become partakers of your heavenly treasure. (Collect for Proper 21)

Only the genuinely powerful can be merciful for mercy is the abridgment of power. God, who has all power, does not focus on judgment and condemnation. God gives us time to learn, opportunity to change, and the grace to recognize the need for growth.

God invites us to partake in the treasures of heaven, and to take our place at the Eucharistic table where we receive the medicine that heals our souls and strengthens us for the race we run.

But ours is not a race that merely exhausts us. Running for the promises of God is an exhilarating experience in which we can feel our bodies, our spirits and our minds functioning as a whole, working in unity, stretching forward toward the goal of knowing God, and of being fully known.

Mystery of Prayer

"Almighty and everlasting God, you are always more ready to hear than we to pray, and to give more than we either desire or deserve." (Collect for Proper 22)

I have recently come up against the paradox of "scheduling prayer." I know that if I did not have the practice of making time each day for morning and evening prayer, and for quiet contemplation, that I would find innumerable excuses for skipping it. On the other hand, the practice of having the time set apart has made it even more obvious to me that the time I spend in prayer is miniscule compared to the time that I spend on the treadmill of worry, and busy-ness.

This collect really speaks to me. Whether I am consciously on my knees in prayer, or leading worship, or hastily throwing intercessions toward heaven between appointments, God is always there, listening, and ready to hear. But that is not all, God already desires to give me much more than I can even imagine, let alone desire or deserve.

Prayer is a mystery. It is an action that joins the human soul to God and opens us to the possibility of being formed into that which God desires us to be. What we often forget is that no matter how much we may ask God to guide, direct, change or inspire us, we can never begin to approach an understanding of the blessings that God already intends for us.

True prayer is this. To put oneself in the presence of God and to ask for God alone. No bargaining, no promises, no desperate pleas. To pray is to say, simply, "Here I am God" and to be open to what God wishes to do.

In my opinion, the best expression of this attitude of prayer comes from Julian of Norwich when she prays:

"God, of your goodness, give me yourself. For you are enough to me, and I can ask for nothing less that is to your glory. And if I ask for anything else, I shall always be in want, for only in you have I all."

Amen. And Amen. And let all the people say "Amen."

Prevenient Grace

Lord, we pray that your grace may always precede and follow us, that we may continually be given to good works; through Jesus Christ our Lord, who lives and reigns with you and the Holy Spirit, one God, now and forever. Amen. (Collect for Proper 23)

The best definition I know for prevenient grace (the grace of God that precedes, accompanies, and follows us throughout our lives) comes from "Carousel." It is an anthem giving voice to the assurance that no matter what happens, God is with us.

When you walk through a storm keep your chin up high
And don't be afraid of the dark.
At the end of the storm is a golden sky and the sweet silver song of a lark.
Walk on through the wind, Walk on through the rain,
Tho' your dreams be tossed and blown.
Walk on, walk on with hope in your heart
and you'll never walk alone, you'll never walk alone.

I know that this song is one that will stay with you the rest of the day, so I will simply invite you to let the words of this Collect join it as you hum your way through the next 24 hours. (I also cannot help but wonder if Rodgers and Hammerstein had read the words of Scripture that inspired this Collect.)

The grace of God does precede and follow us, and God does this out of love for us; but not solely for our safety and reassurance. The grace of God precedes and follows us so that we can "do good works". Those good works are a visible manifestation of the presence of God being made real in the world.

Some of those good works are possible of our own volition. Much good is done in the world simply because someone desires to do good things. But the only way that we can be <u>continually</u> given to good works is to be aware of and to tap into the continually present prevenient grace of God. When we do that, the storms and tempests of life cannot overcome us. And when we are not overcome, we cannot be deterred from doing the good work to which God calls us.

God Goes With Us

Moses said to the LORD, "See, you have said to me, `Bring up this people'; but you have not let me know whom you will send with me. Yet you have said, `I know you by name, and you have also found favor in my sight.' Now if I have found favor in your sight, show me your ways, so that I may know you and find favor in your sight. Consider too that this nation is your people." He said, "My presence will go with you, and I will give you rest." And he said to him, "If your presence will not go, do not carry us up from here. For how shall it be known that I have found favor in your sight, I and your people, unless you go with us? In this way, we shall be distinct, I and your people, from every people on the face of the earth." (Exodus 33:12-16)

I was present one evening when my three year old grandson was having a bed-time melt-down. Each time his mom and dad would tell him goodnight and close the door, he would scream and pitifully plead "Please don't leave me!" until they returned to reassure him that he was not alone. It was nerve-wracking, heart-wrenching, and only partly tantrum. He really didn't want to stay up later. He just didn't want to be alone.

With all due respect to Moses, I think he is having a similar conversation with God. At this point in the Exodus, Moses is tired of standing in the breach between God and the people. His testiness is all the more evident as he realizes that his credibility before the people is fading fast and that he needs some assurance that God is indeed not going to leave him. He seems to be saying, "I really need some help here, God. They won't respect me as a prophet and we won't be known as your people unless you are with us. Please don't leave me."

It's a conversation that we all have with our parents, our partners, our friends, and our God. More than anything else we tend to fear abandonment. And even the Moses types among us need reassurance. Holy Scripture is replete with examples of God's promise that we are not alone, that we will not be abandoned, and that God will never desert us. It is a characteristic of our humanity that we forget and that we doubt. But God's word to us remains: "I am with you always."

A Cleft of the Rock

The LORD said to Moses, "I will do the very thing that you have asked; for you have found favor in my sight, and I know you by name." Moses said, "Show me your glory, I pray." And he said, "I will make all my goodness pass before you, and will proclaim before you the name, `The LORD'; and I will be gracious to whom I will be gracious, and will show mercy on whom I will show mercy. But," he said, "you cannot see my face; for no one shall see me and live." And the LORD continued, "See, there is a place by me where you shall stand on the rock; and while my glory passes by I will put you in a cleft of the rock, and I will cover you with my hand until I have passed by; then I will take away my hand, and you shall see my back; but my face shall not be seen." (Exodus 33:17-23)

Having received God's promise that Israel will be accompanied by the presence of God in its journey, Moses asks for just one more thing. "Show me your glory, I pray." God agrees to show Moses God's goodness and to bestow grace and mercy upon him, but not even Moses, the greatest of all prophets, may see the face of God. There is a lesson for all of us in that. We cannot, in this life, see the face of God and live. We are not yet able to withstand such glory, though we trust that in eternity we may.

And yet, God does not deny Moses the experience of being present as the Divine passes by. Instead, God places Moses in the cleft of the rock. Moses cannot see God's face, but remains on the rock, shielded by the hand of God from the consequences of viewing anything other than God's back.

In such a casual and informal age as ours, when no one and nothing is beyond the scrutiny of public opinion, the concept of the unimaginable Glory of God eludes us. We are casual in our prayers, and in our worship of God, and should we scratch deeply enough we would no doubt discover that we no longer believe in the life-altering power of holiness and glory. Yet each day God, gently, lovingly and providentially continues to shelter us in the cleft of the rock while Glory passes by closely enough for us to touch.

Forgiveness and Consequences

*O LORD our God, you answered them indeed; **
you were a God who forgave them,
yet punished them for their evil deeds. (Psalm 99:8)

It is indeed a hard lesson when we learn that forgiveness does not erase consequences. The slate may indeed by wiped clean of the sum that we owe for our actions but echoes of those actions remain and reverberate throughout our lives.

How would the definition of forgiveness change if it meant that all memory and effect of the sin or injury were expunged along with the guilt of the penitent? It has been said that sin is inevitable the life and experience of human beings. Others have seen sin as one of the injuries of life subject to the healing grace of God in eternity. The fact remains, though, that in this life, the repercussions of sin are not erased even when the sin is forgiven. We bear in our own lives the marks of our sins, just as clearly as we bear the signs of age and illness. They become part of who and what we are. They demonstrate our humanity and our need for God.

Thus, when God hears the pleas of the children of Israel, they are forgiven and restored, but they cannot in this life escape the outcome of their actions.

We may perceive those outcomes as the natural consequences of what we have done; or we may experience them as God's wrath and punishment upon us for the violation of divine law. In either case, the effect will be the same. We will still need compassion and forgiveness; and having faced and endured the results of our willful disobedience, we will be all the more aware of our need for the compassion and mercy of God.

God will, in God's time and grace, heal us; even if part of that healing may be the painful awareness of the cost of our actions. But in the end, as Dame Julian writes, for those who are to be saved (and she believed that all would be saved), all shall be well.

Power and Conviction

For we know, brothers and sisters beloved by God, that he has chosen you, because our message of the gospel came to you not in word only, but also in power and in the Holy Spirit and with full conviction; (I Thessalonians 1:4-5)

When the Good News of God in Christ takes root in a community, its people are changed. Hearing the word of God is only the beginning. It is only when that word is embodied in the life of a people whose conviction is empowered by the Holy Spirit that the message can be proclaimed. No one since the time of Jonah has been moved or converted by a bored or indifferent apostle. And in that humorous example, even Jonah's prophetic petulance is over-ridden by the grace of God.

It is a dangerous thing indeed for a community to consider itself serenely safe in the familiarity of its calm and studied worship. The Holy Spirit moves where it will and awakens those whose spiritual slumber is not yet too deep. And when that happens new life and conviction follow.

Each of us should be prepared to be moved by the Spirit – in whatever form the Spirit chooses. Some are moved toward quiet rededication; others are filled with enthusiasm. Each is evidence of the power of the Spirit moving among the faithful, and each has work to do.

And as powerful as the spoken word appears to be to us today, it is not the final demonstration of the presence of God in a community. Word leads to conviction which in turn leads to action. And action in the world in the name of Christ brings the Gospel to life in the world.

Loyalty Tests

The Pharisees went and plotted to entrap Jesus in what he said. So they sent their disciples to him, along with the Herodians, saying, "Teacher, we know that you are sincere, and teach the way of God in accordance with truth, and show deference to no one; for you do not regard people with partiality. Tell us, then, what you think. Is it lawful to pay taxes to the emperor, or not?" But Jesus, aware of their malice, said, "Why are you putting me to the test, you hypocrites? Show me the coin used for the tax." And they brought him a denarius. Then he said to them, "Whose head is this, and whose title?" They answered, "The emperor's." Then he said to them, "Give therefore to the emperor the things that are the emperor's, and to God the things that are God's." When they heard this, they were amazed; and they left him and went away. (Matthew 22:15-22)

Beware of theologians asking secular questions – especially when those questions masquerade as matters of the spirit.

The Pharisees have no interest in whether or not secular coins may be used to pay Roman taxes. Had they presented a coin from the temple, they might at least have been able to engage Jesus in a conversation about money. As it is, they attempt to trick him into commenting on something that is of very little interest to him. His response if entirely dismissive of their stated question. "Give to the emperor the things that are the emperor's."

But as usual he answers the question that they have not asked: "and to God the things that are God's." What is the use of wondering whether or not it is lawful to pay a secular tax when matters of faith are being ignored?

As we often do when it comes to money, they are attempting to establish a false dichotomy. There is all the difference in the world between paying ones taxes as a citizen and in honoring God by offering all that we are and all that we have to the work of God in the world. They, and we, know that until we are ready to do the latter, we are all merely playing at games of semantics.

Persevering

Almighty and everlasting God, in Christ you have revealed your glory among the nations: Preserve the works of your mercy, that your Church throughout the world may persevere with steadfast faith in the confession of your Name; through Jesus Christ our Lord, who lives and reigns with you and the Holy Spirit, one God, for ever and ever. Amen. (Collect for Proper 24)

For those who take their faith seriously, it has never been easy being a Christian especially when the Church is also the State as in the case of the Holy Roman Empire. Then and now, those who actually sought to follow the teaching and example of Christ were in the minority.

This prayer expresses the hope that Christians everywhere will focus first and foremost on their love and faith in the redeeming work of God in Christ – even if they discover that their proclamation is at odds with the prevailing values of a nation or a culture.

Such a commitment to the Gospel requires that we know what Jesus said, and so much as we are able, that we understand what he meant. The Glory to be proclaimed among the nations is not tied to the government, culture of philosophy of any nation. In fact, the Word of God challenges centralized power unless that power genuinely seeks to serve and sustain all God's people through acts of love and mercy.

To be the Church, the Church must be counter-cultural, for an honest interpretation of the word of God will always present serious challenges to individuals and to institutions – including the Church herself. May God grant us the grace to proclaim the Gospel with power and in steadfast faith.

No One Like Moses

Never since has there arisen a prophet in Israel like Moses, whom the LORD knew face to face. He was unequaled for all the signs and wonders that the LORD sent him to perform in the land of Egypt, against Pharaoh and all his servants and his entire land, and for all the mighty deeds and all the terrifying displays of power that Moses performed in the sight of all Israel. (Deuteronomy 34:11-12)

To say that God knew Moses face to face is not to say that Moses knew God on the same terms. Despite his greatness, Moses remains a human servant of God and his life is a demonstration that the line between humanity and divinity is a clear one.

But Moses is indeed an extraordinary man and a friend of God. He exhibits the full range of human emotion from rage to ecstasy; he flees Pharaoh after killing a man, but has the courage to stand in the breech between the wrath of God and the children of Israel; and he is alternately obedient to the leading of the Spirit and when frustrated, capable of disobedience on a scale that prevents his entering into the promised land. Moses is everyman and no man.

What truly distinguishes Moses from the rest of us is the intimate trust of his relationship to God. While they are not and cannot be equals, Moses is not afraid to be honest with God. Nor is he reluctant to demand a response from God. Abraham bargains with God over the destruction of Sodom, but Moses openly challenges God (the "Your People" passage of Exodus 32 is one of the most endearingly human conversations in Scripture).

In the end, Moses is unequaled as a prophet because even though he recognizes that he is not equal to the task to which God has called him he shows up and does the best that he can do. He is able to be God's instrument for the liberation of Israel because he himself has known the liberating love of God in his own life.

From Age to Age

Lord, you have been our refuge from one generation to another.
Before the mountains were brought forth, or the land and the earth were born,
from age to age you are God. (Psalm 90:1-2)

As in the Gloria Patri (*as it was in the beginning, is now and ever shall be*), the Psalmist mixes verb tenses when speaking of God. You have been, you are now, and you always will be God. Because we are creatures who are captive to time, it is comforting to us to be reminded that God is outside of time. It has been said that while we experience life as a series of moments strung together in what we call the past and present while we anticipate the future, God sees all of creation in a moment. It is not that God is unconcerned with time; God is simply beyond time.

For us, that results in the blessing of divine continuity. God does not change with time – God remains God no matter what our lives, our times, and our experiences may lead us to believe. This also means that time is not our enemy. Even though our experience of life is bounded by what we understand as the passage of time, our salvation and our relationship with God are eternal, full, and complete from age to age and from one generation to another.

Given that our hearts and minds are continually subject to change, we may be misled into thinking that because we have changed God no longer knows us. The truth is that God knows who we were, what we are and what we shall be and that all those states of being are held in the heart and mind of God eternally.

To Please God

For our appeal does not spring from deceit or impure motives or trickery, but just as we have been approved by God to be entrusted with the message of the gospel, even so we speak, not to please mortals, but to please God who tests our hearts.(I Thessalonians 2:3-4)

It may have been fairly easy for St. Paul to say that we are to be about the business of pleasing God rather than mortals, but he was clearly not raised as most of us (especially female) were raised. We were taught, directly and indirectly, that pleasing people, and being a pleasant person were our primary purpose for being here on the planet. No wonder so many of us grew up to be professional people-pleasers, and no wonder people-pleasing is fundamental to the modern life of the church.

How long has it been since your faith community actually said of did something that was not calculated to cause the least social resistance, or the least damage to the budget. The days of boldly proclaiming a gospel of justice and accountability are little more than memory.

The same is true of our personal spirituality. Who among us is willing to confront attitudes and situations which conflict with the gospel? And even more, who among us is willing to be challenged or confronted ourselves?

The Good News of God in Christ is simple, direct and confrontational. "God is with us. Now act like it!" That fact that God is with us is generally received as good news indeed. But the imperative to behave, speak, and live in a manner that conveys that Good News is not so readily accepted. Yet without the latter, the former is easily trivialized and reduced to little more than a platitude on a coffee mug or a pillow.

Speak the truth. Speak the truth in love. But speak!

The Greatest Commandment

When the Pharisees heard that Jesus had silenced the Sadducees, they gathered together, and one of them, a lawyer, asked him a question to test him. "Teacher, which commandment in the law is the greatest?" He said to him, "`You shall love the Lord your God with all your heart, and with all your soul, and with all your mind.' This is the greatest and first commandment. And a second is like it: `You shall love your neighbor as yourself.' On these two commandments hang all the law and the prophets." (Matthew 22:34-40)

People "tested" Jesus because he and his teachings annoyed them. He was not fond of tradition for tradition's sake, and was even less enamored of systems that pitted people against rules. As a result, he was often in conflict with authority. The Sadducees were the conservative keepers of the priestly ritual and liturgy of Judaism, while the Pharisees were the folks who knew and studied the law. This particular lawyer apparently thought that Jesus was an illiterate peasant who had never even been in a synagogue. The "test" question he asks is a fundamental one, the answer to which every practicing Jew would have known. He need not have been surprised that the answer Jesus gives is completely accurate and orthodox.

Things are not so different today. We often assume that anything which rocks the boat of the status quo must be fundamentally flawed; so our first reaction is to question the authority, motive or intelligence of the presenter.

The real irony of this encounter is that the Great Commandment is and always has been in conflict with the status quo. Nothing can be more challenging to a life of settled ease than a commitment to loving God with all our hearts and our neighbors as ourselves – yet how often we manage to say those words without allowing them to penetrate into our hearts and minds.

The real "test" is not whether we are able to recite the law, but whether we obey it.

Any Questions?

Now while the Pharisees were gathered together, Jesus asked them this question: "What do you think of the Messiah? Whose son is he?" They said to him, "The son of David." He said to them, "How is it then that David by the Spirit calls him Lord, saying, `The Lord said to my Lord, "Sit at my right hand, until I put your enemies under your feet"'? If David thus calls him Lord, how can he be his son?" No one was able to give him an answer, nor from that day did anyone dare to ask him any more questions. (Matthew 22:41-46)

Jesus was a master at asking trick questions. And he really didn't do it because he had the answer himself or just because he wanted to make a teaching point. He generally did it to shut people up. He knew that sometimes the only way that we can hear God is to be rendered speechless long enough to have to listen.

Listening, especially listening to God, is a dying art. Most folk these days are so accustomed to continuous noise and stimulation that the idea of quietly paying attention to what is going on in our hearts is terrifying. Even if we are not talking, we are reading, typing, or checking our messages. We are nearly never "offline."

Perhaps Jesus asks the Pharisees an unanswerable question in an effort to get them to think about something other than themselves. Perhaps Jesus is also trying to get us to be quiet long enough to hear what he is saying. Ask yourself, "How much of the noise and worry in my own head are my attempts to avoid being aware of God?" But don't argue about it – just turn it off and listen for God.

All You Need is Love

Almighty and everlasting God, increase in us the gifts of faith, hope, and charity; and, that we may obtain what you promise, make us love what you command; through Jesus Christ our Lord, who lives and reigns with you and the Holy Spirit, one God, for ever and ever. Amen. (Collect for Proper 25)

As a very young child, I learned two songs with the line "the Bible tells me so". The first was "Jesus Loves Me" and the second was "Faith Hope and Charity". Both have stayed with me for over 60 years. And together they teach us nearly everything we need to know as Christians.

"Jesus loves me, this I know, for the Bible tells me so."
"Have faith, hope and charity. That's the way to live successfully. How do I know? The Bible tells me so!"

Jesus does love us. And the three things that we need in order to live a life that demonstrate our understanding of the message that Jesus loves us, are faith, hope, and charity.

We are called to a relationship of trust with God. That's faith. We base that faith on the trust that even though we cannot always see what is happening or what lies ahead, that God is faithful and is working God's divine purpose out in creation. That's hope. And the one thing that undergirds all of creation and holds all life together is love. That's love/charity.

As St. Paul writes in the 13th chapter of 2nd Corinthians, "faith, hope and love abide. But the greatest of these is love."

It is only through the exercise of these virtues that we can glimpse even now the reign of God and live our lives in expectation of the time when the kingdom will come on earth as in heaven.

And so we live in faith, with hope, through love as we await the day of Christ's coming.

May that day come swiftly! Amen.

The Shelter of the Throne

For this reason they are before the throne of God, and worship him day and night within his temple, and the one who is seated on the throne will shelter them. They will hunger no more, and thirst no more; the sun will not strike them, nor any scorching heat; for the Lamb at the center of the throne will be their shepherd, and he will guide them to springs of the water of life, and God will wipe away every tear from their eyes." (Revelation 7:15-17)

Suffering in life is inevitable, and universal. Perhaps that is why every theistic faith to some degree promises cessation of pain and suffering to those who have been faithful and who make their way to the presence of God. Of course, nearly every faith also includes a place of heightened suffering and pain for those who have not been faithful, but that is a topic for another day.

For folks in first century Palestine, an end of suffering would certainly have included enough to eat and drink, relief from heat and blazing sun, safe shelter and the absence of sorrow and grief. The would finally enjoy the protection of a king who would not abuse, enslave or exploit them, and their dignity as human beings would be restored.

For much of the world today the same set of circumstances would apply. But for those of us to do not suffer for want of the basics -- food, water and shelter, and a degree of respect – what does the beatific vision represent? For some it may be a place where they do not plod through time tethered to the treadmill of productivity. For others the shelter of the throne may provide safety from emotional, physical or verbal abuse. And for still others, the Lamb on the throne may free them from the tyranny of class, wealth or physical appearance.

The fact is that we are all enslaved to something, even if it is of our own making. But God knows that and it is God's gracious and loving will to unburden us, wipe our tears away and make a place for us in the sheltering presence of the throne.

Taste and See

*Taste and see that the LORD is good; **
happy are they who trust in him!
*Fear the LORD, you that are his saints, **
for those who fear him lack nothing.
*The young lions lack and suffer hunger, **
but those who seek the LORD lack nothing that is good. (Psalm 34:8-10)

This is one of those "yes, but" passages. It is tempting to think that we are promised all the good things of life if we will only seek God; but many a grand plan has been devastated by the failure to recognize a metaphor.

Yes, we do receive all the good things of Faith when we seek God, but the Psalmist is speaking spiritually not literally. Those who seek God are spiritually happy. They lack none of the spiritual benefits of faith and relationship with God. They do not hunger for the awareness of the presence of God in their lives. They are indeed rich beyond measure. In fact, in the goodness of God, they have all that it is spiritually possible to have.

Will they still encounter want, need, fear and anxiety? Absolutely. And they will have to address those needs as everyone else must. Sometimes they may be prosperous, comfortable and confident concerning their physical future – just as those who are not seeking God may very well be. But sometimes they will suffer as all creatures do.

The difference is that the hunger which drives us to seek God is always satisfied. For God is also, always seeking us and if we seek God we will find and be found by God. Perhaps not as we expect God to be, and most certainly not in terms of our achieving our personal goals. But we will encounter God. And in doing so, we will gradually discover that seeking anything other than God will ultimately leave us bereft; because it is only in God that we find everything.

God of your goodness, give me yourself. For you are enough to me and I can ask for nothing less that is to your full glory. And if I ask for anything less, I will always be in want, for only in you have I all. (Julian of Norwich)

Children of God

The reason the world does not know us is that it did not know him. Beloved, we are God's children now; what we will be has not yet been revealed. What we do know is this: when he is revealed, we will be like him, for we will see him as he is. And all who have this hope in him purify themselves, just as he is pure. (I John 3:1-3)

We've all heard someone say: "Seeing is believing." Those are the practical ones who must have trustworthy, physical verification before they will believe. Others insist: "Believing is seeing." These are the intuitive types who somehow just know things and trust their intuition to direct them.

But this passage seems to suggest that those who start from sight as well as those who start from belief, end up in the same place. "Seeing/Believing is becoming." As children of God (which we already are), we are also in the process of becoming who and what we will be. When that happens, we will see that we are like God. And we and everyone else, will recognize it.

We're used to that already, when we meet someone new it's not uncommon to hear, "Wow, I'd know you anywhere, you look/sound/act just like your sister." But that can't happen if the person we are meeting has never met our sister. We carry the resemblance of those with whom we really share life and relationship. That's what makes is possible for others to see.

But that is not the end of it. Sometimes the resemblance is not so evident. Sometimes it is hidden and must be revealed through the process of getting to know someone. Or as St. John implies, sometimes that resemblance is obscured by distance, time, or estrangement. Being a child of God does not necessarily mean that we look enough like God to be immediately recognizable as such. That is why we are called to imitate Christ in living lives that encourage the comparison.

But in any case, we are all children of God and we are all in the process of being made like God. That is good news for all the saints!

The Key to Happiness

"Blessed are the poor in spirit, for theirs is the kingdom of heaven.
"Blessed are those who mourn, for they will be comforted.
"Blessed are the meek, for they will inherit the earth.
"Blessed are those who hunger and thirst for righteousness, for they will be filled.
"Blessed are the merciful, for they will receive mercy.
"Blessed are the pure in heart, for they will see God.
"Blessed are the peacemakers, for they will be called children of God."
(Matthew 5:2-9)

When Jesus spoke these words to those gathered on the hillside to hear him preach, he was very much aware that few of them had any reason to rejoice because of their life experience. They were the inhabitants of an occupied nation, living under the rule of Rome. Their religious system had been coopted by that same power, and their prospects for a long or healthy life were very dim. None the less, he spoke to them of the blessedness of their experience; and he told them to be happy.

For to be blessed is to be happy. At least that is what Jesus meant when he used the Greek word, markarios as the equivalent for blessed. Happy are the poor in spirit. Happy are the meek. Happy are those mourn.

Why? Because for Jesus, blessedness meant to be in the presence of God, or to partake in the nearness of God. It is only our narrow, and quite self-centered understanding of happiness today that makes us equate being happy and blessed with being comfortable or prosperous. We are not promised an end to suffering and need in this life. But we are reminded that we are not alone in those moments.

When we are poor in spirit, or meek or merciful, we are more clearly aware of the presence of God, and when we partake of the presence of God, we resemble God, and we become like God. It is those moments that we become Children of God.

In Good Company

"Blessed are those who are persecuted for righteousness' sake, for theirs is the kingdom of heaven. Blessed are you when people revile you and persecute you and utter all kinds of evil against you falsely on my account. Rejoice and be glad, for your reward is great in heaven, for in the same way they persecuted the prophets who were before you. (Matthew 5:10-12)

People are persecuted for all manner of reasons, and quite frequently for things over which they have no control. That is not the sort of persecution to which Jesus refers in these verses. He speaks specifically of those who are persecuted for their having stood up for righteousness, and for having remained faithful to him in times and places where it was neither popular nor safe to do so. When that happens, Jesus reminds the persecuted that they are blessed/happy – because they are in very good company.

Even so, while there may be some sense of moral justification in having been persecuted for righteousness sake, we would consider it quite odd that someone would rejoice in or feel blessed by the experience. That sounds a lot like looking for suffering, and we might think that the better response would be to keep a low profile. But for those who are sufficiently committed to the cause of righteousness that sense of blessedness is also a source of strength and comfort in the face of persecution.

Fortunately, most of us have very little experience of persecution. Unfortunately, it is very easy to think that we are being persecuted when we are not. Sometimes we get into trouble because we have done something wrong. Then we take our lumps. But if, as followers of Christ, we find that we are being persecuted for doing the right and loving thing in his name, then we may take comfort in knowing that we are neither the first nor the last to be hated for loving.

Virtuous and Godly

Almighty God, you have knit together your elect in one communion and fellowship in the mystical body of your Son Christ our Lord: Give us grace so to follow your blessed saints in all virtuous and godly living, that we may come to those ineffable joys that you have prepared for those who truly love you; through Jesus Christ our Lord, who with you and the Holy Spirit lives and reigns, one God, in glory everlasting. Amen. (Collect for All Saints Day)

The *elect* in this prayer are the members of the Body of Christ, and therefore, the communion of saints – past, present and future. Some were alive at the beginning of the church in this world, others are alive today, and still others have not yet been born. But all are knit/woven/joined together by Baptism, Eucharist, and profession of faith in Christ Jesus. Some are "S" saints like Francis and Claire, and some are "s" saints like you and me, but all are sealed by the Holy Spirit and marked as Christ's own forever. The joy that we all will share in eternity with God is something that we cannot at this point imagine or begin to understand. It is beyond the power of human expression and so we call it "ineffable."

But it is good. Union and communion with the saints of God is a joy beyond our knowing, and is promised to those who truly or "unfeignedly" love God. Of course, truly loving God is probably just as challenging a concept as is describing the indescribable....or just as difficult as loving all the members of the family of God that we already know. None of us is going to do it perfectly...even those whom we revere as the "S" saints of the faith, and whose example we strive to follow could not do so perfectly. But that is not the point. The point is that we are all part of the family of God, even if we may never in this life know each other. That is the source of its power. We are made one in the body and one in the spirit through the grace of God.

Day of Decision

Now if you are unwilling to serve the LORD, choose this day whom you will serve, whether the gods your ancestors served in the region beyond the River, or the gods of the Amorites in whose land you are living; but as for me and my household, we will serve the LORD." (Joshua 24:15)

Some folks think that one's religion ought to be a private, almost secret matter, freely chosen by the individual and not subject to public attention. To some extent that is true. We are not required to believe, nor are we told what to believe. We get to choose.

But we do have to make a decision, and the choice and practice of our faith are not meant to be secret. Choosing means affiliation, and affiliation requires participation and fidelity. After all, worship involves service and obedience. And that means that what we believe will inevitably become visible to those around us.

A faith that can be kept hidden is hardly a faith at all, because genuine belief results in action.

Joshua knows this. He realizes that everyone must make her/his own decision, and having decided, follow through on it. The practice of faith is a matter of heart, mind and body. It cannot be faked. That's why Joshua gives the people a choice. Choose who you will follow and follow.

But notice, he does not leave it at that. He immediately declares his allegiance so that all will know what he values and what he intends. He does not force others to agree with him, but he does not back down from his own decision. The rest of his life (as well as the lives of his family) will be shaped by his choice to follow Christ, and his actions will bear witness to his decision.

Cause for Belief

"Far be it from us that we should forsake the LORD to serve other gods; for it is the LORD our God who brought us and our ancestors up from the land of Egypt, out of the house of slavery, and who did those great signs in our sight. He protected us along all the way that we went, and among all the peoples through whom we passed; and the LORD drove out before us all the peoples, the Amorites who lived in the land. Therefore we also will serve the LORD, for he is our God." (Joshua 24:16-18)

As they prepare to enter the promised-land, Joshua gathers the children of Israel and asks them who they will worship. He demands that they be prepared to make a decision and then honor it. He also expects that they will be able to articulate why they have chosen as they have.

Their answer is fascinating. They choose the LORD because they know him. They have a relationship with the Lord who freed from slavery in Egypt, protected them throughout their journeys, and who has prepared their way into the future.

In times like ours, where it is so easy to become bored with the tried and true, and tempting to check out what is new and exciting, we often fail to honor the value of relationship. We forget that our lives are not lived in a vacuum. Life is personal, interconnected, and interdependent.

A faith relationship is the same. The children of Israel know that they can trust the Lord. God's providential love and care have been demonstrated in their lives. They choose what they know to be true. They have cause for belief and they are willing to stake their future on it.

We Are Witnesses

Then Joshua said to the people, "You are witnesses against yourselves that you have chosen the LORD, to serve him." And they said, "We are witnesses." (Joshua 24:22)

My mom used to say, “Don’t make promises that you can’t or don’t intend to keep.” She was right. The power of a promise is lost when it is not honored. That is not to say that there may never come a time when we are simply unable to keep a promise we have made – i.e., someone falls and breaks a leg on the way to the winter prom. But promises rely on relationships, and that sort of accident is precisely when the nature and history of the relationship matters most. Reasonable explanations are accepted by reasonable people and breaking your leg on the way to the prom is entirely different from simply not showing up.

But what if we promise when we either don’t fully understand the consequences or we are really not intending to follow through? That’s what Joshua is concerned about in this passage. Do the people understand that this is an all or nothing proposition? Are they aware that they won’t be able to change their minds? Are they willing to be held accountable? If so, then go ahead and promise. If not, you’d better go home and think about it.

Making a promise to God is an utterly serious event. It demands our allegiance and commands our attention. And God remembers. But most of all it is a matter of intention. Do we mean what we are saying and are we ready to give our full attention to following through. That’s why all the prayers and promises of our worship include some variation of “so help me God.” We know that we are not going to be completely faithful on our own, but we trust that with the help of God we will be strengthened to do what we have promised.

Help and Deliverance

*Be pleased, O God, to deliver me; **
O LORD, make haste to help me. (Psalm 70:1)

The greatest tension in the practice of Christianity is the fact that we are to be continually prepared for the coming of Christ, but that we must also wait at the same time. It's sort of like the old adage, "Hurry up and wait." Unlike God, we have very little ability to abide, rest, or remain anywhere. Our attention spans are limited, our ability to engage in delayed gratification is miniscule, and our perspective is so skewed that we are often unable to determine the difference between a real emergency and something that can wait. We seem to have two inboxes in our hearts – "urgent" and "immediate."

But most of all, we really, really do not like uncertainty. We want to know what is going on, how long it is going to last, and what the plan is for taking care of it. When those answers are not immediately evident, we may find ourselves thinking, "If God loves me, then why isn't God fixing this?"

Maybe because sometimes our sense of urgency is there to tell us something. Why does this bother me so much? Why am I in such a rush to get things resolved? What might I learn if I just sat still in the midst of my anxiety and asked God to help me put it into perspective?

It is not that God has other things to do, or that we are not on God's priority list. It is much more a question of why we think that the best solution to a problem is to be delivered from it. If we always get rescued, what do we learn? Typically, we learn to yell, quickly, loudly, and repeatedly for God's help. And to keep on yelling until we get what we want or exhaust ourselves.

It's important to remember that God is always about the work of helping and delivering us. It's just that sometimes the thing from which we are in need of deliverance is our own anxious spirit.

Keep Awake

And while they went to buy it, the bridegroom came, and those who were ready went with him into the wedding banquet; and the door was shut. Later the other bridesmaids came also, saying, `Lord, lord, open to us.' But he replied, `Truly I tell you, I do not know you.' Keep awake therefore, for you know neither the day nor the hour." (Matthew 25:10-13)

It is really difficult to stay alert, prepared and excited if you don't really believe that anything is going to happen. When I was nine I lay awake all night on Christmas Eve waiting for Santa. By the time I was seventeen, I would have slept till noon on Christmas morning. Whether or not Santa had been to our house was a piece of information that would keep until I felt like getting up. Happily my enthusiasm for surprises returned to me in my early twenties, and today I can easily sit up all night watching the sky and thinking about all the Christmases I have celebrated.

Matthew reminds us though, that preparation is a part of enthusiasm. It is not that the foolish bridesmaids weren't excited about the wedding. It's that they weren't excited enough. They had not taken their roles seriously enough to plan ahead for the full experience. They weren't sufficiently invested in their tasks to have considered what might happen if the bridegroom were delayed. So they were ready to party, but not to celebrate.

In my case, it would make no sense to be ready to sit up on the patio watching the December sky all night unless I also remembered to take a blanket and thermos of coffee. Otherwise, I might sit there for ten minutes until I got too cold or sleepy.

Sometimes we forget that a life of faith requires a certain degree of pragmatism. Like the wise bridesmaids, we are in it for the long haul. We don't know what life will throw at us, or what tasks God may have in store, but we can't respond if we are not awake.

Hope of Purity

O God whose blessed son came into the world that he might destroy the works of the devil, and make us children of God and heirs of eternal life: Grant that we, having this hope, may purify ourselves as he is pure; that when he comes again with power and great glory, we may be made like him in his eternal and glorious kingdom... (Collect for Proper 27)

What are the works of the devil? Over the years I have heard a great many suggestions as to what they might be. More often than not, these "works" were described in terms of human morality, and most often in terms of human sexuality. That's pretty racy stuff, and opens the way for some very imaginative descriptions of the devil. But I don't think that is what this means.

The second half of the first clause of this sentence says that Jesus came into the world to make us children of God and heirs of eternal life. So if that is what he came to accomplish, it seems to me that what he came to destroy were those things that would disinherit us from God and deny us the eternal life which is the birthright of the children of God. So how do folks generally get themselves disinherited? By defying or disrespecting their parents – in short, by living such lives that no one wants to claim them as children.

And how might the devil promote such behavior among the children of God? By encouraging us to be arrogant and prideful, and by convincing us that we do not need God or each other. And Jesus, by his life of obedience, prayer and genuine humility, to say nothing about his selfless care for others, very effectively demonstrated the power of love, and the poverty of the works of the devil.

I find it very comforting when things are easy to understand. Jesus came into the world to demonstrate God's love for us and to restore us to our status as children of God and heirs of eternal life. For which we can all say, "Thanks be to God!"

Cycles of the Spirit

The Israelites again did what was evil in the sight of the LORD, after Ehud died. So the LORD sold them into the hand of King Jabin of Canaan, who reigned in Hazor; the commander of his army was Sisera, who lived in Harosheth-ha-goiim. Then the Israelites cried out to the LORD for help; for he had nine hundred chariots of iron, and had oppressed the Israelites cruelly twenty years. (Judges 4:1-3)

Creation. Sin. Judgment. Redemption. This is the cycle of life for the children of Israel, and for each of us as well. When things are bright and new, and all is going well, we tend to lapse into complacency. We are grateful, of course, but we do not dwell on it. The problem is that complacency leads to indifference, and often to arrogance, and spiritually speaking, it is a short step from complacency to sin.

It is also possible to remain oblivious to the power of sin until we begin to reap the consequences, which are often unpleasant enough to make us believe that we are being punished. At that point, we wake up, remember God, and repent –trusting that God will forgive us and restore us.

And so the cycle is repeated; though the condition that we are most apt to remember is the feeling of being punished. It would be far more helpful to realize that what we consider punishment is actually no more than being allowed to experience the consequences of our actions. And that what we experience as redemption – being restored to a right relationship -- is always available to us.

How much time and energy we waste, sliding into trouble and then begging to be saved! Maybe if we could start to learn to pay regular attention to our relationship with God, we wouldn't spend so much time running away from the chariots.

Undivided Attention

*To you I lift up my eyes, **
to you enthroned in the heavens.
*As the eyes of servants look to the hand of their masters, **
and the eyes of a maid to the hand of her mistress,
*So our eyes look to the LORD our God, **
until he show us his mercy. (Psalm 123:1-3)

God has the Psalmist's undivided attention. I wonder what it would take to command our undivided attention. We don't know much about focus. In fact, most of us are in a continual state of distraction in which we spend great amounts of energy attempting to influence the world and those around us. Only the most extreme situations command the sort of focus or hyper-vigilance described in this Psalm. For example, I know that nothing focuses my attention like hope and fear, because in both instances I am acutely aware that I am not in control. I cannot guarantee an outcome. I can only wait. I am anchored to the moment, and dependent upon circumstance that I cannot alter.

The Psalmist finds himself is such a place. His awareness of the need for God's mercy is so overwhelming that it requires his undivided attention. He watches and waits, hoping for mercy, hardly daring to breathe, and unable to look away from the source of his salvation.

But the focus of our undivided attention need not be reserved for such extremes. What might happen if we were to devote five minutes a day to really paying attention and to waiting for God? Could we spare five minutes a day to abide in a place of obedient and watchful trust? That is the whole point of contemplative prayer. In prayer, we are invited to watch and wait for God with the same intentionality displayed by an attentive servant – trusting, obeying and abiding. Such focus is a wonderful gift to God, and prepares us to recognize and receive God's mercy in each day rather than waiting for moments of desperation.

Destined for Salvation

For God has destined us not for wrath but for obtaining salvation through our Lord Jesus Christ, who died for us, so that whether we are awake or asleep we may live with him. (I Thessalonians 5:9-10)

Why is it so difficult for us to understand that God loves us? We are destined for life, not wrath. We are beloved of God, not condemned or forsaken. No matter what happens to us or no matter what we do, God is still with us, still loves us, and still yearns for our love in return.

But it seems that such news is too good to be true. Why should God care for us? How can God overlook our sins? And so we dwell upon all the harsh and condemning tendencies of our own hearts, projecting them back upon God. We speak of a god who is so righteous that only blood and sacrifice will turn aside judgment; and in doing so, we reduce the image and glory of God to that of a frail and petulant human.

The truth is that God has simultaneously destined us for salvation, and provided the means of our receiving it. If that is not good news, I cannot imagine what would be! So cling to the truth that God loves and accepts you. Turn your heart toward seeking and serving God. Open your soul to receive the gifts of salvation and eternal life. And rejoice!

Entering Into Joy

'Well done, good and trustworthy slave; you have been trustworthy in a few things, I will put you in charge of many things; enter into the joy of your master.' (Matthew 25:21)

When at age thirteen, my son first began to perform on stage, he said, "Mom, I live for applause!" Don't we all? We may call it other things – affirmation, appreciation, or self-actualization – but when it comes right down to it, we want to know that we have done a good job and that others, especially those in authority, recognize our accomplishments. We want to hear, "Well done. I'm pleased with you."

Alas, such expressions of approval can be quite addictive. And when we begin to do things specifically for the applause or approval, we miss the point of the original task. The master has given us something to do, and has trusted us with seeing it through. The appropriate response is to do it was well as we are able.

That is what has happened in this passage. The servant has simply done his job. He has done it as well as he can, he has been careful to be thorough and conscientious in the management of those things entrusted to him, and he is prepared to give an accounting for his actions. His reward is that he is brought even closer to the master. He shares not only in the master's approval but in his joy.

God gives each of us things to do. God gives each of us the gifts, talents and means with which to do them. The good and trustworthy servant does the best with what she has been given and abides in the joy of the master.

A Measure of Faith

For to all those who have, more will be given, and they will have an abundance; but from those who have nothing, even what they have will be taken away. (Matthew 25:29)

What kind of point is Jesus trying to make here? The rich get rich and the poor get poorer? It sounds really harsh, and it would be if Jesus were speaking of wealth and prosperity. He isn't of course, but that has not stopped folks from twisting his words to make it seem as though he is.

Jesus is talking about our willingness to invest ourselves in the work of the reign of God.

For to all those who have ______, more will be given, and they will have an abundance. There are innumerable words that can be used to fill in that blank. Try reading it with any of these words inserted: faith, initiative, trust, courage, wisdom, or compassion. The parable hinges on the willingness of the servant to invest her own self in the appointed task, using the gifts she already possesses for the work of the kingdom. By doing that, she grows in faith and ability. She risks much and is greatly rewarded.

But for the servant who allows herself to be defined by a mentality of fear and scarcity and who refuses to risk anything at all, even the gifts with which she started out atrophy from neglect and are lost.

It is not that God is so hard-nosed a manager as to punish those who do not produce. God honors the efforts of those who show up and do their best. The ones who lose out are those who are too timid or fearful to try.

Chewing on Scripture

Blessed Lord, who caused all holy Scriptures to be written for our learning: Grant us so to hear them, read, mark, learn, and inwardly digest them, that we may embrace and ever hold fast the blessed hope of everlasting life, which you have given us in our Savior Jesus Christ; who lives and reigns with you and the Holy Spirit, one God, for ever and ever. Amen. (Collect for Proper 28)

Learning from Scripture is a life-long process. It is one that feeds us daily, and prepares us for the work which God calls us to do. It is also a full-body experience. Much is required to fully incorporate the word of God into our lives. We must hear it. Someone must read and expound it in terms that we can understand. We must read scripture ourselves on a daily basis, and over the years. We must pay attention to what we hear and what we read and allow it to become part of our memory. We must work to make it part of our lives and seek to apply it to our lives. And we must in fact chew on it, digest it, use it as fuel for our spiritual lives, and always be willing to revisit what we have learned.

That is not to say that every word of Scripture is a literal roadmap, or spiritually is wholesome. There is much in Scripture that stands as an object lesson for us in how not to behave. Only by hearing, reading, marking, learning, and inwardly digesting are we able to recognize the truth that Scripture conveys to us. God trusts us with this task, and when we do it, the word becomes alive.

When Scripture becomes alive for us, we are able to receive it as the gift that it is, and we are able to learn and grown from it. We do not do this so that we will be more Biblically literate than anyone else, or so that we will be able to argue over the finer points of the law. We receive the living Scriptures so that we may embrace and enjoy the fullness of eternal life with God.

A Diet of Justice

I will feed them with good pasture, and the mountain heights of Israel shall be their pasture; there they shall lie down in good grazing land, and they shall feed on rich pasture on the mountains of Israel. I myself will be the shepherd of my sheep, and I will make them lie down, says the Lord GOD. I will seek the lost, and I will bring back the strayed, and I will bind up the injured, and I will strengthen the weak, but the fat and the strong I will destroy. I will feed them with justice. (Ezekiel 34:14-16)

Being fed is much more than receiving sufficient food and water. Our souls and our spirits also require the sustaining power of nurture, protection, healing, and encouragement. Specifically, the lack of justice may very easily result in the death of a people. They may starve for want of it.

But in this passage the prophet points out that a diet of justice may also bring destruction. Those who have hoarded, or abused their wealth at the expense of the poor, sick and injured will be force-fed justice and will find that the same food which strengthens the oppressed will choke and destroy them.

As Advent approaches, the focus of our lessons narrows down to issues of ultimate importance. At the end of all things we will all be shown justice in very stark and unmistakable terms. This is judgment. When God reveals what is happening to the poor, God also places responsibility on those who could have helped but did not. We are confronted with our failures and the consequences of our actions.

The end of the Church year is a time of challenge for those of us who are comfortable. Before Advent and the season of preparation for the coming of the Messiah, we must pass through a time of repentance and recommit ourselves to the work of justice.

Between Sheep and Sheep

Therefore, thus says the Lord GOD to them: I myself will judge between the fat sheep and the lean sheep. Because you pushed with flank and shoulder, and butted at all the weak animals with your horns until you scattered them far and wide, I will save my flock, and they shall no longer be ravaged; and I will judge between sheep and sheep. (Ezekiel 34: 20-22)

Jesus speaks of judging between the sheep and the goats, but Ezekiel reminds us that God also judges between sheep and sheep. All are part of the same flock, all are offered the same care and the same opportunities. And all are expected to benefit equally from being part of the flock.

But some of the stronger, more aggressive members have trampled on the rights and needs of the weaker sheep. Some have bullied their way into places of comfort and privilege. Others have discounted and ignored those sheep which could not defend themselves or successfully compete for available resources.

Other than size and weight, there may be little visible difference between two sheep. But God sees and God remembers. God knows that the smaller, younger and less powerful sheep in the flock are especially vulnerable to the selfishness of the older, stronger members.

God has made certain that there is enough to go around. There is an abundance of food, shelter, and time for the growth of a healthy and stable flock. But those who do not trust that abundance and revert to greed and violence to gain more than their share will be most surely be judged.

We Are God's

*Know this: The LORD himself is God; **
he himself has made us, and we are his;
we are his people and the sheep of his pasture. (Psalm 100:2)

God is our Maker. That means that we can trust that we will be protected, fed, led, and sheltered. It also means that God knows us and knows our needs as well as our worth. We belong to God.

But God also does much more. Our Maker is also our shepherd and dwells among us. Far more than simply owning us, our shepherd has a personal investment in the welfare of the sheep, and a love for the flock. He is always with us.

But God's presence and proximity are what we often forget. God does not live at a distance and hire someone to take care of us. God stays with us when the fields are rich with grazing and when the land is wet and frozen. God provides us with shelter against the storms of life, but also encourages us to move about and to explore our environment. God leads us to water, but does not force us to drink.

God is everything to us, and we are expected to know and to remember.

Absolute Power

God put this power to work in Christ when he raised him from the dead and seated him at his right hand in the heavenly places, far above all rule and authority and power and dominion, and above every name that is named, not only in this age but also in the age to come. And he has put all things under his feet and has made him the head over all things for the church, which is his body, the fullness of him who fills all in all. (Ephesians 1:20-23)

How much authority do we give Christ in our lives? Scripture is quite clear that everything belongs to Christ, that he is ruler of all, and sovereign over the universe. Yet, we tend to be very parsimonious in our response. We seem to think that simply acknowledging Christ as savior is enough. But a statement of faith cannot replace of life of faith. Recognizing Christ means putting him at the center of our lives where he reigns with unchallenged power. His teaching becomes the framework of our existence. His power commands our reverence.

When Christ is proclaimed Lord of All, Head of the Church and Author of our Salvation, we are not offering empty praise. Those acclamations are to be lived and embodied in our daily lives. Doing so requires a radical re-orientation of priorities, and a fundamental willingness to remove ourselves from our cherished position at the center of our individual universe.

When we properly understand Christ is first, we recognize that everything else emerges from him. Our values, our cherished relationships, and even our own sense of self all derive from him as the center of our being.

The Family of Christ

`Truly I tell you, just as you did it to one of the least of these who are members of my family, you did it to me.'...`Truly I tell you, just as you did not do it to one of the least of these, you did not do it to me.' (Matthew 25:40, 45)

For good or ill, we are always in the company of Christ the King. We are just not always certain that the person we meet is really standing in for Jesus. If we could be certain that it were him, we would all do the right thing all the time. Instead, we set up our own descriptions and qualifications – loving some of our neighbors and rejecting others. Caring for those we deem worthy, and ignoring the rest. In short, deciding who Christ will be and how or if we will respond. But we really don't have that option.

When we come to terms with the fact that Christ is as present in the poor, the sick and tired as He is in the greatest of saints, we find that we are able to respond to Him in all the myriad ways he comes to us. And so, because we look for him in all people, that is where we will find him, and that is where we will demonstrate our love and make our witness.

Just remember this. When we love, we are loving Christ. When we shun or ignore another, we are ignoring Christ. When we seek Christ, we will encounter Christ. For He is all and is in all.

The Reign of Christ

"Almighty and everlasting God, whose will it is to restore all things in your well-beloved Son, the King of kings and Lord of lords: Mercifully grant that the peoples of the earth, divided and enslaved by sin, may be freed and brought together under his most gracious rule; who lives and reigns with you and the Holy Spirit, one God, now and for ever. Amen." (Collect for Christ the King Sunday)

God's vision for Creation is Unity. Not the sort of unity that erases difference, or finds the lowest common denominator. God's unity is achieved when humanity is reconciled to God and to one another. That unity of accomplished by the working of King the King in all the various ways that we can imagine or describe it.

Christ the Shepherd King
who loves us and searches for us as a shepherd cares for his flock.

Christ the King of Righteousness
who leads us with wisdom and justice.

Christ the Liberating King
who risks everything to free us from sin and death.

Christ the King of Creation
who lives in all and brings us to the fullness of God.

Christ the Messiah
who offers himself as a sacrifice for the sins of all
and who overcomes death for us.

All of these together bring us to Christ the King of Kings. He is the first-born of all creation, the head of the church, and the author of our salvation. And in all his glory he comes to us crucified, risen and ascended in the Eucharist. He is also in our daily lives, in our moments of need and in our times of celebration. And in just a few weeks we will meet him once again as the King of Kings comes to us in the form of a human child, born in a manger.

Giving Thanks

"Almighty and gracious Father, we give you thanks for the fruits of the earth in their season and for the labors of those who harvest them. Make us, we pray, faithful stewards of your great bounty, for the provision of our necessities and the relief of all who are in need, to the glory of your Name; through Jesus Christ our Lord, who lives and reigns with you and the Holy Spirit, one God, now and forever." Amen. (Collect for Thanksgiving Day)

May this day be filled with the light and peace of Christ, along with the warmth of hearth and family. May we all remember those who have labored to make our feasting possible, those who have loved us and opened their hearts and homes to us, those who are working this day, and those who are lonely or sick or hungry.

Although only a slight majority of folks in this country profess a belief in God and are affiliated with a faith community, this is the one day of the year when most people in the nation will actually say a prayer of thanksgiving before eating. For that I say, "Thanks be to God." Perhaps doing so on this day will start a habit of living with gratitude each day. But for those of us who are accustomed to saying grace before meals, I have an additional suggestion. At some point during the day, thank someone in person for what they are in your life. Look at them, make eye contact and tell them why you treasure them. Such communication is truly sacramental as it brings the love and presence of Christ into our relationships.

And remember, you are a precious child of God and a bearer of the light of Christ. Live joyfully and love abundantly.

Notes: